I0901604

THE MINNEAPOLIS MILLERS

OF THE

AMERICAN ASSOCIATION

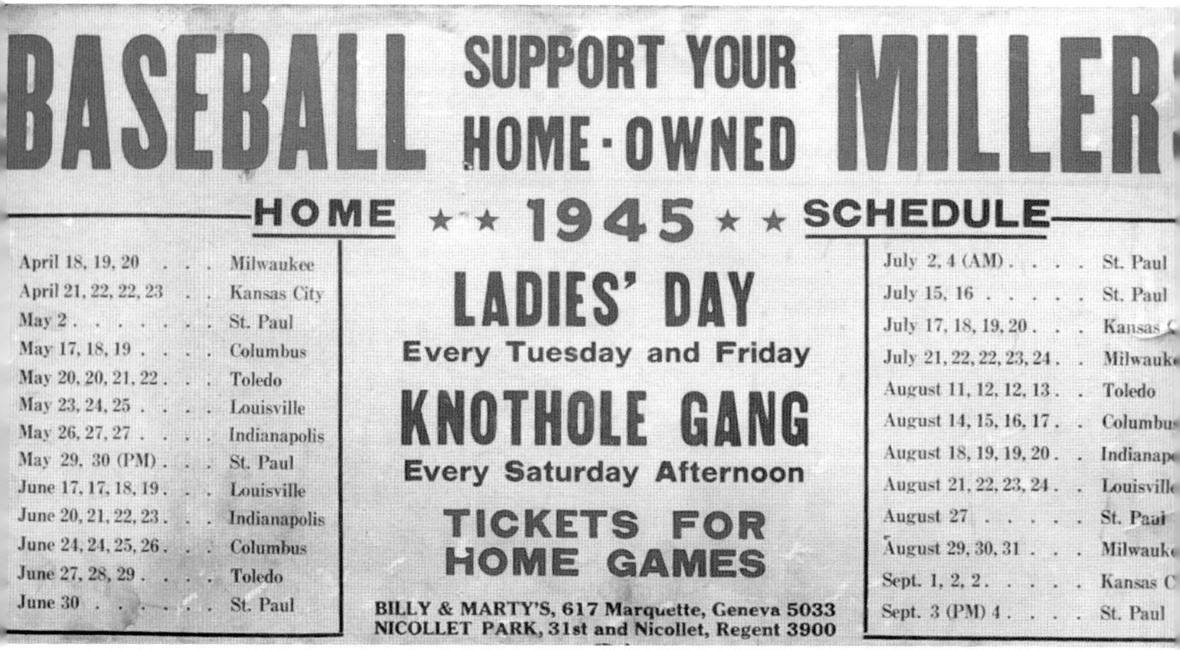

1945 Home Schedule. This two-color display piece, which runs two feet from side to side, describes the Millers as "your home-owned" club. As the major leagues continued to develop their farm systems, fewer clubs could make this claim. Many "Greatest Generation" fans remember buying Millers tickets at Billy and Marty's, as well as participating in the Knot Hole program sponsored by the ball club. Gone are the days when teams would play a five-game series, as the Millers did against the Milwaukee Brewers from July 21 to 24. (Author's collection.)

Front Cover: Known by fans as "Unser Choe" ("Our Joe" in German), Joe Hauser (1932–1936) was one of the most prolific sluggers in league history. For more information, please see page 71. (Author's collection.)

Cover Background: This view of the interior of Nicollet Park was taken sometime around 1945, the beginning of the greatest attendance surge in the park's history. For more information, please see page 8. (Courtesy the Minnesota Historical Society.)

Back Cover: Long a fixture at Thirty-first Street and Nicollet Avenue on the south side of Minneapolis, Nicollet Park's Tudor-style ticket office was the primary portal for Millers fans seeking access to their beloved boys of summer. For more information, please see page 126. (Author's collection; gift from Don Palmer.)

THE MINNEAPOLIS MILLERS OF THE AMERICAN ASSOCIATION

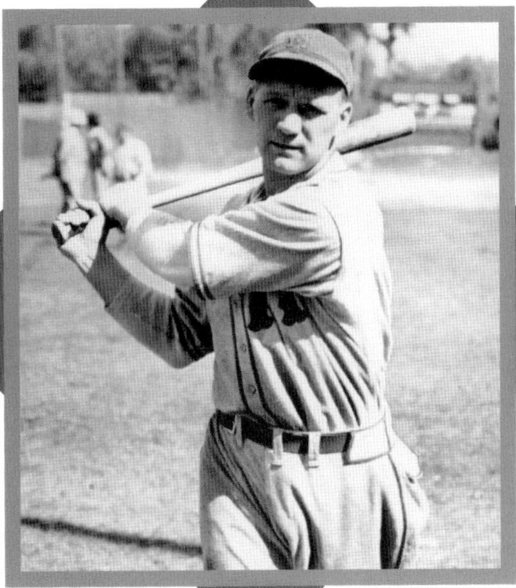

Rex Hamann

ARCADIA PUBLISHING

Copyright © 2015 by Rex Hamann
ISBN 978-1-4671-1347-2

Published by Arcadia Publishing
Charleston, South Carolina

Printed in the United States of America

Library of Congress Control Number: 2015930412

For all general information, please contact Arcadia Publishing:
Telephone 843-853-2070
Fax 843-853-0044
E-mail sales@arcadiapublishing.com
For customer service and orders:
Toll-Free 1-888-313-2665

Visit us on the Internet at www.arcadiapublishing.com

This book is dedicated to the memory of my father-in-law, Dr. Keith E. Lucas, the old Missourian and St. Louis baseball fan whose enthusiastic and unflagging support of my baseball writing inspired this work. With Keith's passing to the "Great Majority" on April 13, 2014, baseball lost a great fan, and the world lost a great man.

CONTENTS

Acknowledgments 6

Introduction 7

1. Deadball-Era Millers: 1902–1920 9

2. Recapturing Their Glory: 1921–1940 45

3. The War Years Take a Toll: 1941–1960 103

ACKNOWLEDGMENTS

The staff at the Hennepin County Library Special Collections granted me their assistance in a variety of ways. In particular, I wish to acknowledge the support I received from Bailey Diers and Gail Wolfson. In addition, my wife, Keitha, was a valued and reliable partner in this endeavor.

INTRODUCTION

Imagine strolling through the woods on a sunny day without a care in the world—looking for nothing, simply open to the possibilities of nature—when suddenly, dangling from a tree branch, a big, brown envelope seems to emerge from the sky. You look at it in amazement—such an unexpected event in so quiet a place—and decide to open it. Inside, you find a treasure trove of vintage family photographs. Nothing can describe how you feel about this serendipitous discovery, but you decide you must share it with the world. Such is how I felt after I came upon the wonderful collection of Minneapolis Millers photographs at the Hennepin County Library, located in downtown Minneapolis, in the summer of 2013.

In this, my second book for Arcadia (I completed a volume on the American Association Milwaukee Brewers in 2004), I have brought many examples from this expansive array to the public eye. Perhaps the most difficult part of the project was the process of selection. In the Milwaukee book, we were dealing with a small, private collection. In this one, the number of photographs could have been double that which made it to the book you now have in your hands. After many hours of making scans, I have attempted to make the selections according to player prominence and artistic quality in order to bring forth the best possible examples. Many of the unpublished photographs will be posted on my American Association website (www.almanacfield.com).

I grew up in a family that more or less supported my incessant need to surround myself with baseball. After my teaching career came to a close some 15 years ago, I dedicated myself to researching and writing about baseball history. Growing up in Madison, Wisconsin, my interests revolved around regional teams, including the old Milwaukee Brewers, and from there my passion in the American Association as a whole slowly grew. I have developed a considerable degree of knowledge with respect to the Association, including the Minneapolis Millers and St. Paul Saints (whose rivalry I describe in a book recently published by McFarland: *The Millers and the Saints: Baseball Championships of the Twin Cities Rivals*). In describing these select photographs, I have made every effort to present things in a way that will inspire curiosity. Through these pages, the reader is invited to look back upon the past with a sense of wonder toward the game of baseball as it was.

Please observe the dates (in parentheses) following the name of each player in the caption titles; these indicate the years spent as an active player with the Minneapolis Millers.

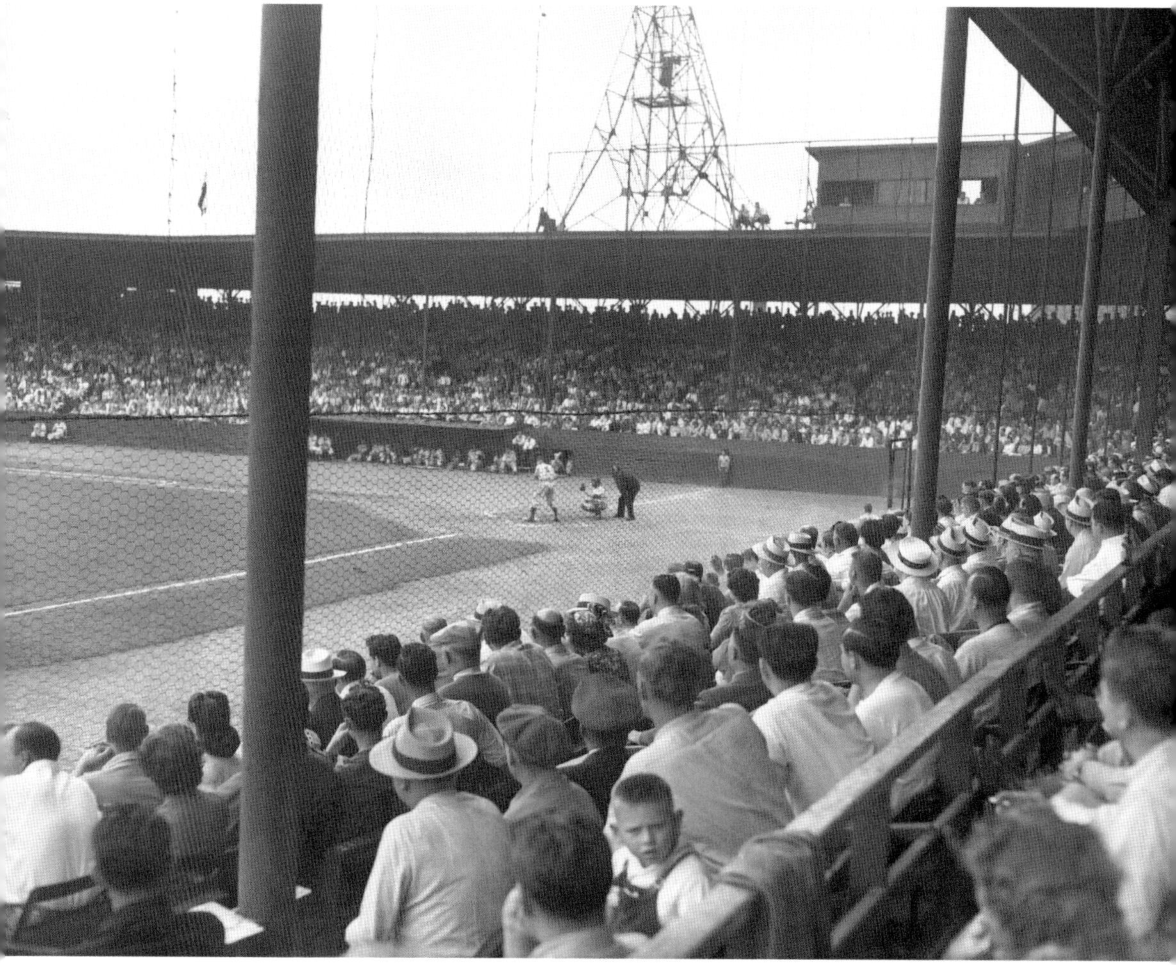

INSIDE NICOLLET PARK. The photographer of this c. 1945 image sat, accompanied by the murmur of the crowd, in the third-base grandstand, aiming the camera lens in the direction of home plate. Originally built in 1896, Nicollet Park sported an all-wooden grandstand, a parking area beneath the facility, and the shortest right-field line in the league. For many years, it was believed that the distance from home plate to the right-field corner was just over 279 feet. However, in 1949, a reporter for the *St. Paul Pioneer Press* determined it was actually 258 feet. To center field, the distance was a healthy 435 feet, and down the line in left it was 336 feet. The stands had a capacity of 10,000. The best five-season attendance total, 232,152, came right after World War II between 1945 and 1949. The first American Association game at Nicollet Park was played on Saturday, May 10, 1902, against the Louisville Colonels. The Millers struck first with four runs in the first inning, going on to win 9-4. Manager and right fielder Walter Wilmot had three hits in four at-bats, and Fred Luther was the winning pitcher. (Courtesy the Minnesota Historical Society.)

1

Deadball-Era Millers 1902–1920

In 1902, the American Association formed in part as a response to the introduction of the American League in 1901. Minneapolis was one of eight clubs that belonged to the American Association, and the Millers were joined by their neighboring St. Paul Saints, the Milwaukee Brewers, the Kansas City Blues, the Columbus (Ohio) Senators (later, Red Birds), the Indianapolis Indians, the Louisville Colonels, and the Toledo Mud Hens. These eight teams remained a cohesive circuit for five decades before the reach of major league organizations began to infiltrate Association nests.

The Millers held fast as members of the league, remaining a steady contestant after the departure of the Milwaukee Brewers in 1952 and enjoying some of their best seasons in the twilight of the league. But the early years set things in motion for fans of the Mill City Nine. After a slow start as a league contestant, Minneapolis enjoyed its first solid season during the 1904 campaign under the leadership of William H. Watkins. The following year, the Millers had one of their finest runs of the next two decades, posting a record of 88-62 and finishing in third place. But in 1910, the doors blew off thanks to a magical combination of superb pitching and powerful hitting. It was during that year, the first season under the managerial purview of "Pongo Joe" Cantillon, that the Millers achieved a club-record 107 wins, losing 61, while running away with the American Association pennant. It was their first of nine first-place finishes during their six-decade stint in the circuit.

During what was typically known as the "deadball era," the Millers came away with four league championships through 1920, narrowly missing out against the Milwaukee Brewers in 1913 when they recorded 97 wins against 70 losses. The 1915 race, perhaps the most intriguing in American Association history, came down to the two local rivals, the Millers and the Saints, but Minneapolis captured the crown that year by a mere game and a half. From 1902 to 1920, the Millers posted a win-loss record of 1,516-1,379 for a winning percentage of .524 (a percentage that would match their 59-season record).

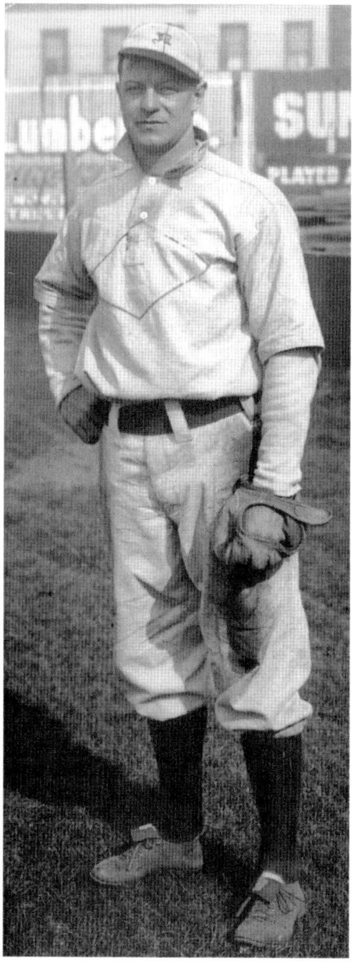

LEE QUILLIN (1902, 1908–1909). Born in North Branch, Minnesota, on May 5, 1882, Leon Abner Quillin was one of the few Minneapolis players with local ties. He originally came to the Millers as a mere lad of 20, batting .217 in 97 games for the 1902 Millers. The Chicago White Sox gave him a look in 1907 when he squeezed out 29 hits in 151 at-bats (.192). In 1908, the versatile Quillin played 70 games as a third baseman and 28 in the outfield, batting .204 with 20 stolen bases. (Courtesy of Hennepin County Library Special Collections.)

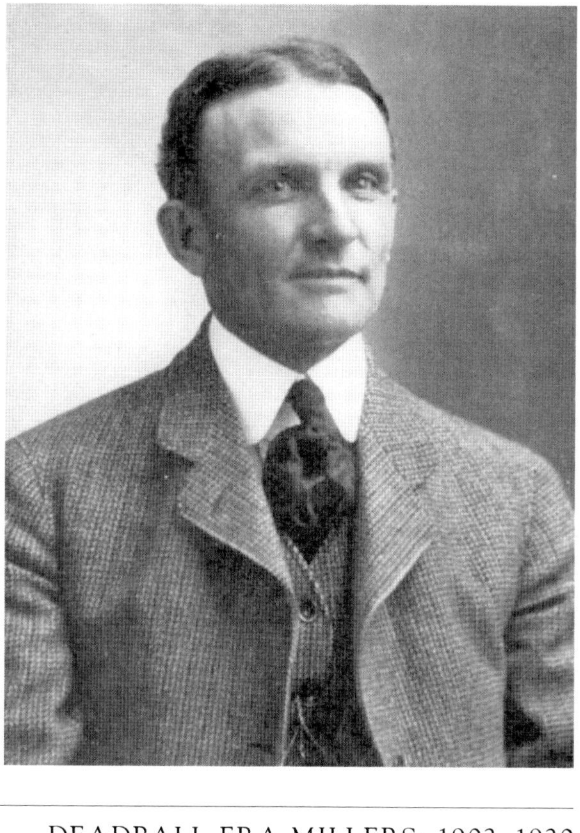

WALT WILMOT (1902–1903). At the age of 38, Wisconsinite Walt Wilmot took the reins of the Minneapolis Millers during their first season in the American Association. Playing right field in addition to his managerial duties in 1902, Wilmot batted .262 with a club-leading 33 doubles while appearing in 135 of the club's 140 games. Wilmot's final resting place is at the Plover Cemetery in central Wisconsin, located about three and a half hours east-southeast of Minneapolis. (*Reach's Official American Association Base Ball Guide* for 1903.)

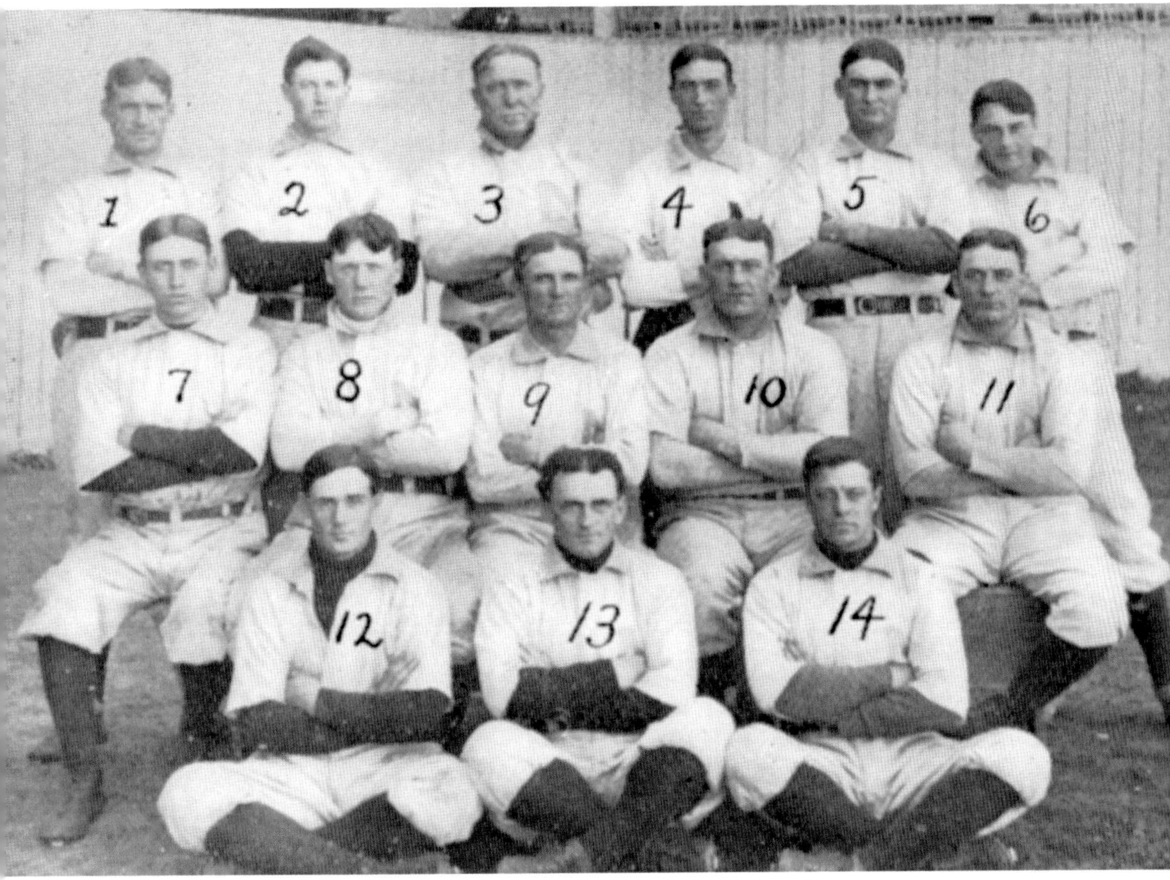

THE 1902 MINNEAPOLIS MILLERS. Pictured from left to right are (first row) Denny Sullivan (center fielder), Angus Grant (second baseman), and Lee Quillin (shortstop); (second row) Walter Mullin (pitcher), Mike Lynch (third baseman), Walt Wilmot (manager/left fielder), Bill Byers (catcher), and George Yeager (catcher); (third row) Dan Lally (left fielder), Otto Newlin (right-handed pitcher), Perry Werden (first baseman), Dave Martin (right-handed pitcher), Cy Torrence (pitcher), and Joseph "Lefty" Sporer (left-handed pitcher). The Millers finished in seventh place with a record of 54-86 under Wilmot in 1902 as the first American Association season got underway. (*Reach's Official American Association Base Ball Guide* for 1903.)

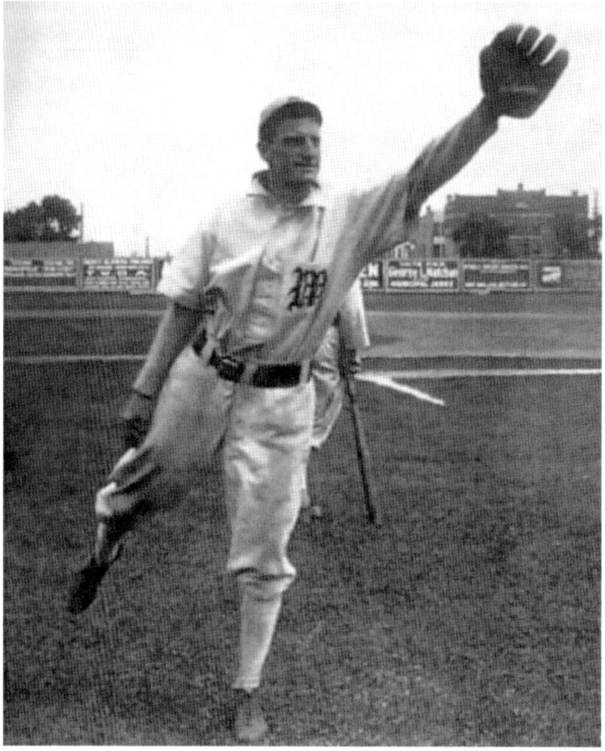

BILL FOX (1904–1906). Fox poses for the camera at Nicollet Park in 1904 in this exceptional vintage photograph. A native of Sturbridge, Massachusetts, the second baseman came to the Millers in his 12th professional season. After tasting big-league play during two abbreviated seasons, Fox became a charter member of the Indianapolis Indians during their first American Association season in 1902. His years in Minneapolis were characterized by strong fielding but weak hitting. His most noteworthy season came in 1904, when he batted .222 with 19 doubles in 149 games. William Henry Fox died at 74 in 1946 and is buried at St. Mary's Cemetery in south Minneapolis. (Author's collection.)

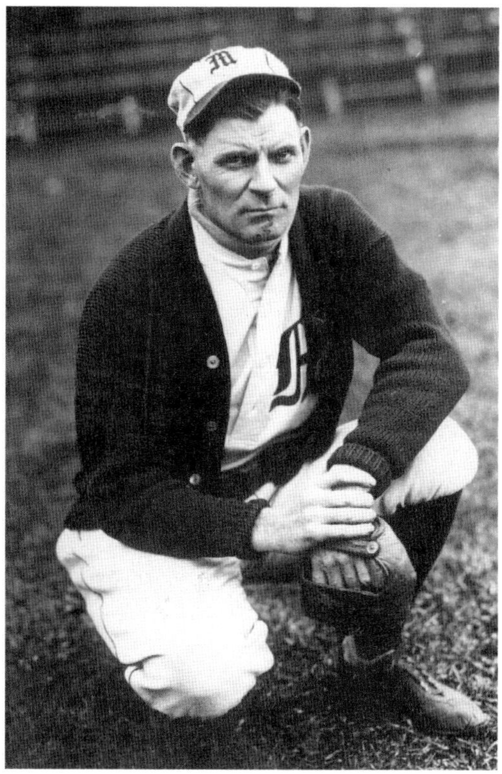

FORREST "FROSTY" THOMAS (1903–1907). As a 22-year-old, Missouri native Thomas lost 20 games in 1903, winning just eight. But the right-hander turned it around the very next year, picking up 21 victories against 15 losses as the Millers surged from a seventh-place finish into the fourth slot, thanks to the work of Thomas and fellow hurlers Gene Ford, Archie "Lumbago" Stimmel, and Cy Morgan. Thomas and Stimmel both struck out 118 men that year. The minor league career of Frosty Thomas was essentially a draw, with 147 wins and 146 losses. (Courtesy of Hennepin County Library Special Collections.)

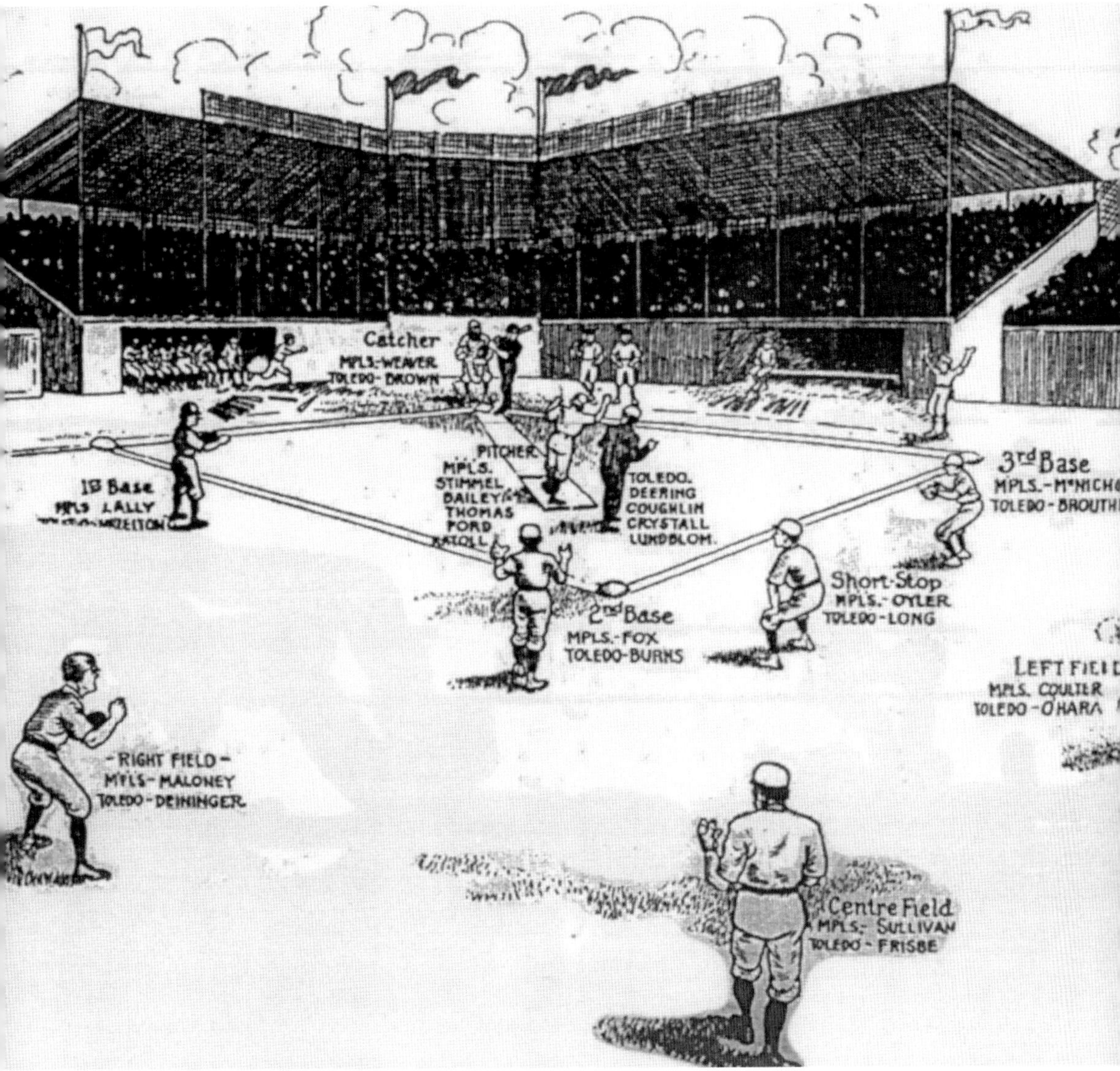

MATCH-UPS: TOLEDO VS. MINNEAPOLIS. The May 6, 1904, edition of the *Minneapolis Tribune* included this detailed representation of Nicollet Park, where the Millers were scheduled to open the season at home in a series against the Toledo Mud Hens. According to the graphic, the following match-ups were in place. Paired off in right field were Billy Maloney, for Minneapolis, and Otto Deininger, for Toledo; in center field, Denny Sullivan and Charlie "Bunt" Frisbe [*sic*; Frisbee]; in right, Art "Cy" Coulter and Bill O'Hara. At first base, Dan "Bud" Lally was paired with Willard Hazleton; at second, Bill Fox with John Burns; at shortstop, Andy Oyler with Herman Long; and at third base, Frank McNichol with Art Brouthers. The scheduled catchers were Art "Buck" Weaver and Sam Brown. The starting pitchers for the afternoon's contest were Archie "Lumbago" Stimmel and Bill Crystall [*sic*; Cristall]. The only change from the depiction was the placement of catcher Charles Reading in place of Brown in the actual lineup that day. Toledo won the affair 4-2. (Author's collection.)

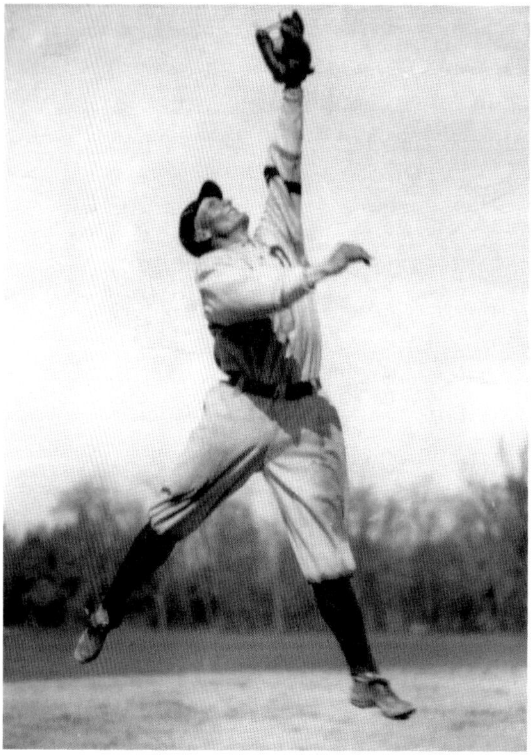

DAVY "KANGAROO" JONES (1905). Active in four major league seasons (nearly 400 games) before joining Minneapolis in 1905, Jones, a Wisconsin native, had his best season with the Chicago Cubs prior to becoming a Miller as an outfielder. Under manager William Watkins, Jones worked wonders with the bat, hitting at a .346 clip with 18 doubles and 210 total bases for the third-place Millers. His club-leading 33 stolen bases underscored his value to the team; he led the league with 126 runs. It was good enough for him to head back to the major leagues the next season, this time to Detroit. (Courtesy of Hennepin County Library Special Collections.)

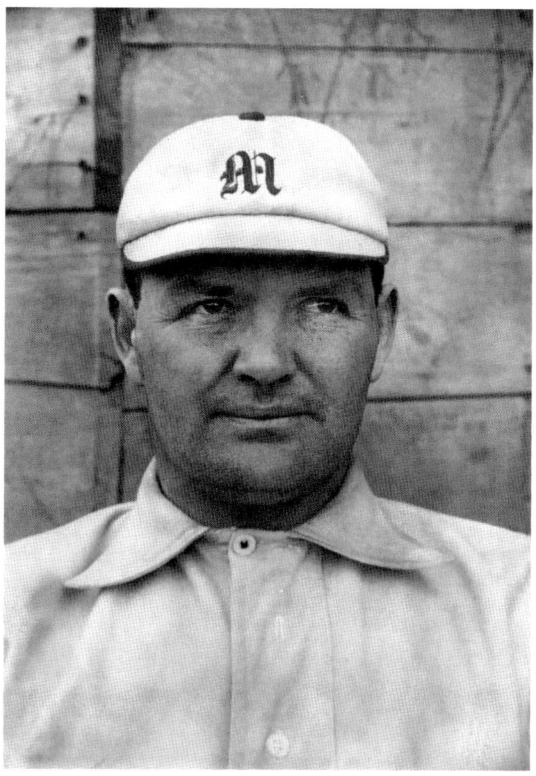

ED "BATTLESHIP" GREMMINGER (1904–1907). Although he appears somewhat distracted in this rare 1905 photograph, Gremminger was anything but since his first season as a Miller in 1904, when he played in 52 games and batted .278. The stocky Canton, Ohio, native had his best year in a Millers uniform at the age of 32 in 1906, when he appeared in 144 games, most of them at third base, hitting .302 with 216 total bases. It was a career year for the former National Leaguer. The Millers finished in third place with a record of 79-66 under Mike Kelley. (Courtesy of Hennepin County Library Special Collections.)

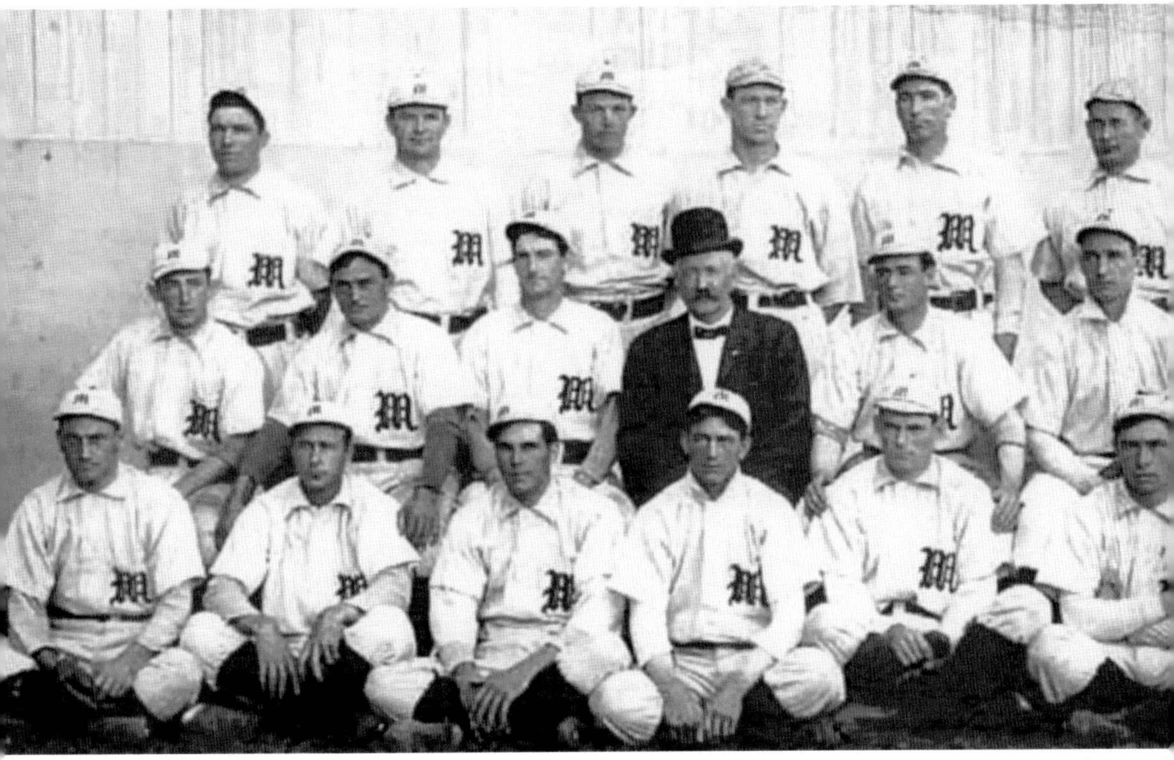

The 1905 Minneapolis Millers. After winding up in seventh place its first two seasons, and landing fourth in 1904, Minneapolis was on the rise. With William H. Watkins in his second year at the helm, the Millers finished third in the race, 11 games behind the Columbus Senators. The identification of this photograph, originally published in the *Minneapolis Tribune*, proved particularly challenging, as it was found that the players were misidentified. From left to right are (first row) Win Kellum (left-handed pitcher), Ed Siever (left-handed pitcher), Gene Ford (right-handed pitcher), Jesse Stovall (right-handed pitcher), Frosty Thomas (right-handed pitcher) and Peaches Graham (outfielder/right-handed pitcher/first baseman/shortstop); (second row) Andy Oyler (shortstop), Boss Schmidt (catcher), Billy Fox (second baseman), William Watkins (manager), Denny Sullivan (outfielder), and Davy Jones (outfielder); (third row) Bill Friel (third baseman/outfielder), Ed Gremminger (third baseman), Jerry Freeman (first baseman), Doc Marshall (catcher), Cy Coulter (outfielder), and Mike Kahoe (catcher). (Author's collection.)

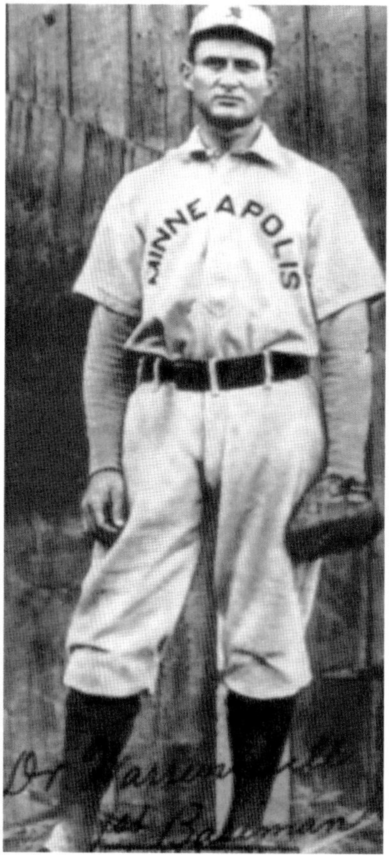

WARREN "DOC" GILL (1909–1912). First baseman Gill spent six minor league seasons in Classes B and C before making the leap to the Class A Millers in 1909 at the age of 30 (the league would alter its classification system in 1912, when the American Association became a Double-A league). While Gill never hit above .263 in his four years under Joe Cantillon, he was a base-stealer extraordinaire, swiping 41 sacks his first year to lead the club. He led the league in steals in 1911 with 55 snatches to his credit, helping the Millers "steal" their second straight league championship. (Courtesy of Hennepin County Library Special Collections.)

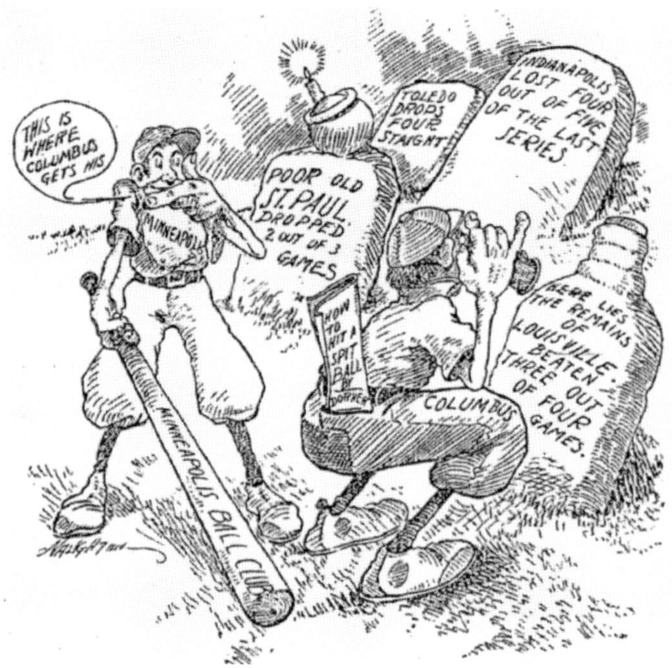

THE NEXT VICTIM. Subtitled "Columbus Making Another Discovery," this symbol-laden comic depicts the Columbus (Ohio) Senators about to receive their comeuppance from Minneapolis. The artwork expresses a darkly humorous viewpoint of the league race as it entered the final weeks of the 1905 season with Columbus on the verge of taking its first of three straight pennants. (*Minneapolis Tribune*, August 29, 1905.)

BILL "TIP" O'NEILL (1907–1910). After performing for the 1906 World Series champion Chicago White Sox under Fielder Jones, in 1907, O'Neill appeared with Minneapolis in 146 of 154 contests, batting .296 with 24 doubles and stealing 39 bases, the league's third-best mark. He suffered from typhoid fever during the off-season of 1909–1910, delaying his appearance with the Millers during his final season in professional ball in 1910, when his contract was picked up by the Louisville Colonels for a portion of the season. In 1920, he died at the age of 40, a victim of tuberculosis. (Author's collection.)

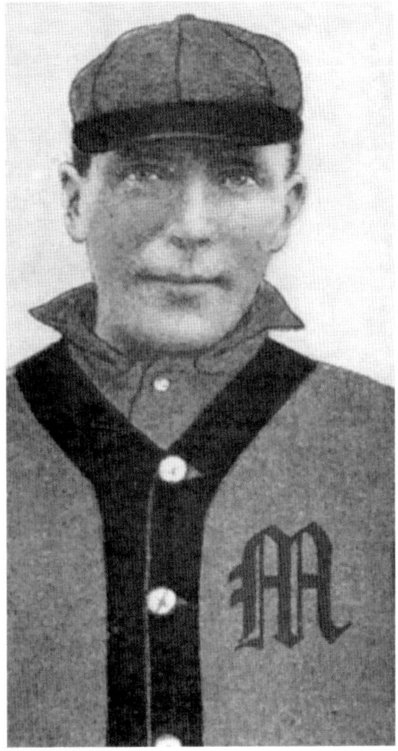

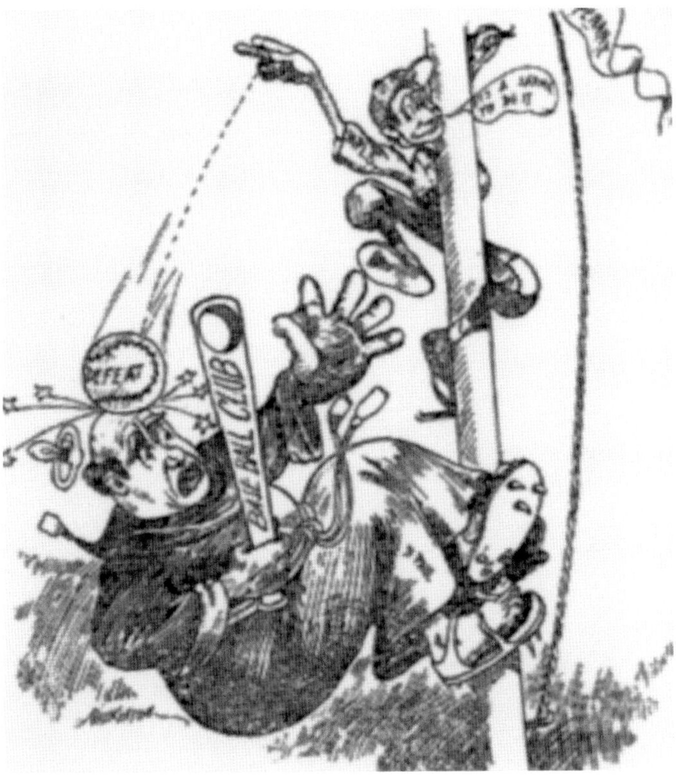

"POOR OLD ST. PAUL." The Twin Cities of Minneapolis and St. Paul were home to one of the most intense and long-lived rivalries in professional sport: the Minneapolis Millers and the St. Paul Saints. As evidenced by this drawing from the pen of artist Naughton, the Millers were getting the upper hand against their eastern neighbor at that point in the 1905 season. (*Minneapolis Tribune*, August 19, 1905.)

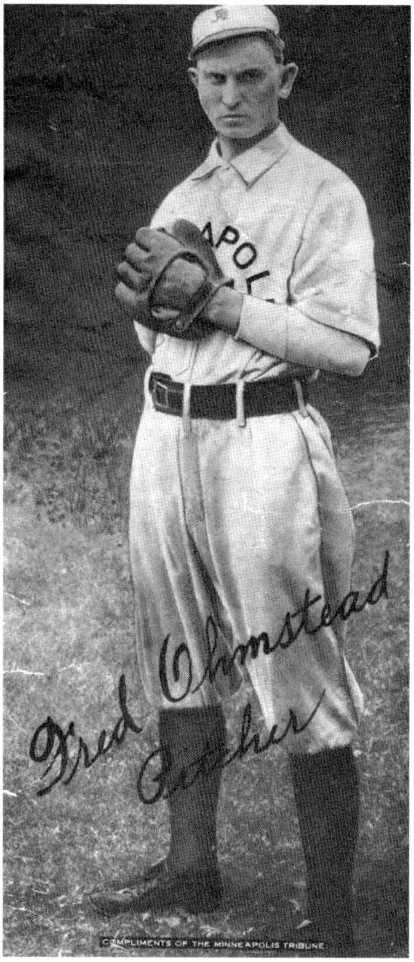

FRED OLMSTEAD (1909, 1912–1913). This photograph of Olmstead was originally featured, along with images of other Millers, as a sort of promotional item in the *Minneapolis Tribune*. In his first season with Minneapolis in 1909, the 27-year-old right-hander helped push the Millers to a second-place finish with his club-best 24 wins against only 12 losses, leading the league with a .667 winning percentage under Jimmy Collins, the team's regular third baseman. The Millers were in the race right up until the season's final week, when the Louisville Colonels pulled away and became the American Association champions. (Author's collection.)

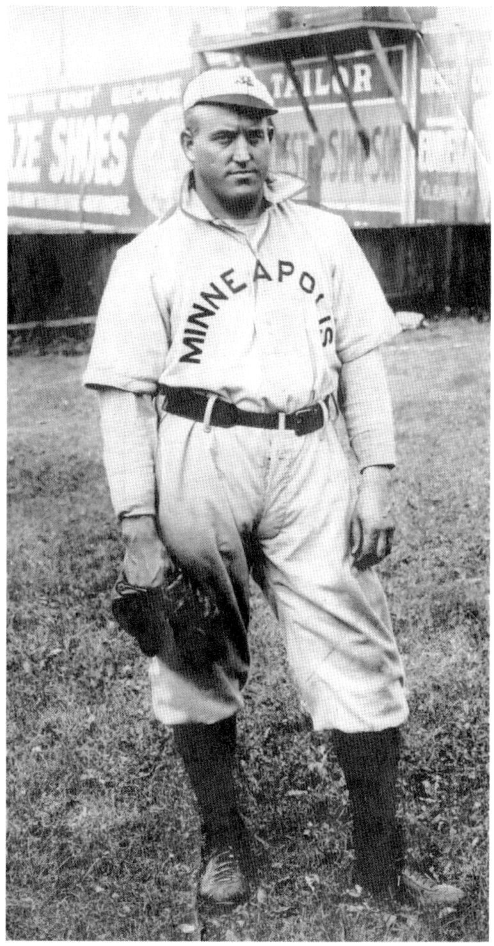

IRVING "YOUNG CY" YOUNG (1909, 1912–1913). The stocky left-hander lit up the local scene for Minneapolis with 23 wins in 1909, but Fred Olmstead's 24 victories led the club that year. That combination brought the Millers to within a week of the pennant, but Louisville captured the flag. The next year, Young was with the Chicago White Sox under Hall of Famer Hugh Duffy, scratching out a 4-8 record. When he returned to Minneapolis, the Maine native appeared in a career-high 51 games, winning 16 against 14 losses. The Millers sent Young to Milwaukee in 1913, where he finished his minor league career. (Courtesy of Hennepin County Library Special Collections.)

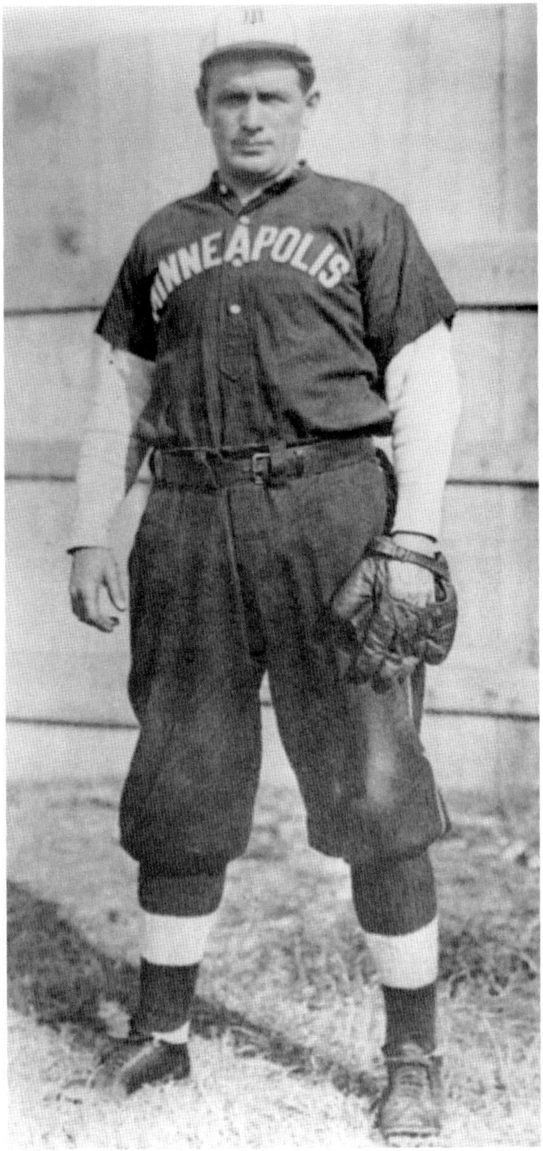

Roy Patterson (1908–1914, 1917–1919). Known for his effective spitball, the "St. Croix Boy Wonder" posted 22 wins against 12 losses, combining with Tom Hughes for a powerful one-two punch in the Millers' rotation to set the course for their first championship season in 1910. After getting his start in professional ball as a member of the St. Paul Apostles/Saints of the Western League in 1899, he spent 10 seasons in a Minneapolis uniform beginning in 1908, amassing 218 decisions with a record of 134-84 (.615). After his first seven seasons with Minneapolis, Patterson pitched and managed in the Class C Northern League before returning to the Millers for abbreviated stints. He is known for throwing the inaugural pitch at the start of the American League in 1901 as a member of the Chicago White Sox. The final resting place of this former great lies within the picturesque grounds of the St. Croix Cemetery near the town of St. Croix Falls, Wisconsin, just an hour's drive northeast of Minneapolis. (Author's collection.)

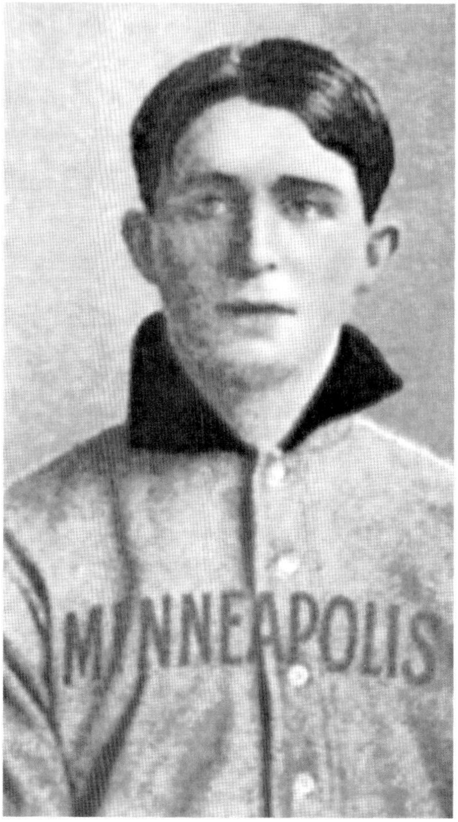

Red Downs (1909). While his fielding average of .924 was worst among league second basemen, Downs made up for his mistakes by hitting 44 doubles and 11 triples, with a .271 batting average to boot, just after playing for the Detroit Tigers. He was later a star of the Pacific Coast League and helped start the Professional Ballplayers of America organization to help baseball's sick and needy former players, eventually acting as its director. The Great Depression took its toll on Downs, and he fell into criminal activity, robbing a jewelry store in Los Angeles in 1932 and serving three and a half years prison time. He died of cirrhosis of the liver in Council Bluffs, Iowa, at the age of 56 in 1939. (Author's collection.)

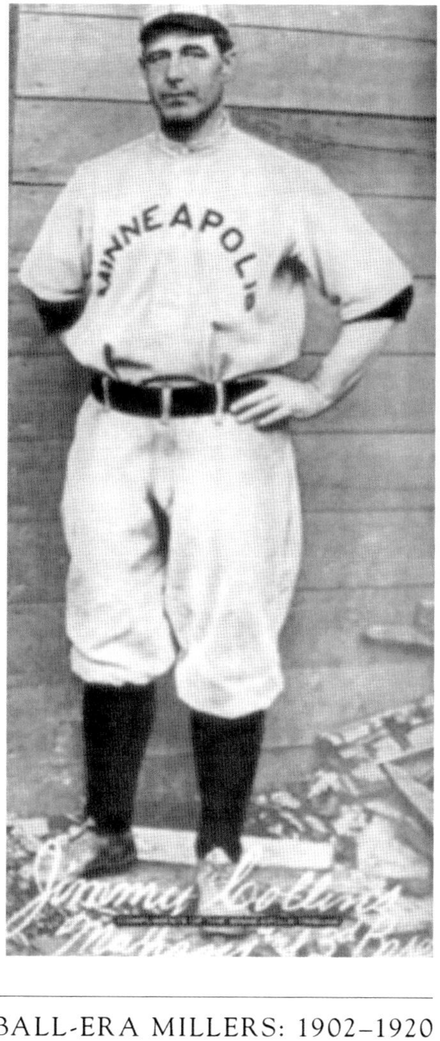

Jimmy Collins (1909). Acting as player-manager for Mike Cantillon's Millers, future Hall of Famer Jimmy Collins fielded what was arguably the Millers' most competitive club to date. Appearing in 153 of their 167 games in 1909, Collins covered the hot corner, batted .273 with 21 doubles, and managed the team to a third-place finish with a record of 88-79, just a few games behind the Louisville Colonels. Collins, 39, whose reputation as a fielder for the Boston Americans preceded him, finished the season with a rather subpar .919 fielding average based on 45 errors in 152 games. The Buffalo, New York, native was "a magician with the glove and a terror with the bat," not to mention a "feared clutch hitter for the Boston clubs," according to the National Baseball Hall of Fame and Museum website. (Author's collection.)

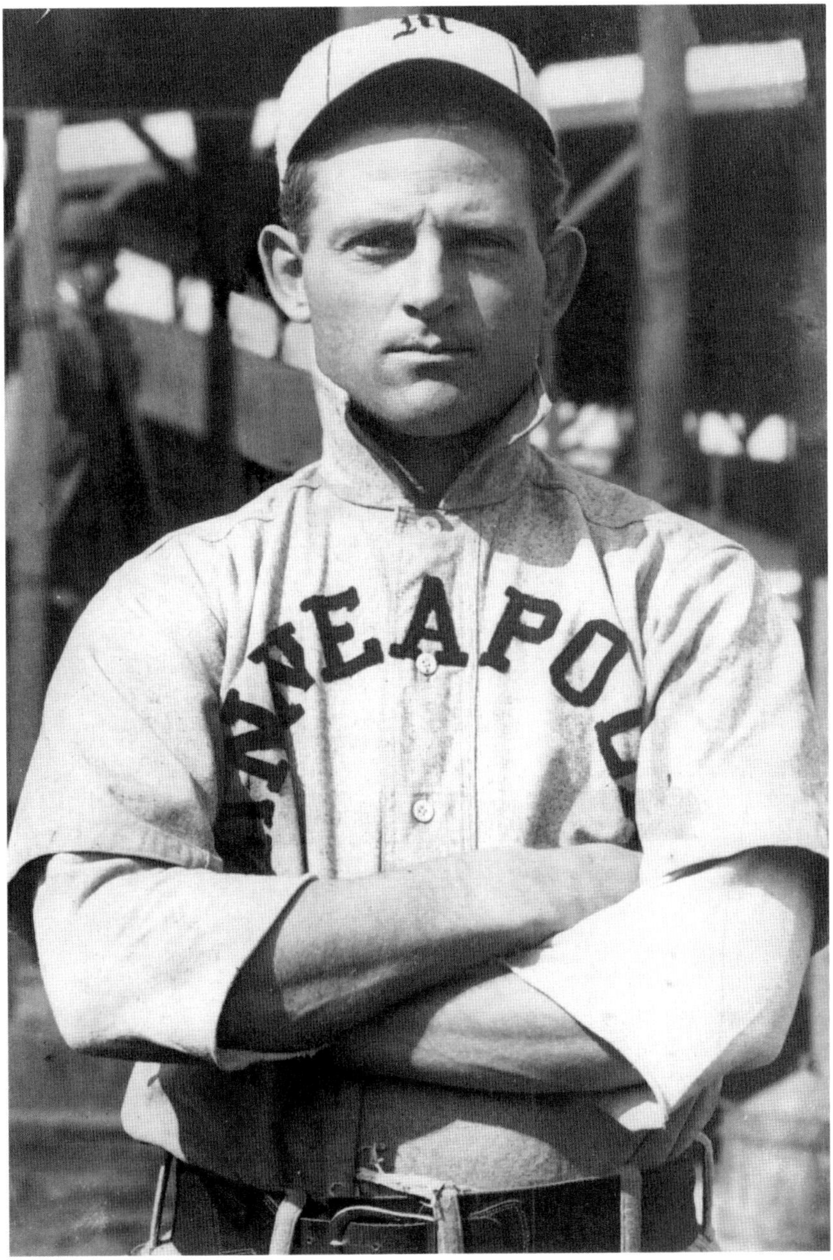

GAVVY "CACTUS" CRAVATH (1909–1911, 1922). The son of a Southern California prune farmer, Cravath came east after banging up the Pacific Coast League and strutted his stuff for three years in a Millers uniform. His quintessential claim to fame was establishing the new American Association home run record in 1911, swatting 29 long balls and demolishing the old record (set by Buck Freeman of the Millers with 18 in 1907), while batting .363 with 53 doubles. He became a member of the big leagues with the Philadelphia Phillies in 1912, remaining there through the 1920 season. When he returned to the Millers after over a decade, he had lost a step or two but still thrilled crowds with his bat. (Courtesy of Hennepin County Library Special Collections.)

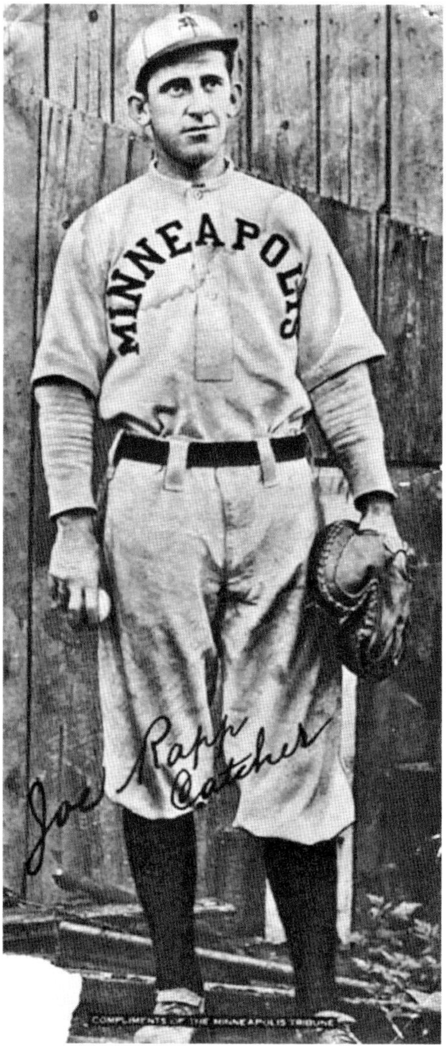

Joe Rapp (1909). Like the Olmstead photograph, this early rotogravure image was originally featured as a promotional item in the *Minneapolis Tribune*, perhaps for clipping by scrapbook dedicatees. These images appeared in the Sunday paper in order to help acquaint fans with the players. While Rapp appeared in only 28 games in Miller garb, he had the good fortune of being one of the featured players in 1909. However, he also had the misfortune of being the backup backstop to John "Bruno" Block, an iron man behind the plate who appeared in all but a handful of games (146), leaving Rapp little playing time. (Courtesy of Hennepin County Library Special Collections.)

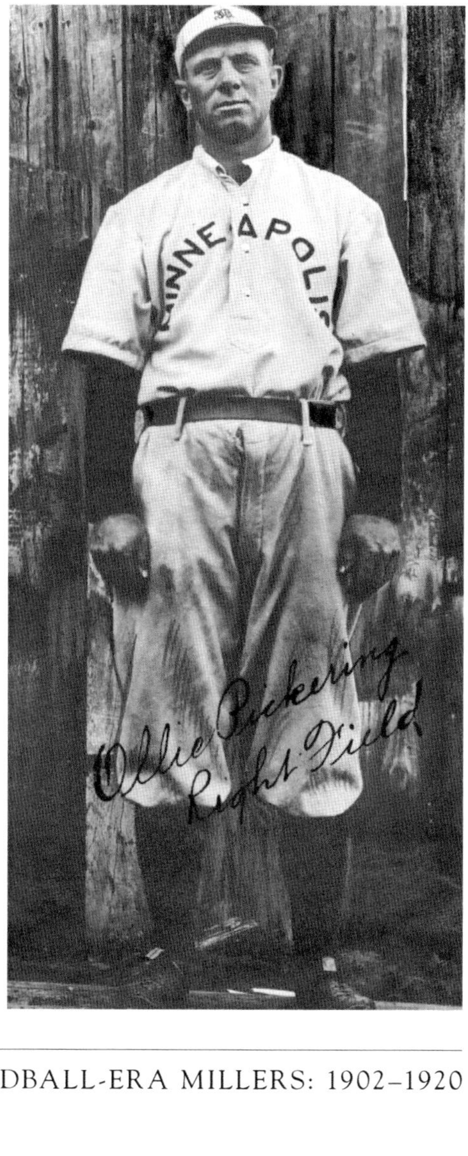

Ollie Pickering (1909–1910). After completing eight years of service in the major leagues with a variety of teams, Pickering came to Minneapolis in 1909 at the age of 40, appearing in 70 games and batting a modest .213, a mark below his major league career mark of .271. The right fielder was traded to Louisville in July 1910 for former Miller Bill "Tip" O'Neill. (Courtesy of Hennepin County Library Special Collections.)

Dave "Filipino" Altizer (1910–1918). After a cup of coffee with the Toledo Mud Hens in 1903, "Daredevil Dave" Altizer perfected his game at the major league level with the Washington Senators. He returned to the Association with Minneapolis in 1910, batting an even .300 with a league-leading 65 stolen bases. During his nine-year tenure with the Millers, Altizer batted .305 with 299 stolen sacks. The Illinois native's participation in the Spanish-American War and military record overseas must have helped mold him into the superb athlete he became on the baseball field. (Author's collection.)

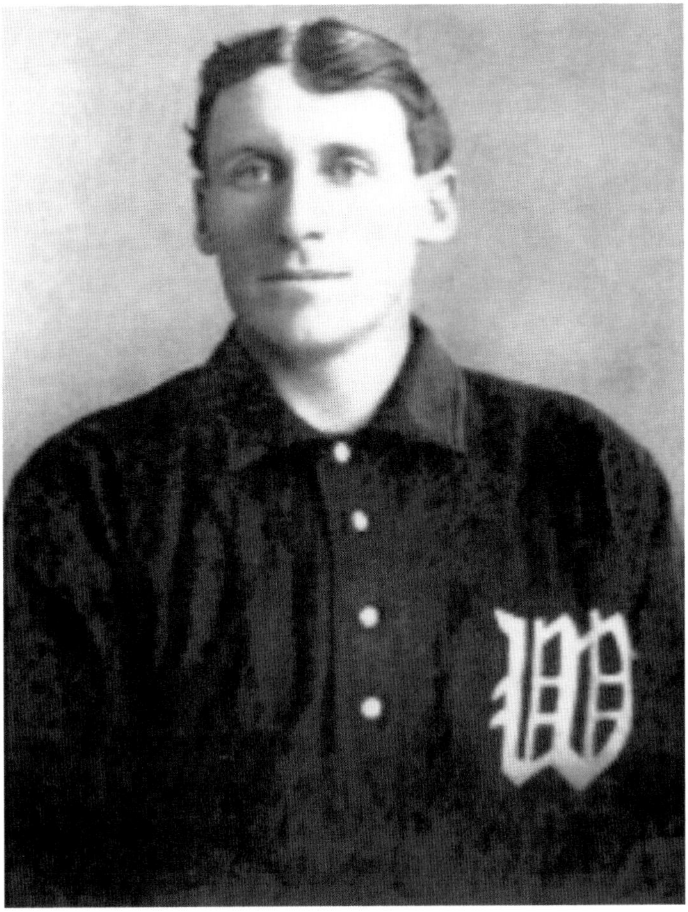

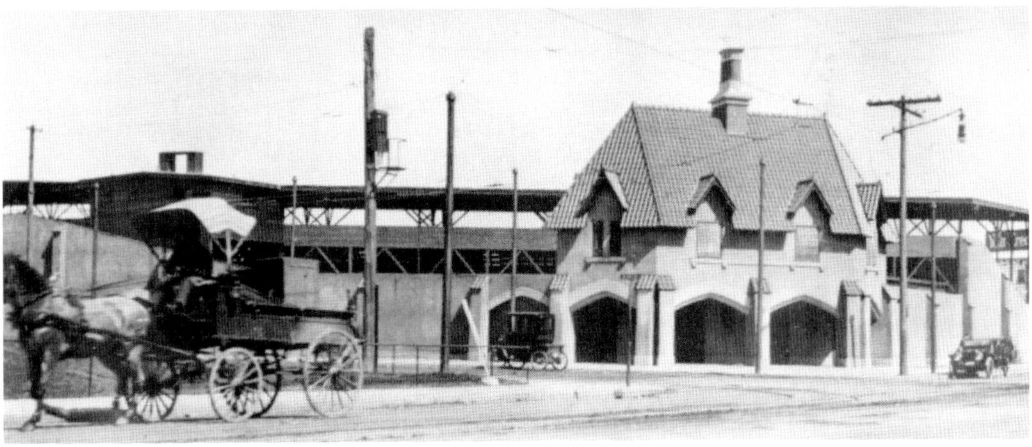

Nicollet Park, 1912. Modes of transportation around the city of Minneapolis contrasted sharply during the first season after a Nicollet Park renovation. The distinctive ticket office, adorned with its clay-tile roof, elegant dormers, and gracious Tudor styling, was a recognizable fixture at Nicollet through the 1955 season. In later years, it sported colorful signage to draw patrons toward the park. (Author's collection.)

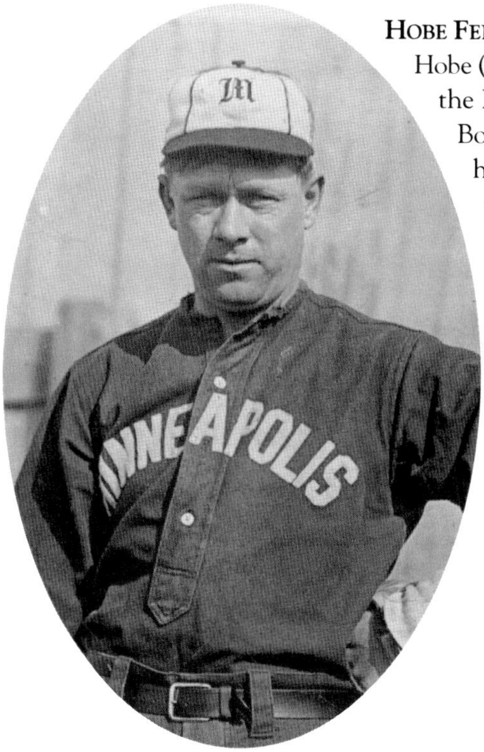

HOBE FERRIS (1910–1912). Known locally as "the Billiken," Hobe (pronounced "HO-bee") Ferris was a central figure in the Millers' three-year championship run (1910–1912). Born Albert Samuel Ferris in Great Britain in 1874, he was a longtime Boston Red Sox second baseman prior to his arrival in Minneapolis. In his first year as a Miller, Ferris played third base in 125 games, having converted to that position with the St. Louis Browns two years before. In 1911, Ferris had his best season as a professional ballplayer, batting .303 with 14 home runs and 34 doubles (fourth-ranked on the club) and tying with outfielder Claude Rossman with 273 total bases (fourth-ranked on the club). (Courtesy of Hennepin County Library Special Collections.)

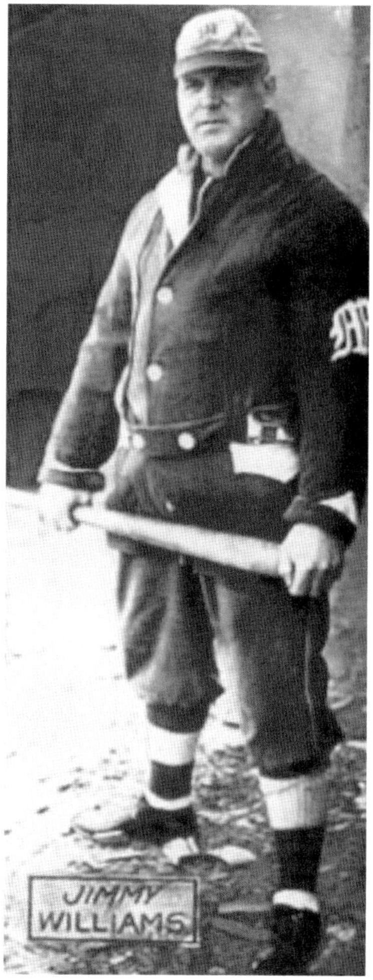

JIMMY WILLIAMS (1910–1915). Williams provided steady work at the keystone sack during his lengthy stay with Minneapolis. An 11-year career in the major leagues was behind him when he became a fixture in the Miller infield. During his first season under Joe Cantillon, Williams, 33, appeared in 148 games at second base, batting .315 with 37 doubles as Minneapolis captured its first American Association championship. The next year, he took his swinging supremacy a step further by hitting 43 doubles, six triples, and seven home runs while producing a .332 batting average over the course of 162 games. (Courtesy of Hennepin County Library Special Collections.)

Joe Cantillon (1910–1923). Born in Janesville, Wisconsin, in 1861, Cantillon played his first season of professional ball at the age of 24. In 1890, he went west to play in the California League and remained a fixture there for the next few years; it was there that his moniker "Pongo" came about. His first American Association season came with Milwaukee in 1903, when he managed the Brewers to a 77-60 third-place finish. Cantillon was hired by his brother Mike to manage the Minneapolis Millers, a post he held from 1910 until the end of the 1923 season, amassing 1,108 wins against 935 losses. (Courtesy of Hennepin County Library Special Collections.)

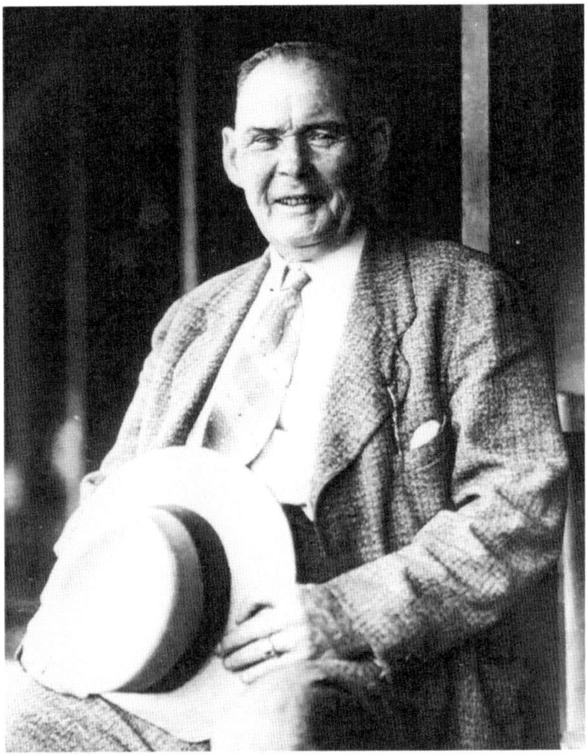

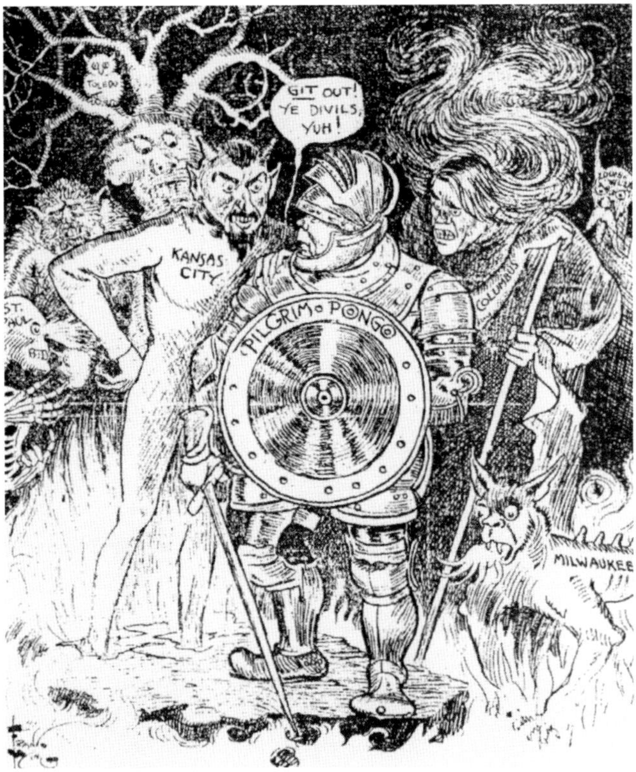

Pilgrim Pongo and the Night Terrors. Enough to spook any reader, this intricate caricature of the various league members confronting Millers manager "Pongo Joe" Cantillon during the 1911 league race seems more suited to a Halloween edition of the newspaper, but the season was in full swing when it appeared in the *Minneapolis Journal* on August 2, 1911. The grammatically skewed caption accompanying this drawing reads, "Pilgrim Pongo and his cohorts in the invasion in which is depicted the terrors confronting which starts westward tonight." (Author's collection.)

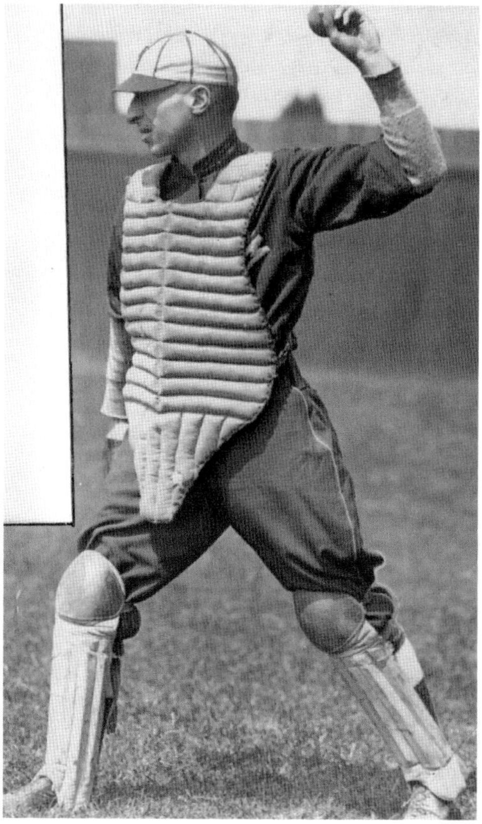

WIB SMITH (1910–1914). Wilbur Floyd Smith began his professional career as a catcher at the age of 19 in 1906, coming to Minneapolis in 1910. Valued primarily for his skills as a backup catcher, Smith appeared in a combined 357 games for the Millers. During the club's 1912 pennant drive, Smith appeared in 80 contests, batting a career-high .288. As the club's primary catcher in 1914, he swatted 14 doubles in 109 games. Smith, a Michigan native, is buried at the famous Lakewood Cemetery in Minneapolis. (Courtesy of Hennepin County Library Special Collections.)

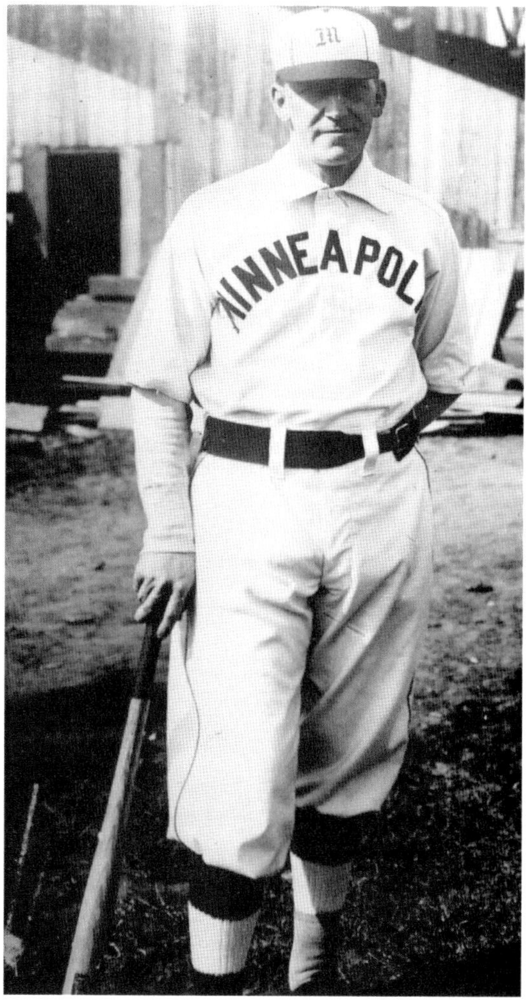

OTIS "GRUMP" CLYMER (1909–1915). Only after he turned 38 did the Pennsylvania speed merchant finally begin to slow down, and he was consequently let go early in the 1915 season. But had it not been for his ability to get on base with supreme consistency out of the leadoff position, the Minneapolis championship machine would have been missing a vital valve. From 1910 to 1912, a time frame corresponding with the club's three consecutive championships, Clymer stole 150 bases. Clymer was killed when he drove his automobile off the Seventh Street viaduct in St. Paul, Minnesota, the night of February 27, 1926, one month after his 50th birthday. (Author's collection.)

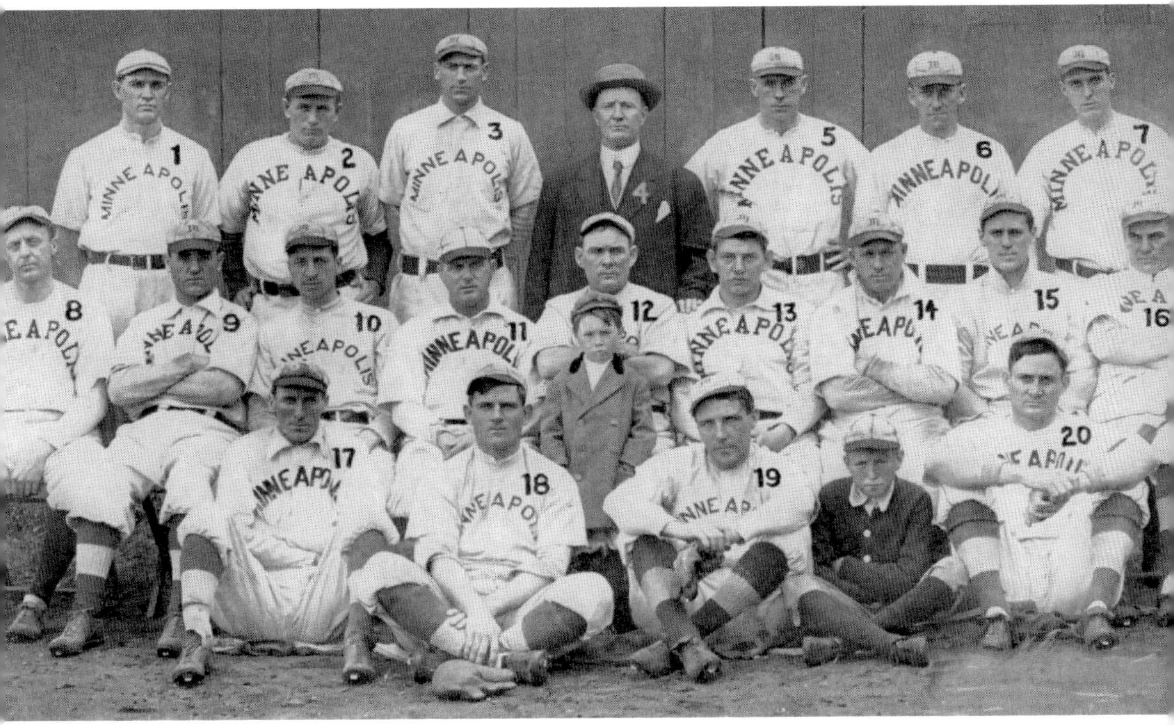

The 1910 American Association Champion Minneapolis Millers. The children in this photograph are unidentified; the men are, from left to right, (first row) Dave Altizer (shortstop), Gavvy Cravath (outfielder), Tip O'Neill (outfielder), and Doc Gill (first baseman); (second row) Lou Fiene (right-handed pitcher), Barry McCormick (second baseman), Wib Smith (catcher), Jimmy Williams (second baseman), "Pongo Joe" Cantillon (manager), Nick Altrock (left-handed pitcher), Hobe Ferris (third baseman), Frank "Yip" Owens (catcher), and Claude Rossman (outfielder); (third row) Leo Sage (right-handed pitcher), Roy Patterson (right-handed pitcher), Hub Dawson (catcher), Mike Cantillon (owner), Tom Hughes (right-handed pitcher), Otis Clymer (outfielder), and Bill Lelivelt (right-handed pitcher). The Millers won their first league championship in 1910, posting an all-time club record of 107-61, the most wins by a league contestant to date. (*Reach's Official American League Base Ball Guide* for 1911.)

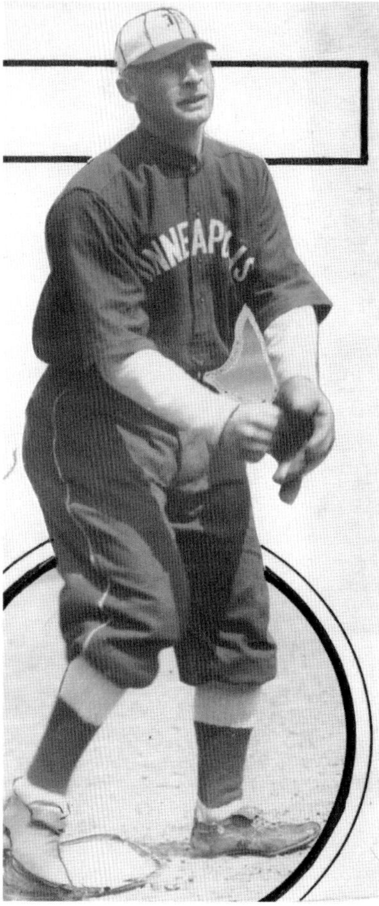

LEE TANNEHILL (1913–1914). The younger brother of former National League pitching ace and former Minneapolis pitcher Jesse Tannehill, Lee Tannehill came to Minneapolis to play third base after 10 straight seasons with the Chicago White Sox. After splitting the 1913 season between the Millers and the Kansas City Blues, the 33-year-old finished the 1914 campaign covering the hot corner in all 170 games the Millers played, sharing the league lead for games played with teammate Dave Altizer, who played all 170 games at shortstop. (Courtesy of Hennepin County Library Special Collections.)

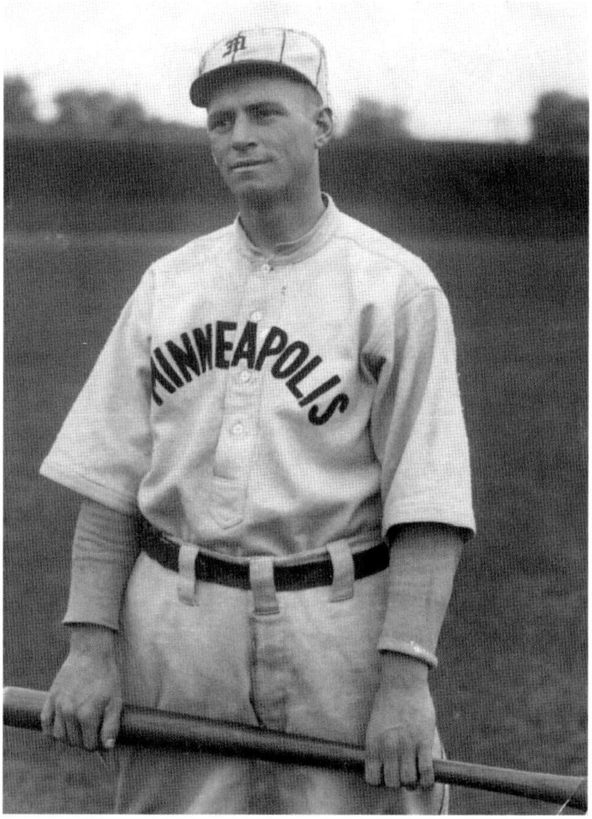

HENRI RONDEAU (1913–1924). The lefty-batting, righty-throwing pride of Danielson, Connecticut, carries the all-time record for most seasons played as a Miller. Beginning at the age of 25, just after a brief major league debut, Rondeau became a Miller outfielder. By the time his tenure at Minneapolis was through, Rondeau had an impressive record: a .295 batting average, 259 doubles, 108 stolen bases, and even one life saved. On July 4, 1922, near his home in Minneapolis, he rescued a young girl whose clothing was ablaze from a fireworks accident. (Courtesy of Hennepin County Library Special Collections.)

IRA HOGUE (1914–1915). Kentucky native Hogue's one full season with the Millers came in 1914, his first year at the Double-A level. He appeared in 48 games with Minneapolis, winning 12 and losing 17. This photograph was likely taken at the farm of manager Joe Cantillon, near Hickman, Kentucky, where preliminary spring-training exercises were conducted at the time. (Courtesy of Hennepin County Library Special Collections.)

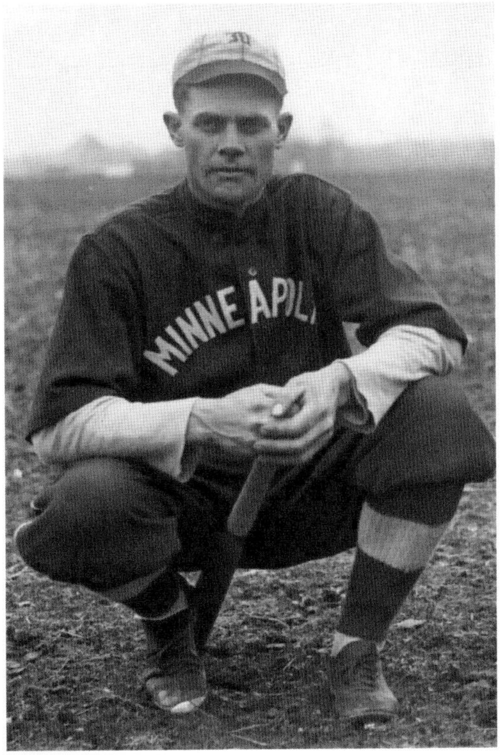

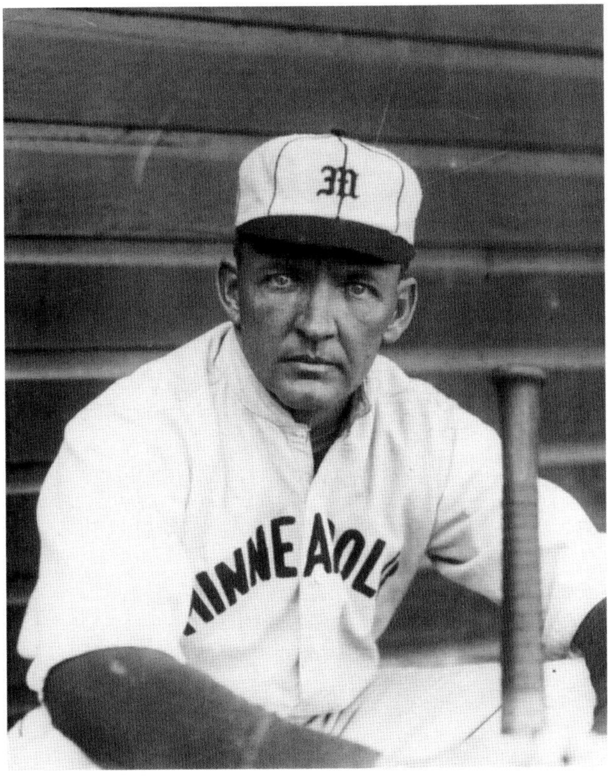

BILLY SULLIVAN SR. (1915). A 16-year major league career catching, including 12 straight seasons with the Chicago White Sox, was not enough to discourage Billy Sullivan Sr. from playing one more professional season. The Wisconsin native coupled with the Minneapolis Millers for the honor of his final season in professional ball. The five-foot, nine-inch, 155-pound backstop was an influential contributor to the Millers' pennant drive as Minneapolis captured its fourth flag in six years. Batting a relatively low .215, the 40-year-old maintained plenty of his former iron man status, catching in 104 games. He was behind the plate during Harry Harper's no-hitter in May 1915. (Courtesy of Hennepin County Library Special Collections.)

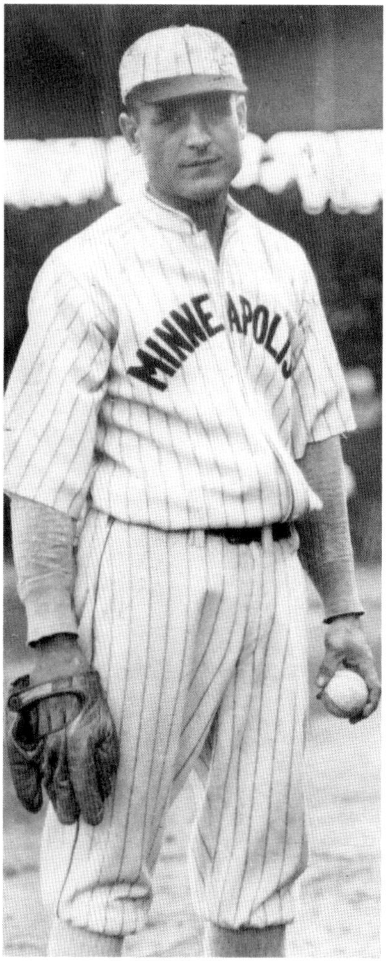

Earl "Chink" Yingling (1915–1916, 1921–1923). Yingling's two exceptional seasons with the Toledo Mud Hens (1910–1911), during which he won 40 games, put the stamp of success on his early career path. With Minneapolis, the southpaw contributed to the Millers' championship season. With a record of 19-17, the native of Chillicothe, Ohio, led the league with a 2.17 ERA in nearly 300 innings of work. A strong hitter as far as pitchers go, Yingling was a valuable asset that year, but his stock was improving. In 1916, he won 24 games, losing 13 as the Millers finished third under Joe Cantillon. (Courtesy of Hennepin County Library Special Collections.)

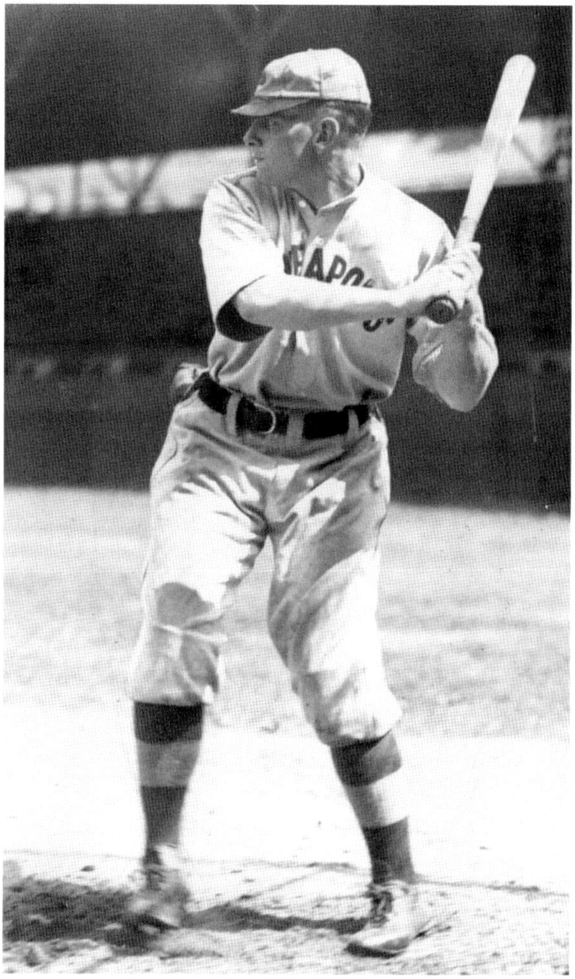

Jack Bentley (1915–1916). Bentley, a Maryland-born lefty, made his Miller debut at age 20, pitching in 36 games and compiling a 7-4 record his first year, 8-6 the next. He then had several successful seasons with the Baltimore Orioles of the International League—after his conversion to first base. In 1921, he batted an astounding .421 in 141 games for the Orioles. Bentley returned to the major leagues as a pitcher in 1923 for the New York Giants, appearing in 52 games, posting a record of 13-8, and batting .427! (Courtesy of Hennepin County Library Special Collections.)

HARRY HARPER (1915) NO-HITS SAINTS. A young—and very wild—right-handed pitcher, Harry Clayton Harper, was responsible for throwing the only no-hitter to take place between the Minneapolis Millers and St. Paul Saints in their six-decade rivalry. This box score provides a summary of events from the May 19, 1915, game, in which the Millers defeated their downriver neighbor 4-0. An exceptional leaping catch by shortstop Morley Jennings in the second frame robbed Saints first baseman Lee Dressen of a hit. At the age of 20, Harper, from Hackensack, New Jersey, was in his first and final season in the minors. (Author's collection.)

SAINTLY CIPHERS

Minneapolis.

	AB.	R.	H.	PO.	A.	E.
Massey, cf	3	0	0	1	0	0
Jennings, ss	4	0	0	5	2	0
Altizer, rf	4	1	1	1	0	0
Cashion, 1b	3	1	0	6	1	0
Rondeau, lf	4	1	2	1	1	0
Williams, 2b	2	1	0	2	1	0
Smith, 3b	3	0	0	0	1	0
Sullivan, c	3	0	1	11	4	0
Harper, p	3	0	1	0	2	0
Totals	29	4	5	27	12	0

St. Paul.

	AB.	R.	H.	PO.	A.	E.
Niles, 2b	1	0	0	2	4	1
Martin, ss	4	0	0	1	4	1
Riggert, cf	4	0	0	4	0	0
Cruise, lf	3	0	0	2	0	0
xKarger	0	0	0	0	0	0
Dressen, 1b	2	0	0	12	1	0
Miller, rf	3	0	0	0	0	0
Johnson, c	3	0	0	3	0	0
Dyer, 3b	3	0	0	0	3	1
Liefield, p	1	0	0	0	5	1
Totals	24	0	0	24	17	4

x—Karger batted for Cruise in ninth.

Minneapolis	0	0	0	1	0	3	0	0	x	—4
St. Paul	0	0	0	0	0	0	0	0	0	—0

Sacrifice hit—Cashion. Double play—Martin to Niles to Dressen. Left on bases—Minneapolis, 5; St. Paul, 6. First base on errors—Minneapolis, 4. Earned runs—Minneapolis, 3. Bases on balls—Off Harper, 7; off Leifield, 3. Struck out—By Harper, 12; by Leifield, 3. Hit by pitched ball—By Harper—Niles and Karger. Balk—Harper. Time of game—1:40. Umpires—Owens and Knapp.

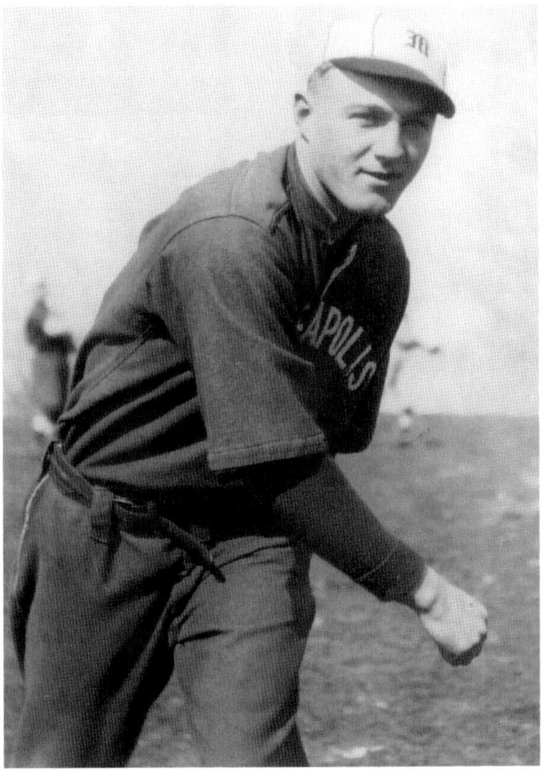

JOE ENGEL (1915). Engel, a 22-year-old southpaw from Chattanooga, Tennessee, came to Minneapolis after three seasons with the Washington Senators. In his lone season with the Millers, he was 5-3 in 15 games. Engel was lucky to have a winning record, posting a 6.47 ERA. After a subpar season in 1914, the Millers won their fourth American Association championship, nosing out their archrival St. Paul Saints by just a game and a half in one of the league's most heated finishes. (Courtesy of Hennepin County Library Special Collections.)

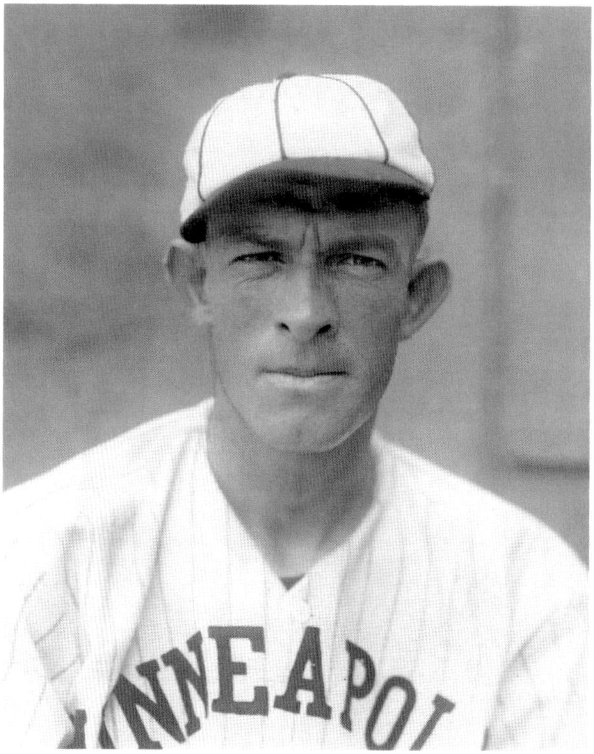

Mutt Williams (1915–1919). Shown here in a 1917 photograph, the 22-year-old opened a few eyes around the league with his amazing 29-win season in 1915 for Joe Cantillon's league champions. Born David (possibly Davis) Carter Williams on July 31, 1892, the six-foot, three-inch, 195-pound Arkansan gave the Millers the ticket they needed to make a late push against the St. Paul Saints that year. He earned his trophy record of 29-14 the hard way, appearing in 64 games and putting in a near-record 441 innings. (Courtesy of Hennepin County Library Special Collections.)

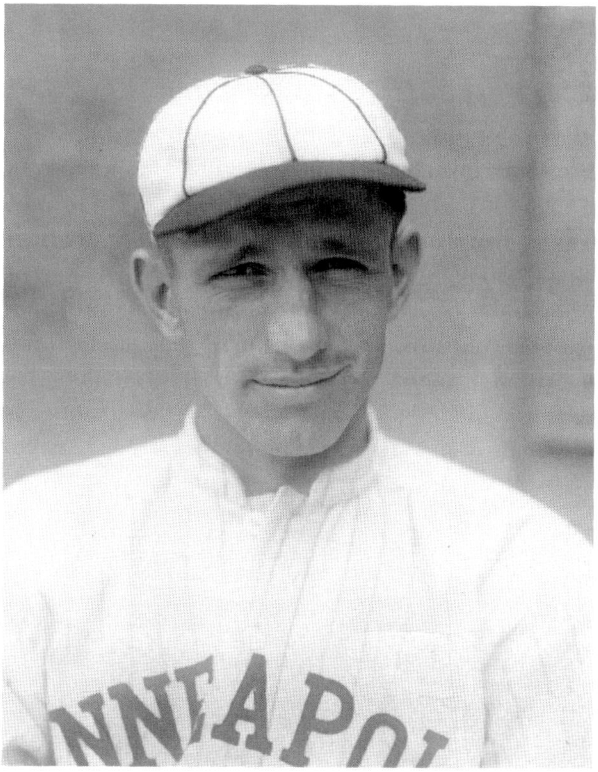

Morley Jennings (1915–1922). Born January 23, 1890, in Holland, Michigan, Jennings never played below Class A during his nine-year baseball career (he spent eight years with Minneapolis). With exactly 3,200 at-bats in 874 games in a Millers uniform, the shortstop averaged .278 at the plate, with 888 hits. His most productive season came at the age of 26 in 1916, with 203 total bases and a .286 batting average. He hit .307 in his first year as a Miller, appearing in 127 games with 24 doubles. Jennings was inducted into the College Football Hall of Fame as a coach in 1973. (Courtesy of Hennepin County Library Special Collections.)

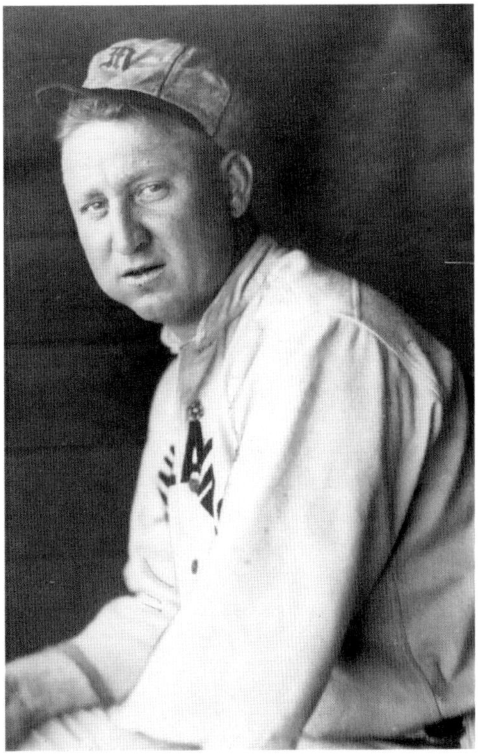

Grover Land (1916). The Kentucky-born catcher began his professional career in 1904 at the age of 19 before starting an 11-year career (1905–1917) in the American Association. Appearing in 774 Association games, Land hit .235, with just one home run. Hitting 83 doubles, 14 triples, and 66 stolen bases, the six-foot, 190-pound catcher was a bit of a speedster. Splitting the 1916 season between the St. Paul Saints and the Millers, Land appeared in 96 games, batting .259, his career best matching his average from 1906. In seven years of major league duty, Land batted .243. (Courtesy of Hennepin County Library Special Collections.)

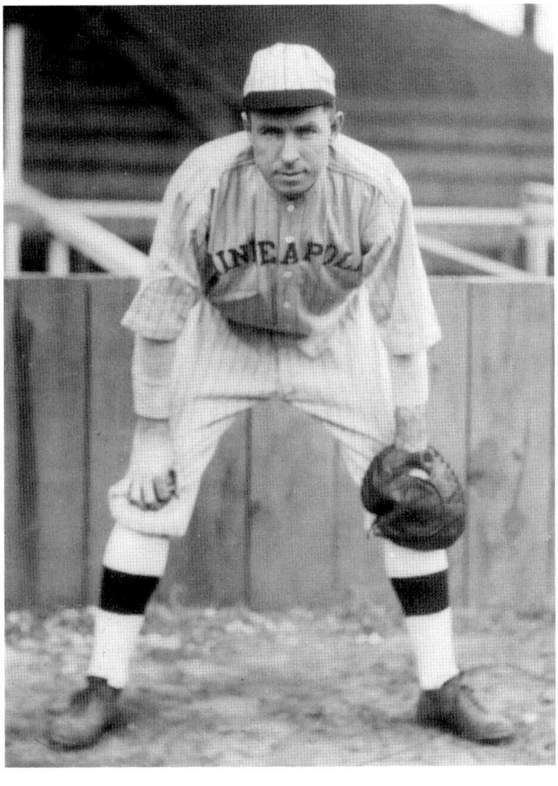

Wally Smith (1915–1916, 1918, 1920–1921). During his initial season as a Miller, 27-year-old Philadelphia native Smith covered third base in all 154 games for the league champions, batting .315 and leading the club with 31 doubles under Joe Cantillon. In 1920, he converted to first base and batted .287 with 27 doubles. Smith was just 42 when he died of tuberculosis in Florence, Arizona. (Courtesy of Hennepin County Library Special Collections.)

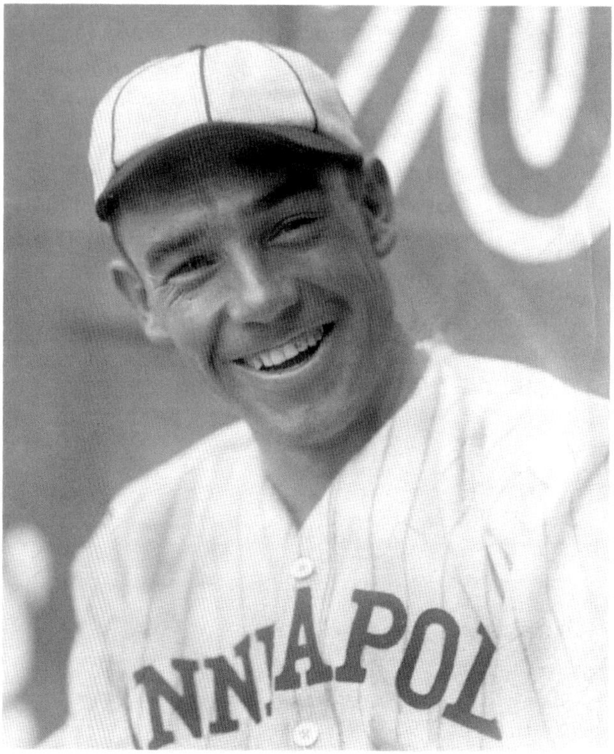

Carl "Huck" Sawyer (1917–1920). Sawyer, a native of Seattle, came to Minneapolis in 1917 at the age of 26, playing the entire season at second base and batting .244 with 27 doubles. He would entertain patrons before games with his comedic antics and agility as an acrobat. In his final season with the Millers, Sawyer approached the club's single-season record for doubles with 50, three short of Gavvy Cravath's 1911 mark; he is one of only six players to hit 50 or more doubles in a season. Sawyer batted .282 and covered second base that year. (Courtesy of Hennepin County Library Special Collections.)

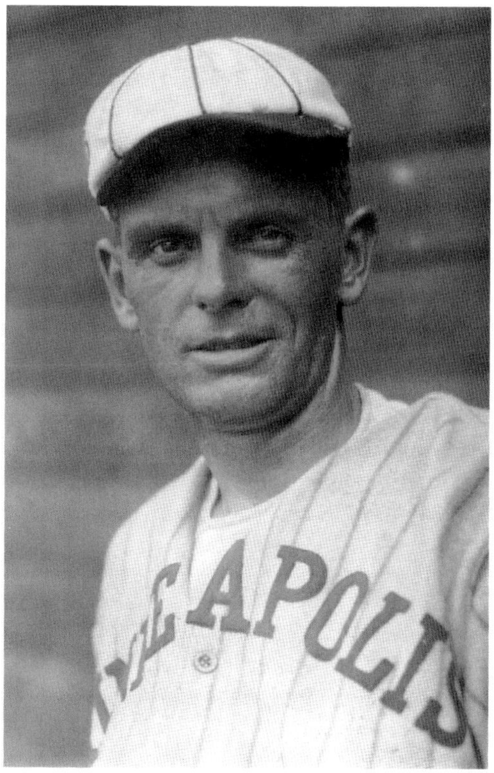

Sandy Burk (1916–1917, 1919). After a very brief season with the Federal League's Pittsburgh Rebels in 1915, the 29-year-old pitcher from Columbus, Ohio, posted a record of 21-16 for the third-place Millers, with a club-high 333 innings of work (ranked second in the league). His mound mate Earl Yingling led the league with 24 wins and was the next man in line with 323 innings toiled. Burk served his country during World War I in 1918 before returning to the Millers for a short stint in 1919. It was at that time that the former soldier became known locally as "Sergeant Burk." (Courtesy of Hennepin County Library Special Collections.)

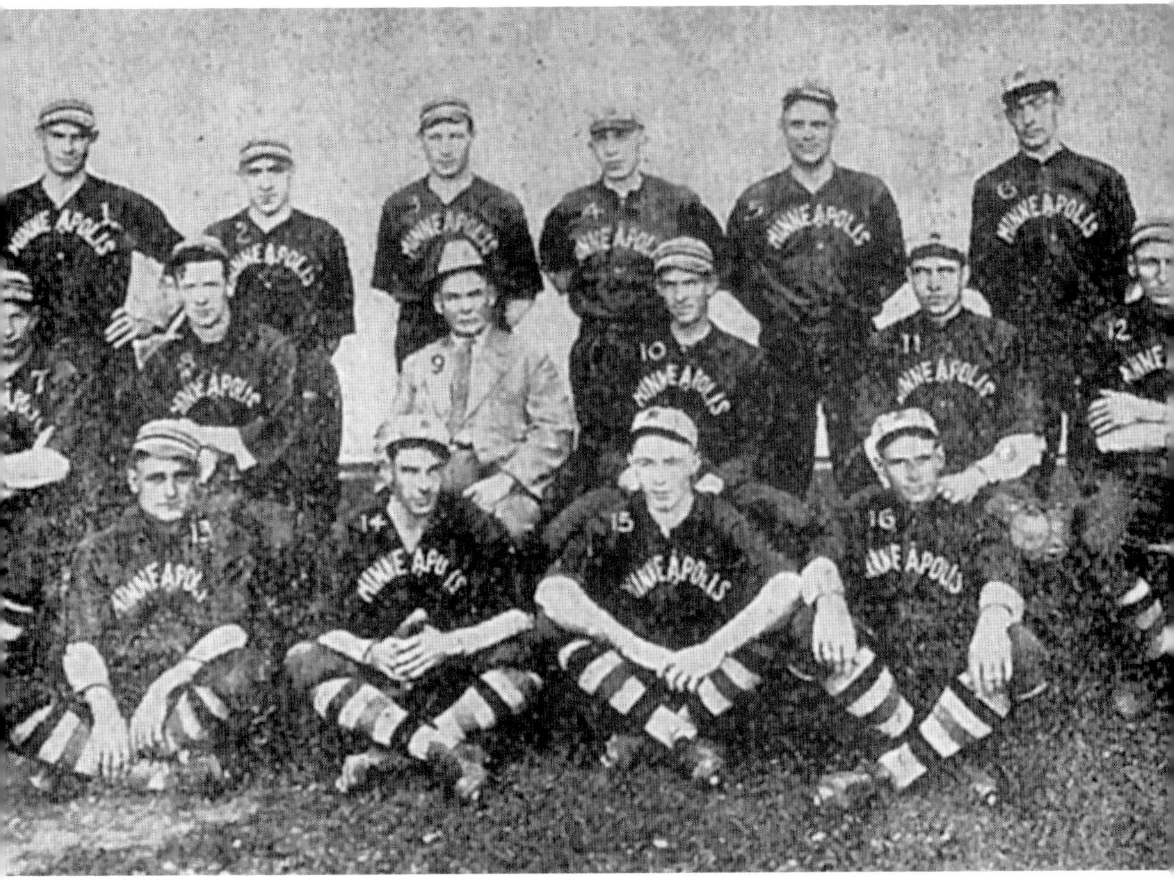

THE 1917 MINNEAPOLIS MILLERS. After winning three straight championships from 1910 to 1912, the Millers continued to battle but could not ascend the league ladder as they had at the start of the decade. Minneapolis landed in sixth place with a record of 68-86, still under the tutelage of "Pongo Joe" Cantillon. Apparently, flashing those jailbird socks did little to distract the opposition that year. Pictured from left to right are (first row) Earl Yingling (left-handed pitcher), Carl Sawyer (second baseman), Sam Crane (third baseman/shortstop), and Henri Rondeau (left fielder); (second row) Red Massey (center fielder), Jack Knight (first baseman/third baseman), Joe Cantillon (manager), Mutt Williams (right-handed pitcher), Clarence Tiffany (pitcher), and Dave Altizer (third baseman/right fielder); (third row) Charlie Boardman (right-handed pitcher), Lou Bachant (catcher), Jeff Thieman (pitcher), Les Stevenson (pitcher), Yip Owens (catcher), and Claude Thomas (left-handed pitcher). (Author's collection.)

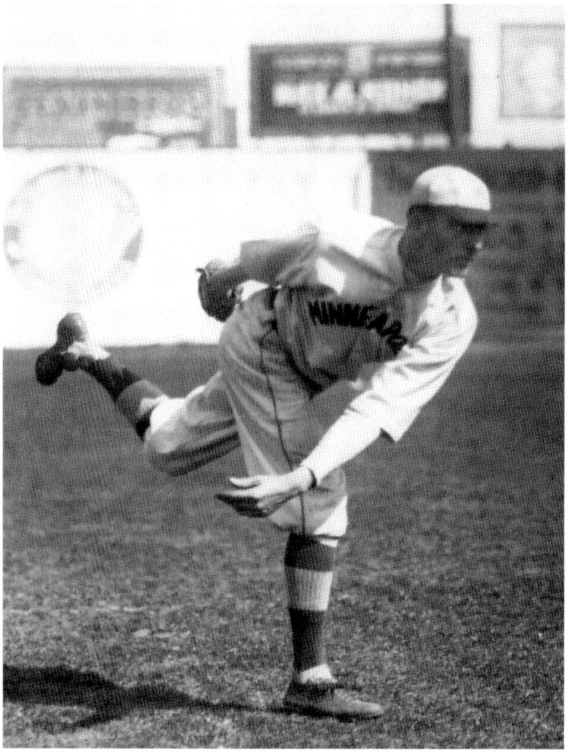

CLAUDE "LEFTY" THOMAS (1917–1918). Shown here completing his warm-up tosses, Thomas demonstrates the fine form that stuffed 20 wins into his basket during the 1917 season. Thomas, who hailed from the "Show-Me State," Missouri, showed a vigorous will to compete after a disappointing stint in 1916 with the Washington Senators, during which he won just one game. Instead of backing down from that experience, Thomas put the culmination of eight professional seasons to his advantage, finishing the season with a 20-24 record for the sixth-place Millers. He showed meritorious resiliency by leading the league in appearances with 62, compiling 374 innings of work. (Courtesy of Hennepin County Library Special Collections.)

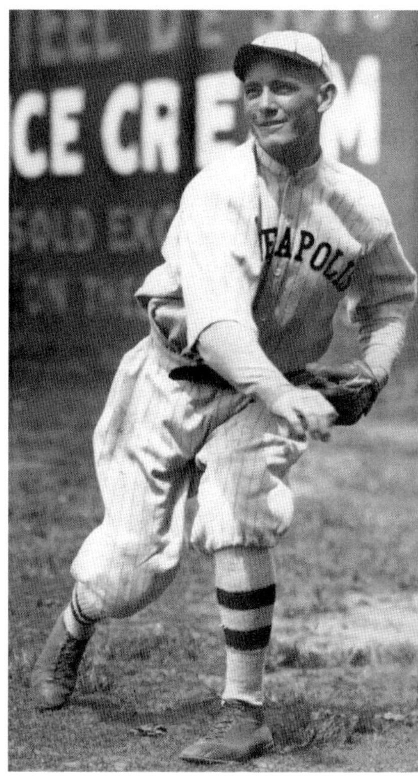

CHARLIE ROBERTSON (1918–1921). A 22-year-old in 1918, Charles Culbertson Robertson left the Millers to serve in the US Army Air Service. When baseball resumed its full slate of games the following year, the Texas lad took up again with the Millers, putting up 11 wins and losing 13. Robertson posted winning records for Minneapolis in each of the next two seasons, showing amazing endurance by pitching 322 innings on his way to an 18-16 record in 1920. During the next year, he amassed exactly 300 innings of work, striking out 175 (second-ranked in the league) on his way to a 17-15 record. (Courtesy of Hennepin County Library Special Collections.)

Dolly Gray (1918). The former star pitcher in the Pacific Coast League, Gray converted to catcher and caught on with the Millers during the war-shortened 1918 season, batting .262 in 27 games. A left-hander, William Denton Gray was born in Houghton, Michigan, and was 39 years of age in 1918. (Courtesy of Hennepin County Library Special Collections.)

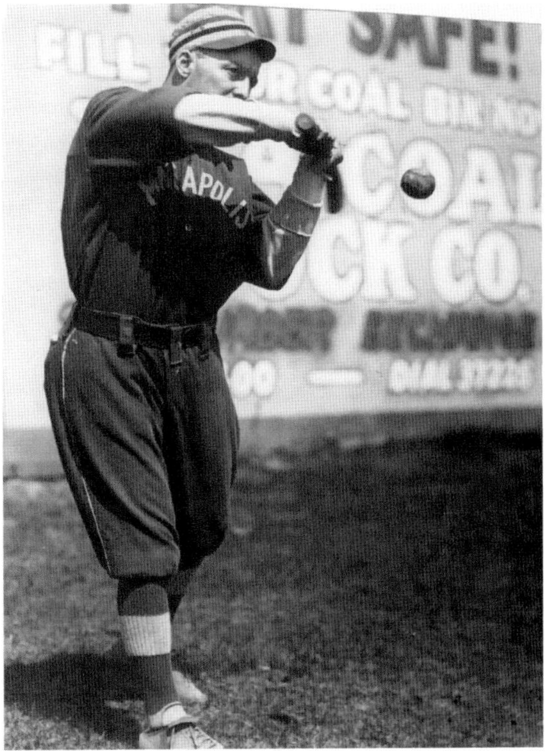

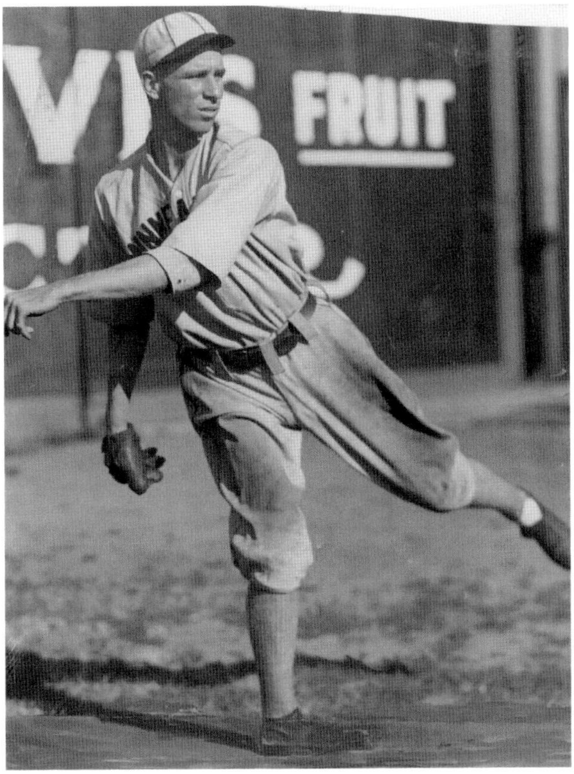

Emilio "Pal" Palmero (1918–1919). Palmero, a native of Cuba, found a home in the American Association at an early age, first pitching for the Louisville Colonels in 1916 and compiling a record of 11-6 at the age of 21. The southpaw came to Minneapolis in the war-shortened season of 1918, going 3-1 in nine games. He split the 1919 season between Louisville and Minneapolis, posting a combined record of 4-11 in 25 games with a 3.39 ERA. He later became one of the better pitchers in the Association, helping pitch the Toledo Mud Hens to their first and only championship with a 14-5 record in 1927. (Courtesy of Hennepin County Library Special Collections.)

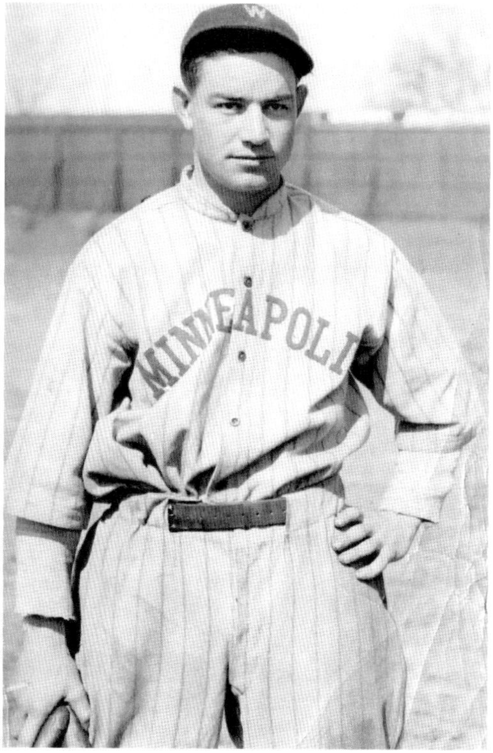

IKE DAVIS (1919–1920). Ike Davis, a five-foot-seven, 140-pound third baseman from Pueblo, Colorado, became a Miller in 1919, batting .258 in 107 games. The next season, the 25-year-old upped his game, posting a .290 average with 34 doubles in 163 games while improving significantly in the field. (Courtesy of Hennepin County Library Special Collections.)

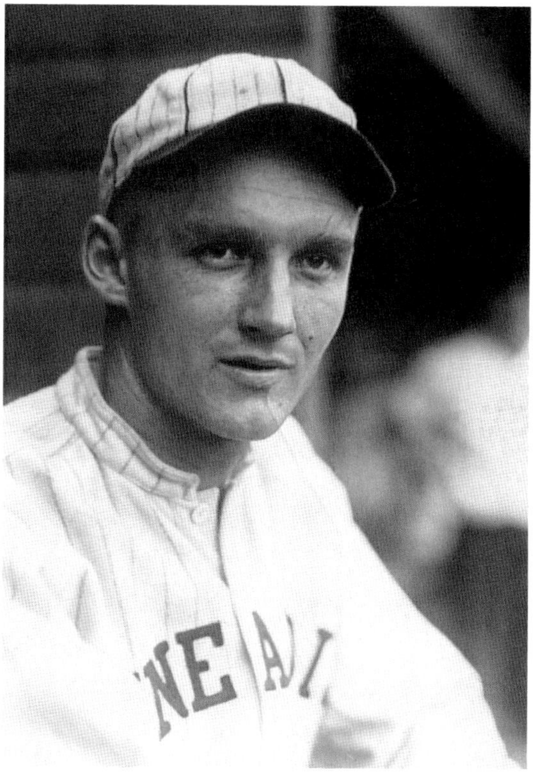

FRANK SHELLENBACK (1919–1920). A big Joplin, Missouri, native, Shellenback had talent from the get-go, starting his professional career as a pitcher in 1917 at the age of 18 with two Double-A teams: the Providence (Rhode Island) Grays and the Milwaukee Brewers. After making just three appearances for Minneapolis in the abbreviated 1918 season, Shellenback pitched in 20 games in 1919, winning seven and losing three with a 3.22 ERA for the fifth-place Millers under Joe Cantillon. Because he threw the spitball, Shellenback was banned from the major leagues in 1920, but he put up an incredible 315-192 record in his 21 years in the minors. He could not resist the call of the upper Mississippi when he returned to the Millers as their manager for a portion of the 1948 season at the age of 49. (Courtesy of Hennepin County Library Special Collections.)

MOLLY CRAFT (1919–1920). Born Maurice Montague Craft in 1895 in Portsmouth, Virginia, Craft first became a professional ballplayer at age 19 in 1915. As a member of the fifth-place Millers in 1919, Craft pitched 18 games, winning six and losing seven. In 1920, he played for both the Millers and the Toronto Maple Leafs of the International League, earning a 6-7 record for Minneapolis in 22 games and then going 8-0 for the Maple Leafs later that season. (Courtesy of Hennepin County Library Special Collections.)

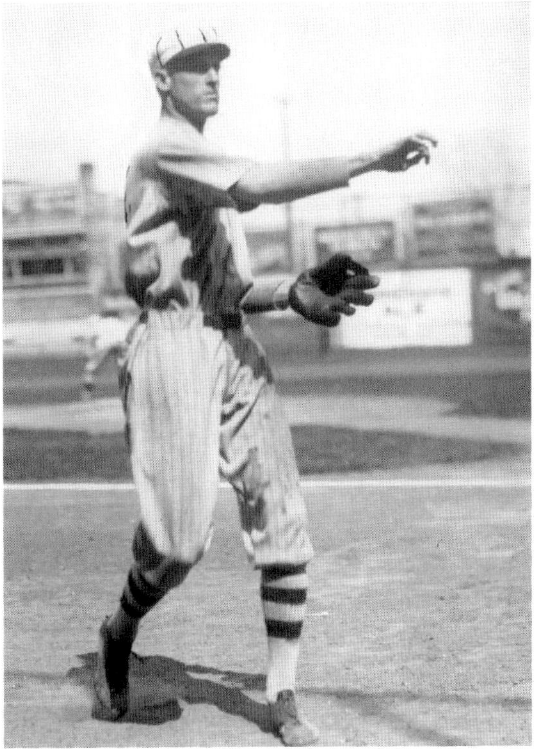

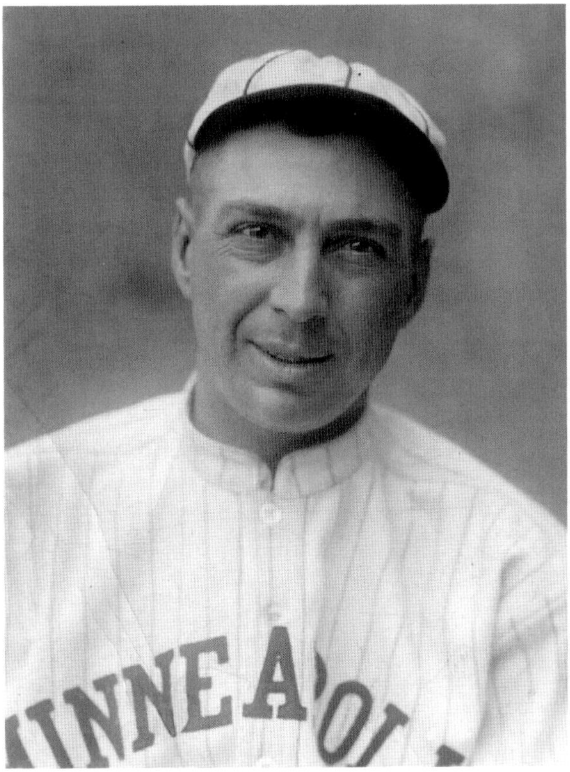

JACK LELIVELT (1919). Several years after his brother Bill last pitched for the Millers in 1912, the Chicago-born outfielder came to Minneapolis in 1919 at the age of 33 in his 15th professional season. After appearing in three seasons with the Kansas City Blues and one with Louisville Colonels, Jack proved an expert with the bat, hitting .346 with Kansas City in 1915 and .325 during the war-shortened season of 1918. In what was essentially his final season at the Double-A level, he batted .287 and swatted 34 doubles with Minneapolis, appearing in 153 games with exactly 600 at-bats. His professional résumé was impressive: in 18 minor league seasons, he batted .332 with 531 doubles and a combined sum of over 3,700 total bases. (Courtesy of Hennepin County Library Special Collections.)

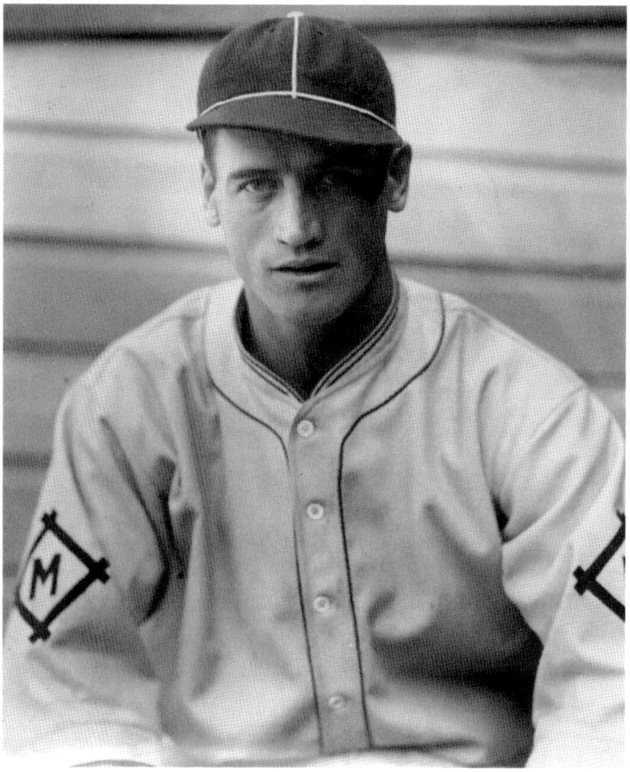

SHOWBOAT FISHER (1919–1920, 1924–1926). Born George Aloys Fisher in Wesley, Iowa, in 1899, the lefty-batting, righty-throwing outfielder was hitting the cover off the ball in the Class D South Dakota League before getting his first look in Minneapolis, a trend he continued in the American Association. After batting .309 in 112 games in 1924, he boosted his average to .350 with 19 home runs and 23 doubles in 1925 for Mike Kelley's fourth-place Millers. Fisher died in 1994 in St. Cloud, Minnesota. (Courtesy of Hennepin County Library Special Collections.)

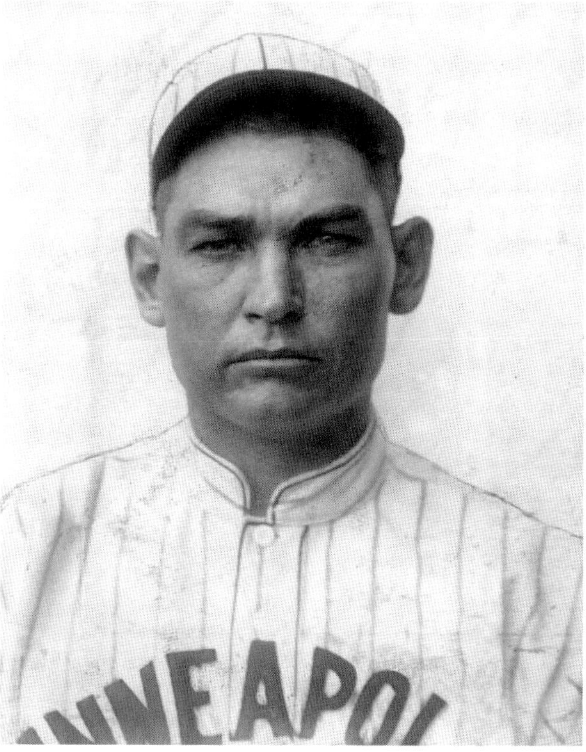

REB RUSSELL (1919–1922). The former star pitcher for the Chicago White Sox converted to outfielder when he joined the Millers in 1919, later establishing himself as a home run hitter (having given up very few while pitching for the Sox). After hitting a combined 15 home runs his first two seasons in Minneapolis, his inner slugger emerged, belting 33 circuit clouts in 1921 and leading the club with 132 RBI. The Mississippi native's American Association numbers were exceptional, with a .332 batting average, 166 long balls, 219 doubles, and 85 triples (1919–1923, 1925–1929). (Courtesy of Hennepin County Library Special Collections.)

TED JOURDAN (1919, 1922–1925). The five-season Miller first baseman was off with a bang after hitting .302 with 30 doubles in 1919, allowing him to return to the Chicago White Sox (with whom he spent a combined four seasons). Standing six feet tall and weighing 175 pounds, the native of New Orleans seemed built to play first base, a position at which he improved over time as a Miller. In 1925, he fielded .992, an excellent mark and his best in Minneapolis. A strong hitter throughout his tenure in the Mill City, Jourdan's most productive season came in 1922, when he hit .312 with 302 total bases. (Courtesy of Hennepin County Library Special Collections.)

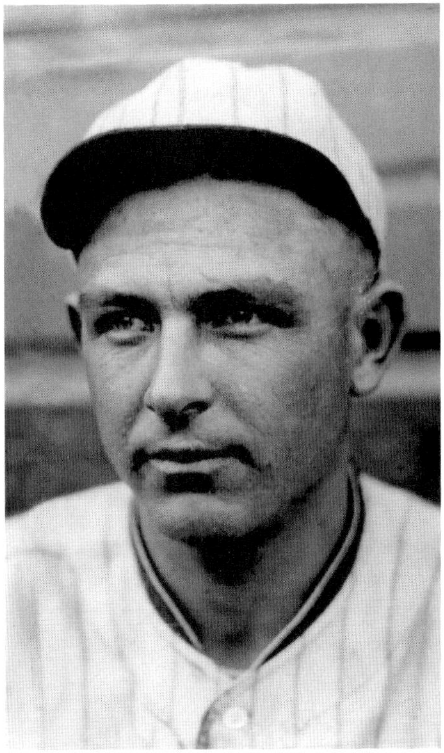

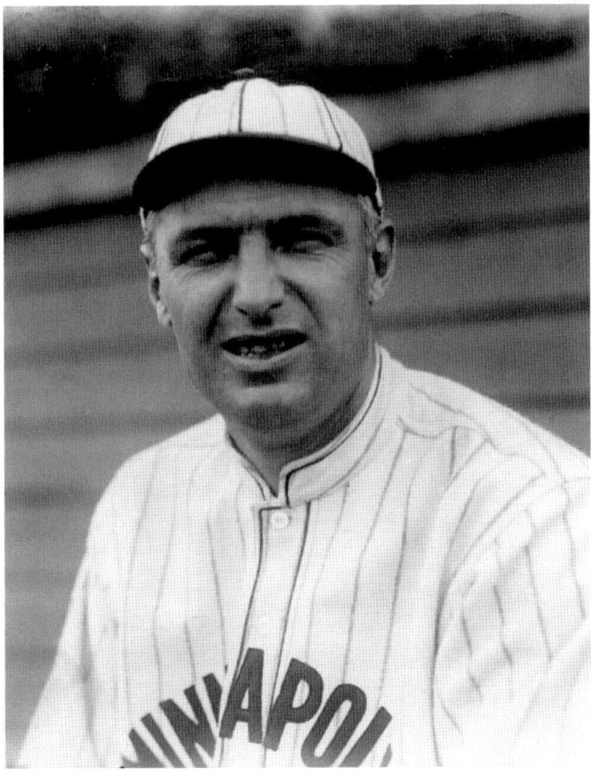

BILL "BIG BILL" JAMES (1920–1921). James came by his nickname honestly: at six feet, four inches tall and 195 pounds, he was built for success as a pitcher, and he used his natural gifts to the utmost, achieving 21 wins during his opening season as a Miller. The 33-year-old Detroit native logged nearly 300 innings in 1920, sharing the club lead in appearances (45) with Charlie Robertson. His club-leading 149 strikeouts and 3.22 ERA provide some insight into his abilities. As a switch-hitter, James enjoyed his best season at the plate that year as well, hitting .286 with three home runs. (Courtesy of Hennepin County Library Special Collections.)

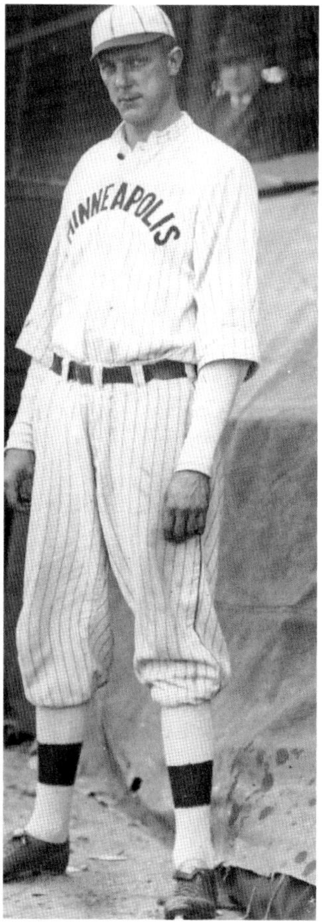

GROVER "SLIM" LOWDERMILK (1920–1921). Nine-year major league veteran Lowdermilk joined the Millers at the age of 35 after successful seasons with the American Association's Louisville Colonels (1912–1914) and piling up 25 wins with the Columbus Senators in 1917 before heading for St. Louis to pitch for the St. Louis Browns. In his first season with Minneapolis, the six-foot-four Hoosier native won 14 games and lost 12, with an ERA of 2.99, for Joe Cantillon's crew, following it up with an 11-9 record the following year. (Courtesy of Hennepin County Library Special Collections.)

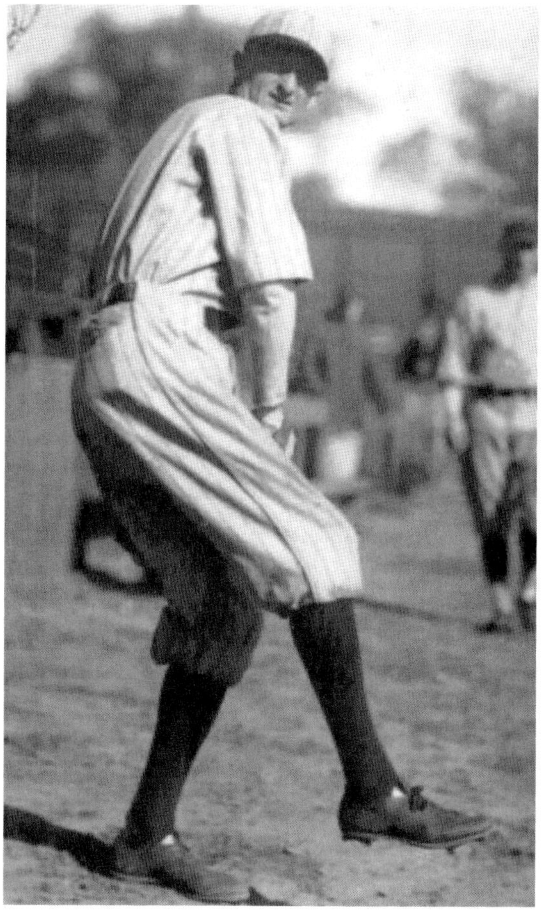

LEFTY GEORGE (1920–1921). The Minneapolis Millers represented a mere stepping-stone for Thomas Edward George, who began his 35-year baseball career in 1909 at the age of 22. George was still playing ball at the age of 57 with the Class B York (Pennsylvania) White Roses, with whom he spent many seasons. Joining the Millers in 1920 after spending part of the year with the Association's Columbus Senators, the string-bean southpaw posted a combined record of 12-19. In 1921, he assumed a full-time role with the Millers, appearing in 42 games with a 10-8 record as Minneapolis finished in second place, four and a half games behind Joe McCarthy's Louisville Colonels. (Author's collection.)

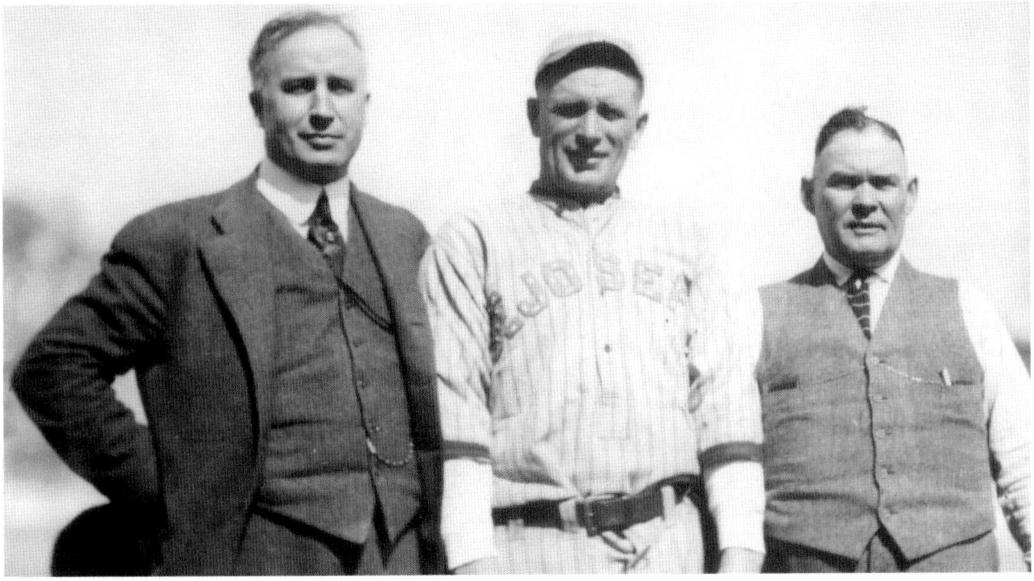

TIP OF THE SPEAR. From left to right in this photograph are Millers president George Belden, former ace Minneapolis pitcher Roy Patterson— who managed the 1916 St. Joseph (Missouri) Drummers of the Western League—and Millers manager Joe Cantillon. The photograph is dated 1921, but it was likely taken earlier. (Courtesy of Hennepin County Library Special Collections.)

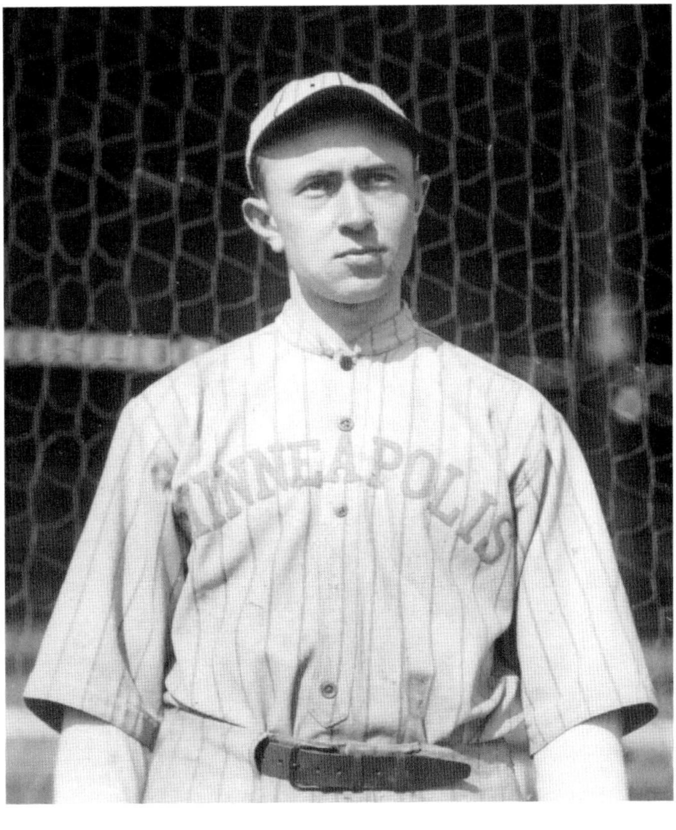

DICK "RIP" WADE (1920–1922). The lefty-batting, righty-throwing native of Duluth, Minnesota, had three strong seasons in succession as a key cog in the Miller machine. As an outfielder, he showed considerable improvement in each of those seasons. His performance in 1921 stands supreme in his lengthy professional career. Amassing 339 total bases, the 23-year-old ranked third on the club, outflanked only by slugger extraordinaire Reb Russell's 372 and Bob Fisher's 352. Wade was second in slugging with a .569 mark with 37 doubles and 31 home runs. (Courtesy of Hennepin County Library Special Collections.)

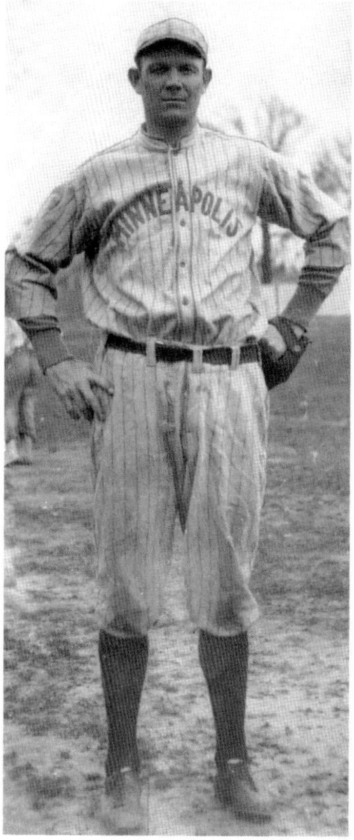

Walt Smallwood (1921–1922). After two scant seasons with the New York Yankees, the six-foot-two righty won 12 and lost eight for the second-place Millers in 36 games in 1921, posting the club's best winning percentage (.600) at the age of 28. Among his mound mates were Charlie Robertson, Grover Lowdermilk, and Lefty George. Smallwood ran his record to 189-194, pitching well over 3,000 innings in 16 seasons of minor league ball, and wrapped up his career managing in the Western League and New York–Pennsylvania League. (Courtesy of Hennepin County Library Special Collections.)

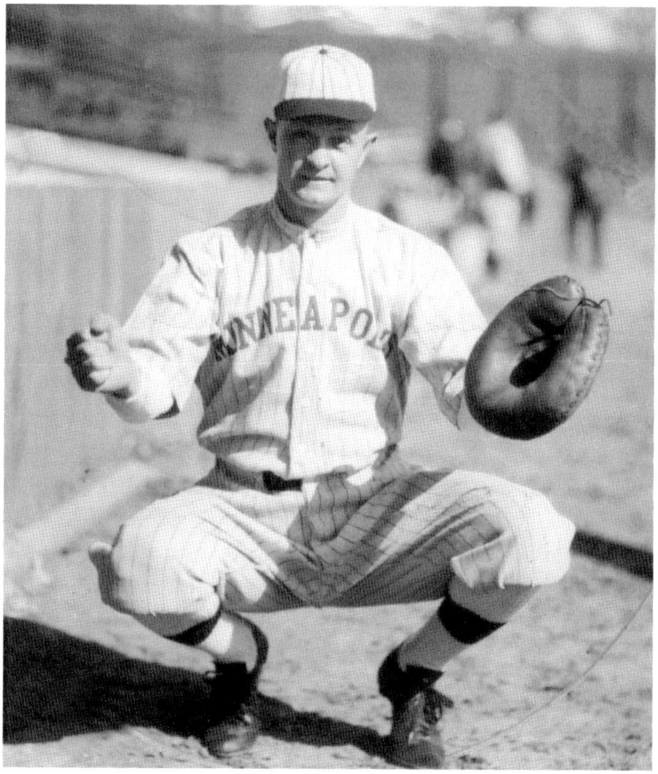

George Shestak (1921). Posing for the camera during spring training, Shestak appears ready to receive any and all curve balls, fastballs, or any other kinds of pitches. Shestak batted .235 in 45 games for Joe Cantillon's second-place Millers in 1921, platooning next to Wally Mayer (110 games catching, .277 batting). (Courtesy of Hennepin County Library Special Collections.)

2

Recapturing Their Glory 1921–1940

With World War I in the rearview mirror and Prohibition in place, the Millers began a new era that established their reputation as a perennially powerful team—but it did not happen overnight. The club started the decade of the 1920s with a bang, winning 92 games in each of the first two seasons and finishing in second place. It was a magical time for baseball around the nation, which was experiencing an economic resurgence. Baseball fever was in the air, and the Millers were one of the hottest items among diamond competitors. But two straight second-division finishes put an end to the magic. Joe Cantillon continued to lead the club through the 1923 season, but a somewhat ironic twist took place when Mike Kelley, the longtime manager of the archrival St. Paul Saints, took the reins in 1924. While his forays as field general were for the most part unsuccessful, he became the president and general manager of the team and was closely associated with the Millers through the time of his death in 1955.

After a sixth-place finish in 1931, the Millers performed a feat of magic rare in the annals of professional sport at such a high level, winning the Association championship in 1932. It was the managerial debut of Owen "Donie" Bush, who had considerable managerial experience with his hometown Indianapolis Indians and had piloted at the major league level. It was the last time the Millers won 100 games.

Under future Hall of Famer Dave Bancroft, the Millers slipped to second place the following season, but in 1934, Donie Bush returned, and the burners were lit once again. The club was poised to grab its sixth league championship. After finishing in first place, Minneapolis met the second-place Columbus Red Birds under a postseason playoff arrangement designed to determine the league champion. Columbus defeated the Millers four games to two, and the hearts of Minneapolitans fell.

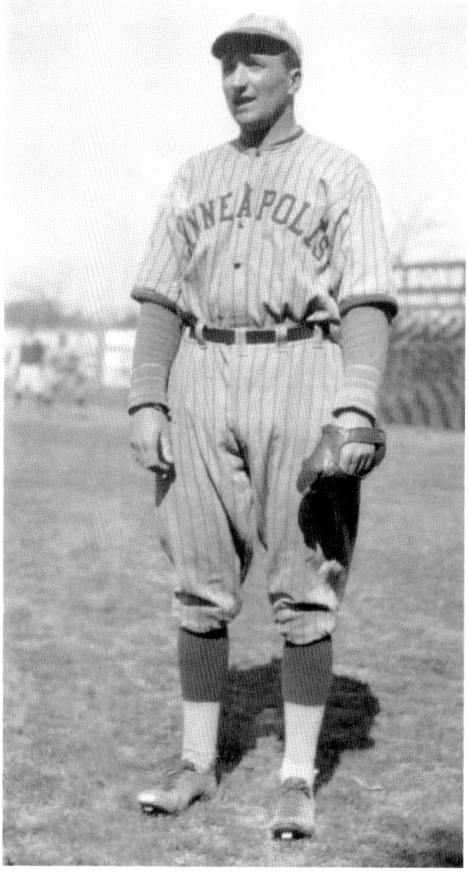

Bill Morrisette (1923). Having completed most of his 11-year minor league career, Morrisette became a Miller at the age of 28 in 1923, producing a record of 8-5 with a 4.66 ERA in 36 games. The Maryland native had one more season left in his right wing before calling it a career with the Dallas Steers in 1924. (Courtesy of Hennepin County Library Special Collections.)

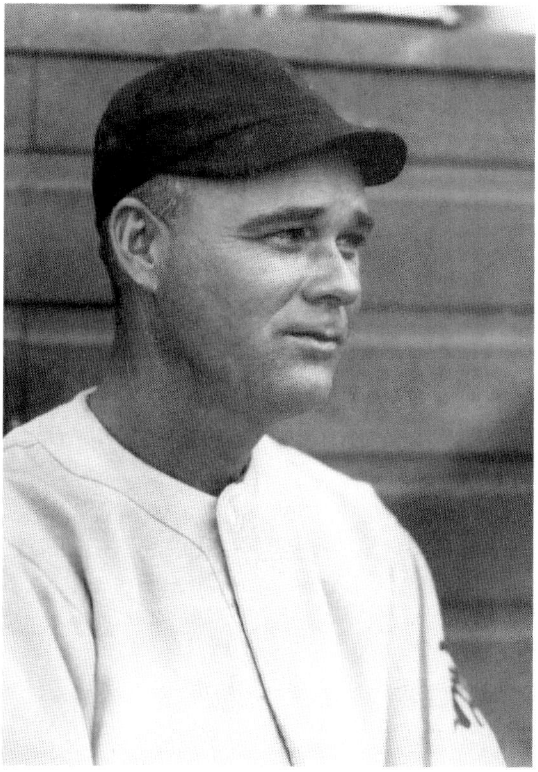

Carl East (1923, 1928). East had the advantage of the "live ball" when he produced 31 circuit clouts in 1923. In 157 games, most of them spent playing outfield, East slapped 223 hits, drove in 151 runs, and batted .375. With 43 doubles and 12 triples, the image of a Triple Crown winner began to emerge. The Georgia native's ratio of strikeouts to walks, 29-87, did not fit the typical slugger mold. For single-season performers, East ranked eighth on the Millers' all-time list with 383 total bases, tied with Ab Wright (1940) and just four fewer than Cravath (1911). (Courtesy of Hennepin County Library Special Collections.)

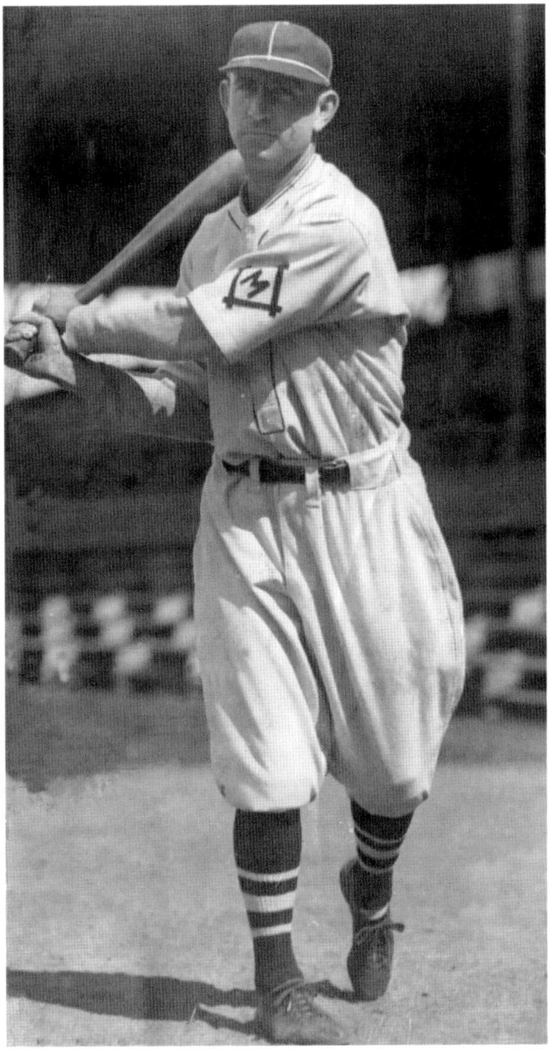

EARL "SHERIFF" SMITH (1922–1930). One of just 45 players in American Association history (1902–1962) to spend 10 or more seasons in the league, the native of south-central Ohio played a lot of ball in his career, including 18 minor league seasons, with a batting average of .294 in more than 2,100 games. After joining Minneapolis in 1922, the five-foot-eleven outfielder flourished as a hitter, batting .316 in 48 games, then repeating that performance in 139 games the following season. But in 1924, he ignited the Millers with a team-leading .353 batting average, 23 home runs, and a circuit-topping 64 doubles, the Minneapolis single-season record. Shown here in a 1925 photograph, Smith had another outstanding season that year, topping his number of total bases from the previous season by 10, pushing it to 377 at the age of 34, second only to Milwaukee's Bunny Brief and his 403. One of the premier Miller players for eight and a half seasons, Earl Smith became a plumber after his baseball career. He died prematurely of an intestinal obstruction at the age of 52 on March 14, 1943. His simple granite grave marker is located at Memorial Burial Park in Wheelersburg, Ohio, near the Ohio River just east of Portsmouth. (Courtesy of Hennepin County Library Special Collections.)

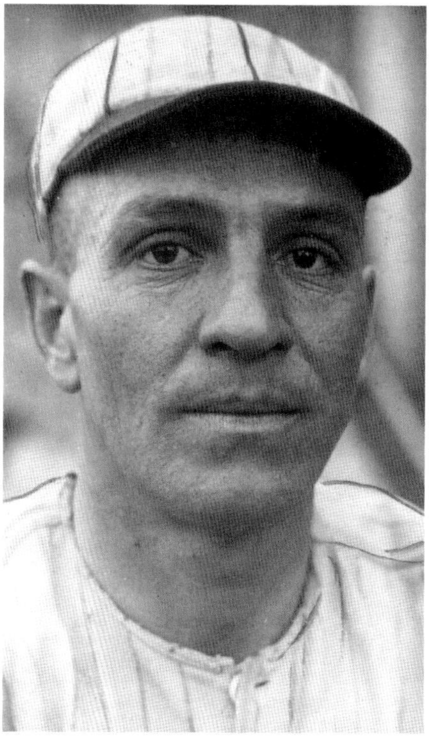

DAN "RUSTY" TIPPLE (1923). Pitching for the Indianapolis Indians, Tipple registered a no-hitter against the Association's Cleveland Spiders on June 25, 1915. In 1923, Tipple, 33, appeared in 39 games, earned 16 victories, and suffered 17 defeats in 240 innings for Minneapolis. The club's leading pitcher in wins, Tipple had not yet solved his issue with wildness, a factor that plagued him during his season with Indianapolis, walking a league-high 170 batters. His 141 strikeouts, however, just under teammate Eric Erickson's 148, ranked fourth in the league for the sixth-place Millers. (Courtesy of Hennepin County Library Special Collections.)

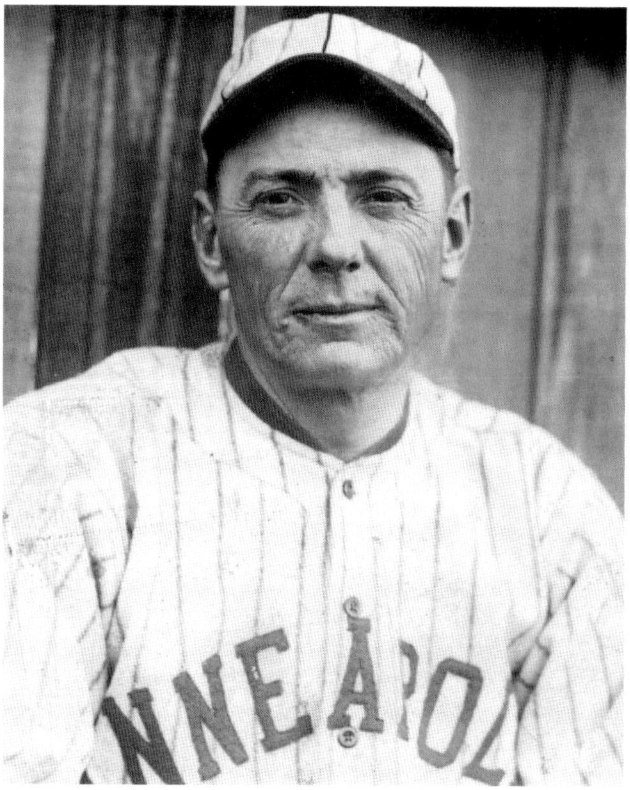

CLYDE "DEERFOOT" MILAN (1923). One year after spending 16 consecutive seasons with the Washington Senators, Milan (pronounced "Millen") stepped up to the plate for the Millers, appearing in 101 games, 77 in the outfield, at the age of 36. Batting .296, Milan had 12 doubles, four triples, and three home runs. After having essentially trademarked the stolen base as his own private purview during his time with Washington (495 swipes), he was no longer a leader in that department in the Association, stealing just two sacks. (Courtesy of Hennepin County Library Special Collections.)

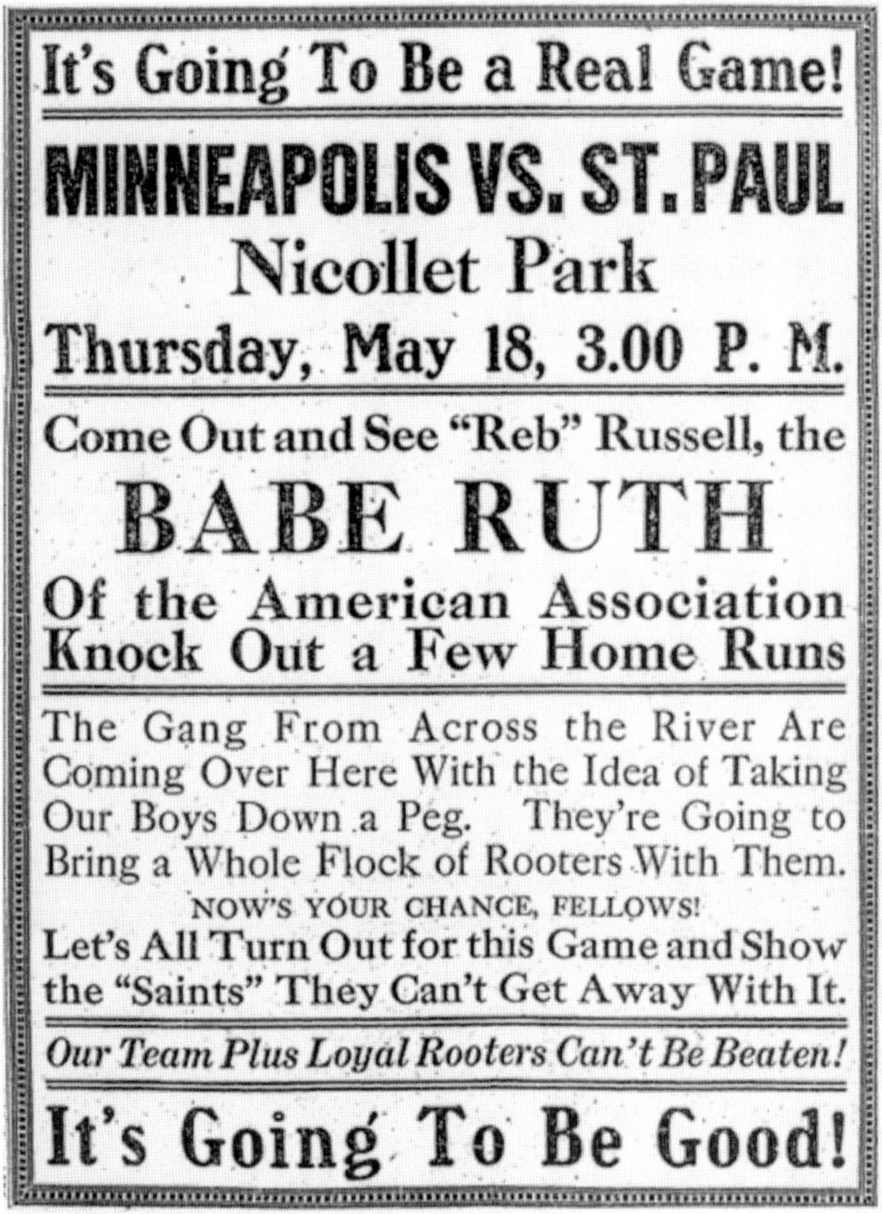

A Real Game! This 1922 newspaper advertisement played up the intensity between the Millers and the Saints. When the *Minneapolis Tribune* came out with this full-page graphic for the game of May 18, 1922, the season was entering full swing. Ewell Albert "Reb" Russell, a converted pitcher from his days with the Chicago White Sox, was an American Association "Sultan of Swat" after belting 33 home runs as the runner-up in the Association's 1921 home run derby. Kansas City Blues outfielder Bunny Brief walloped 42 long balls that year, a new league record. Russell was homerless in the game, with one hit in one at-bat, as the Millers defeated St. Paul 7-6 to even the overall series at a game apiece. (Courtesy of the microfilm collection of the Wilson Library, University of Minnesota.)

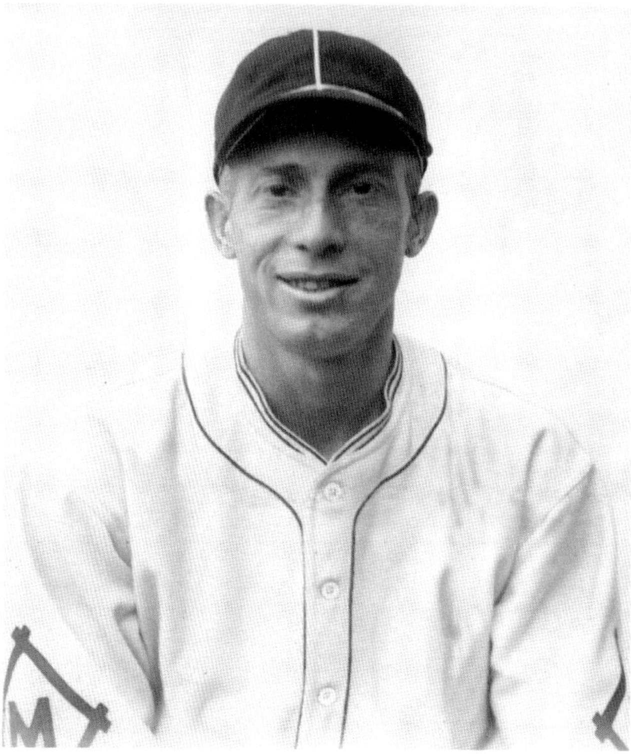

CHARLIE "CHAD" SEE (1924–1925). See spent the final two seasons of his professional career with Minneapolis. He pitched and played outfield both seasons, in 1924 posting a 7-7 record as a right-hander and batting .317 in 104 games, with nine home runs and 18 doubles from the left side. He was primarily an outfielder (22 games) and pinch hitter the following year and continued to hit the ball hard, batting .319 in 80 games. See died at the age of 51 aboard his boat, the *Loretta*. (Courtesy of Hennepin County Library Special Collections.)

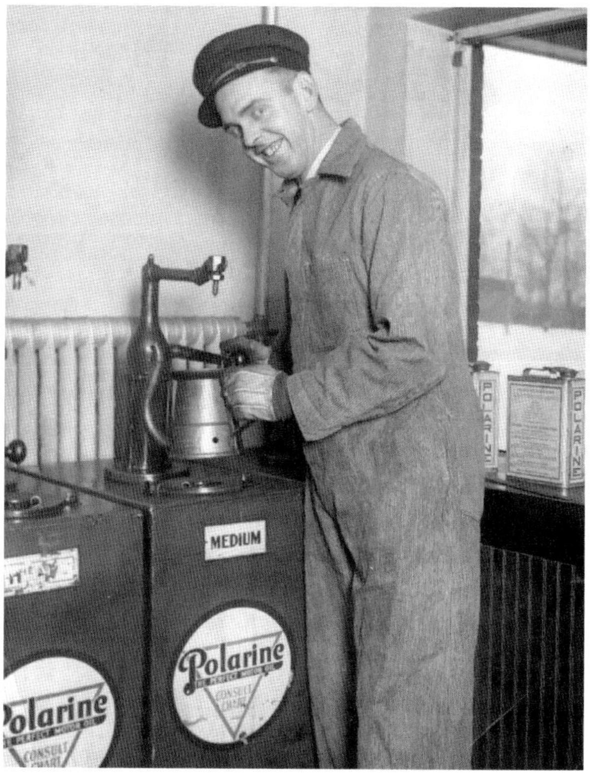

DOUG "BUZZ" MCWEENY (1924). Pictured in about 1925, pitcher Doug McWeeny plies his off-season trade at the filling station he owned near Chicago. One can just imagine the conversations he had with customers while checking the oil under the hood or washing the windshield. McWeeny came to Minneapolis at the age of 27 in 1924 after a few trials at the major league level and as a pitcher with the San Francisco Seals of the Pacific Coast League, winning 35 games between 1922 and 1923. The big righty from Chicago did not fare as well as a Miller, posting a record of 6-9 with a 5.58 ERA in 26 games. (Courtesy of Hennepin County Library Special Collections.)

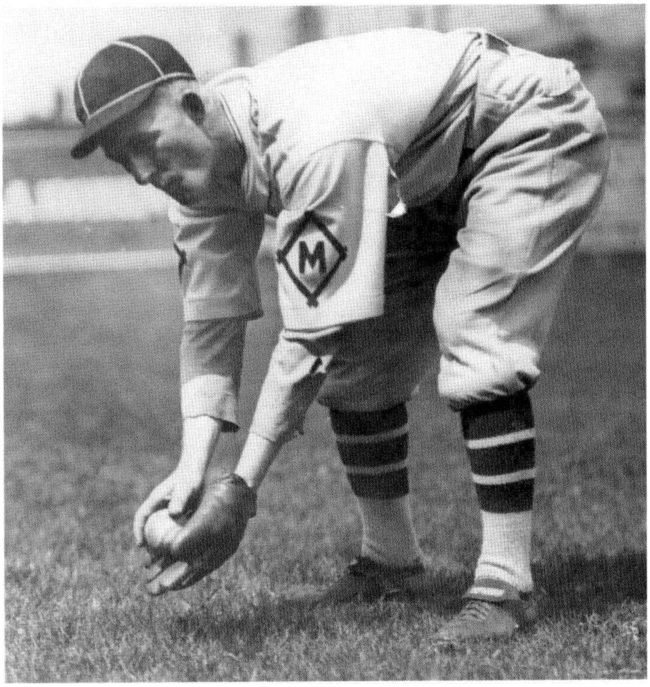

Johnny Mitchell (1924). Mitchell played shortstop in 97 games, sharing duties with Ray French (both French and Mitchell hit below .250 for the sixth-place Millers). Mitchell was a former New York Yankee and Boston Red Sox infielder before coming to Minneapolis at the age of 29, spending a portion of the 1924 season with the Brooklyn Robins. The Detroit native finished his professional career in the Pacific Coast League, where he performed well for an assortment of teams. (Courtesy of Hennepin County Library Special Collections.)

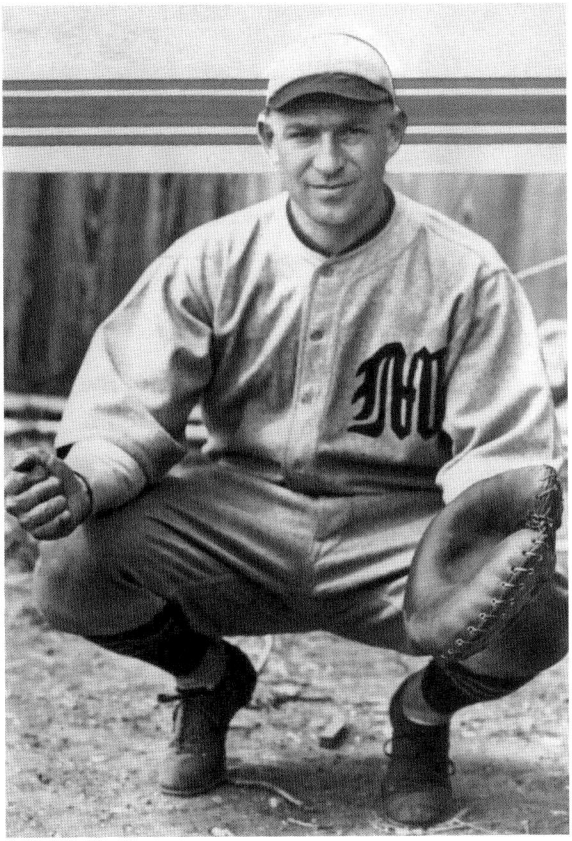

Fred Sengstock (1924–1925). Fred Sengstock joined the Millers as a catcher at the age of 26 after getting his American Association introduction with the Milwaukee Brewers in 1921. Sengstock backed up Eddie Ainsmith, a 15-year major league veteran, behind the bat, but his hitting was a liability for the fourth-place Millers; in 61 games, he batted .211, while Ainsmith hit .332 in 107. (Courtesy of Hennepin County Library Special Collections.)

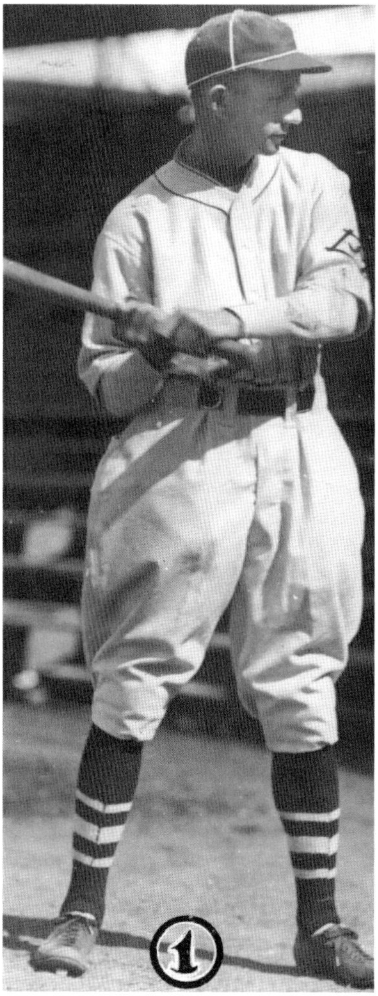

Carl Schmehl (1925). Appearing in just three games with the St. Paul Saints in 1921, the utility infielder then maintained a solid batting record with Class A teams in Connecticut before coming to Minneapolis in 1925. The diminutive Brooklyn native appeared in 123 games for Minneapolis in 1925, playing the outfield in 23 tilts, shortstop in 44, and second base in 33, hitting .287 with 23 doubles and 12 stolen bases. (Courtesy of Hennepin County Library Special Collections.)

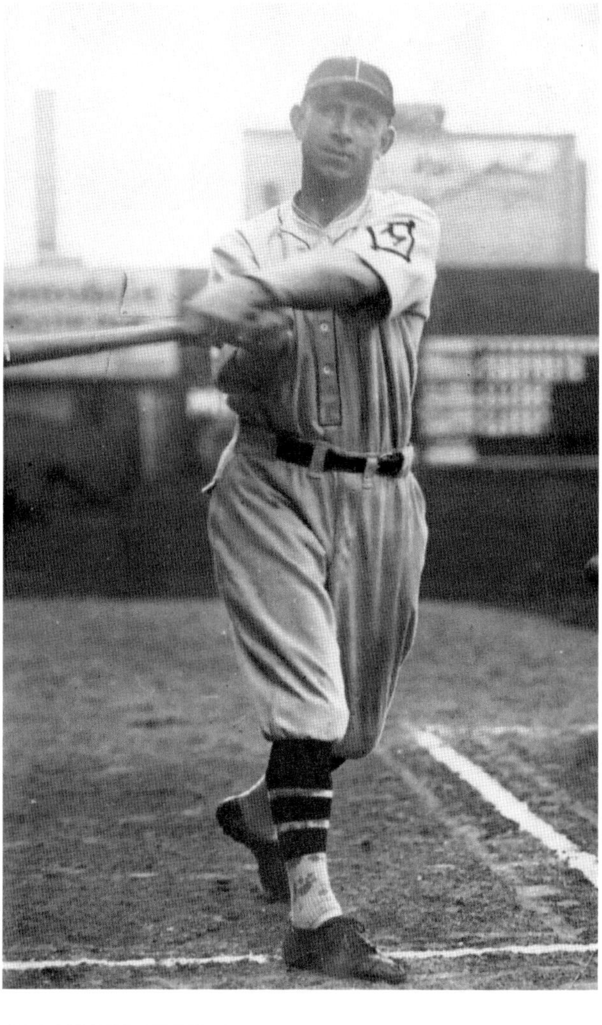

Tillie Walker (1924–1925). Coming to Minneapolis with 13 seasons of major league experience (averaging .281 at the plate with 244 doubles), Clarence William Walker played outfield in 51 of his 70 games during his first season as a Miller, hitting .313. The Tennessee native left the Millers after just 30 games the following year. (Courtesy of Hennepin County Library Special Collections.)

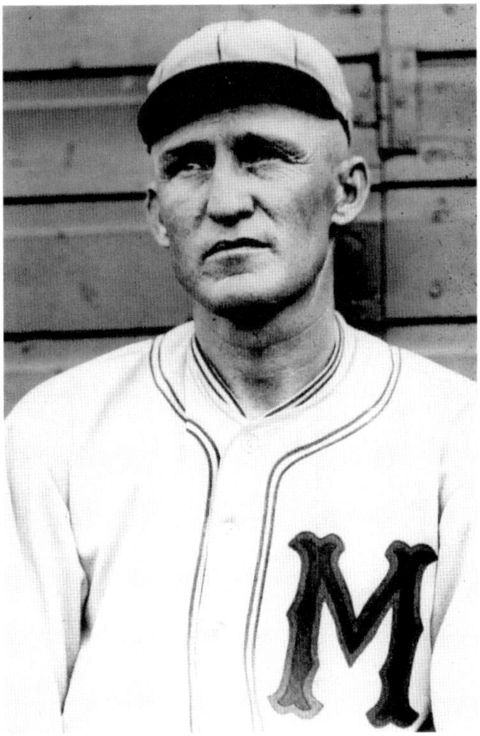

Johnny Butler (1925, 1929). Butler came to Minneapolis at the age of 32 after performing the previous five seasons for the Wichita (Kansas) Western League club. The Kansas-born infielder was a real asset to the Millers in 1925, primarily playing shortstop (81 games) but also adapting to the hot corner (44 games) and first base (22 games). Hitting .339 with nine home runs and 33 doubles helped pave the way for Butler's advancement. The next year, he finally made the majors, a rookie at the age of 33, playing for the Brooklyn Robins. (Courtesy of Hennepin County Library Special Collections.)

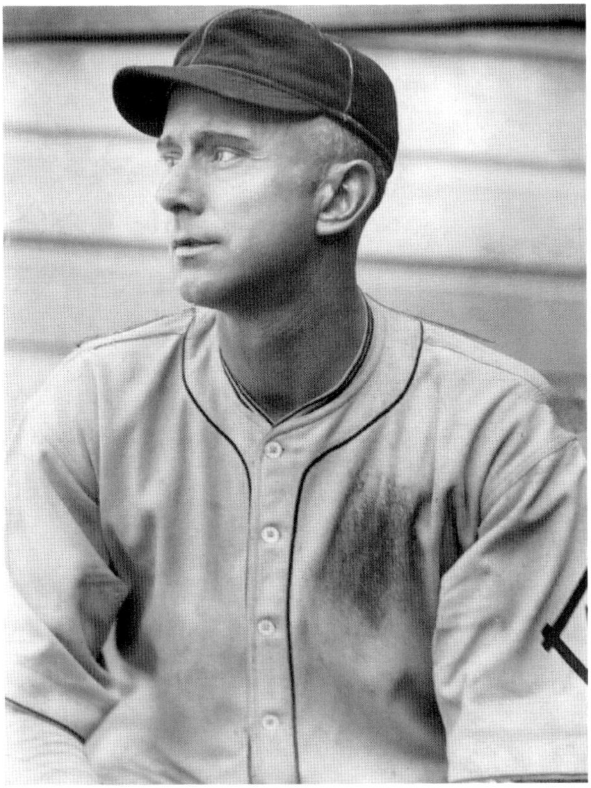

Jim "Rifle Jim" Middleton (1925–1927, 1929). Middleton lit up American Association charts in 1916 with 21 wins and nine losses for Louisville after going 12-14 the year before as a Louisville Colonel. Middleton blew the doors off the circuit in 1920 with Toledo with 26 wins and 14 losses at the age of 31. He first came to Minneapolis in 1925, posting a yeoman-like 12-7 record; then, in 1926, he achieved 20 wins against 15 losses in 53 appearances, the league's top mark, despite walking more batters than he struck out (100-87). (Courtesy of Hennepin County Library Special Collections.)

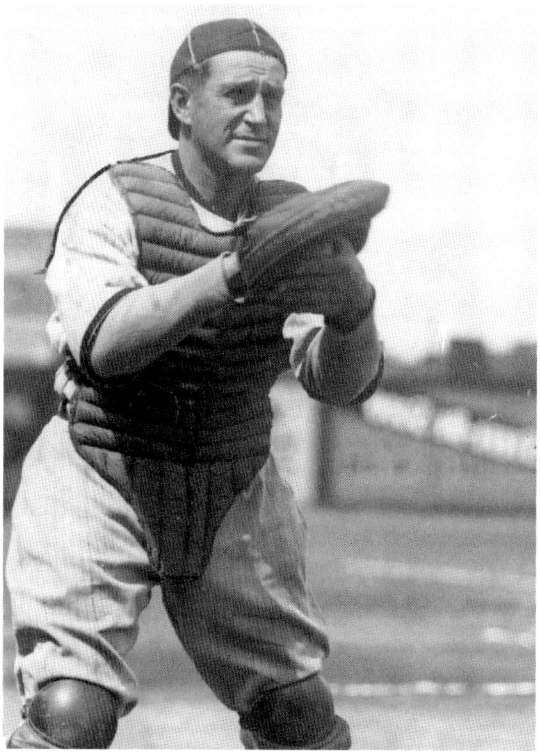

ERNIE KRUEGER (1926–1928). After Krueger's eight-year major league career was over, the beefy Chicago-born catcher was an American Association fixture during the 1920s, playing for Indianapolis from 1922 to 1925. Joining the Millers in 1926 at the age of 35, he was the lead backstop (62 games), platooning alongside Butch Byler (54 games) and former longtime Columbus Senator Hank Gowdy. Swinging from the right side, Krueger batted .265 with a .967 fielding percentage. Minneapolis finished in seventh place with a record of 72-94 under Mike Kelley that year. (Courtesy of Hennepin County Library Special Collections.)

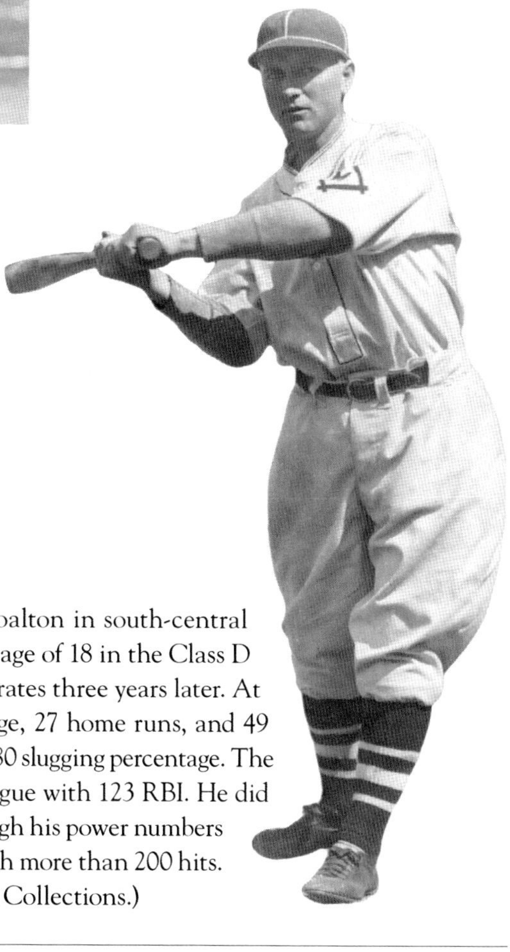

PAT DUNCAN (1925–1929). The native of Coalton in south-central Ohio broke into professional ball in 1912 at the age of 18 in the Class D Ohio State League and joined the Pittsburgh Pirates three years later. At 31, the outfielder's bat sizzled with a .345 average, 27 home runs, and 49 doubles, leading the fourth-place Millers with a .580 slugging percentage. The following season, he batted .351, leading the league with 123 RBI. He did himself one better by batting .352 in 1927, although his power numbers were down. It was his second of three seasons with more than 200 hits. (Courtesy of Hennepin County Library Special Collections.)

DICK LOFTUS (1926–1927). Donning the Minneapolis pinstripes, 25-year-old outfielder/first baseman Richard Joseph Loftus, a former Brooklyn Robin, hit .294 without a home run in his first season with the Millers, appearing in 119 games. The club finished in seventh place with a record of 72-94 under Mike Kelley in 1926. (Courtesy of Hennepin County Library Special Collections.)

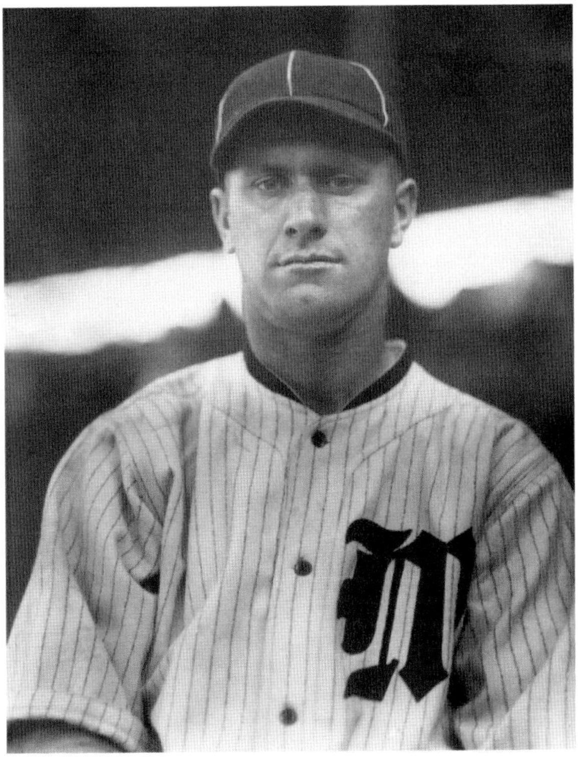

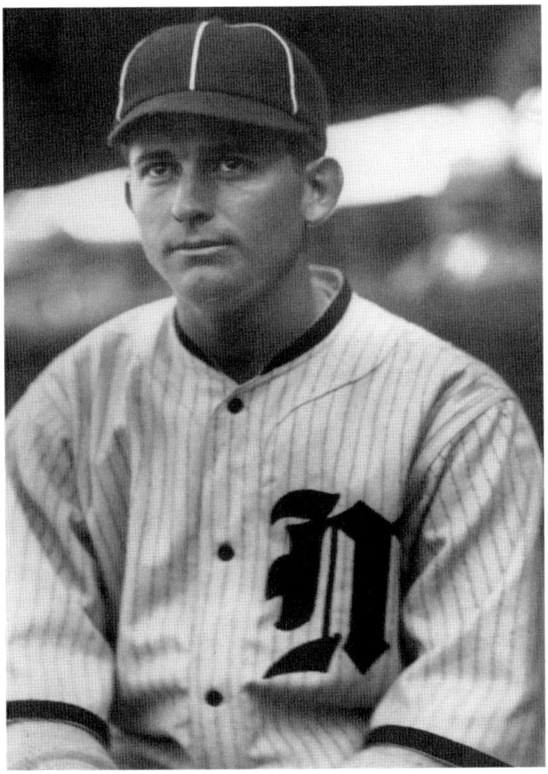

TEX WILSON (1925–1927). Born Gomer Russell Wilson in Trenton, Texas, this southpaw first pitched for Minneapolis in 1925, losing the decision in his only appearance. He returned in 1926, when his record was 6-10 in 39 games, but the best was yet to come. In 1927, Wilson was 12-9 in 37 games, working 203 innings and striking out 77 batters. Wilson later worked for Texaco, and he died at age 45 of a heart attack. (Courtesy of Hennepin County Library Special Collections.)

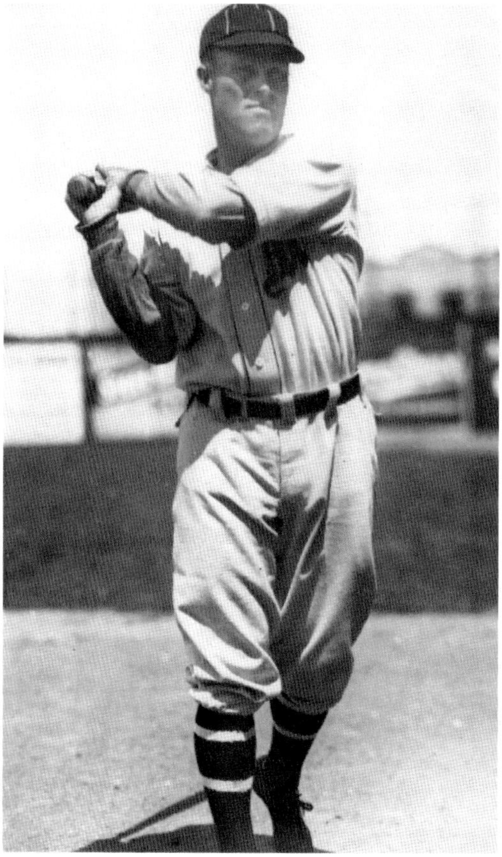

OLLIE "TARZAN" TUCKER (1927). The 25-year-old outfielder from Radiant, Virginia, helped shine a light on the season for the fifth-place Millers in 1927. After a cup of coffee with the Washington Senators that year, he was among a cluster of four Minneapolis players—including fellow outfielders Earl Smith and Pat Duncan, with catcher Eddie Kenna—who batted at least .340. Tucker appeared in 123 games, drilled 24 home runs, swatted 19 doubles, and drove in exactly 100 runs while batting from the left side. Tucker's stellar hitting was on display throughout his 13-year minor league career, nearly all of which was spent at Class A and Class AA, finishing with a .333 batting average and exactly 200 home runs. Tucker died at his home in Radiant after surgery to remove a brain tumor; he was 38. (Courtesy of Hennepin County Library Special Collections.)

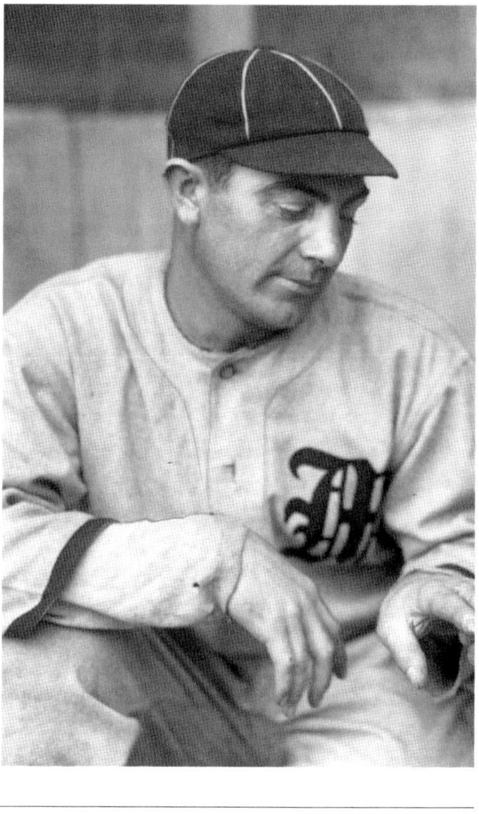

LEO "LEFTY" MOON (1926–1928). After starting his career in 1924 at the age of 25, Moon was still developing his professional résumé in 1926 when he boarded the Miller express, appearing in six games. But in 1927, he led the Association with 55 appearances on his way to a 16-22 record as a regular part of the Minneapolis rotation, which included fellow North Carolinian Rube Benton, Pat Malone, and Jim Middleton. Moon spent 16 seasons in professional baseball. (Courtesy of Hennepin County Library Special Collections.)

Frank Emmer (1926–1931). The five-foot-eight, 150-pound shortstop from Crestline, Ohio, appeared in 59 games for Minneapolis in 1926, batting just .240. But as the team's regular shortstop the following season, his batting improved dramatically. Appearing in a club-high 164 games, the 31-year-old batted .330, walloping a league-leading 32 home runs and scoring a league-high 154 runs. Emmer, with 213 hits, was one of three Millers to reach the 200-hit plateau that year. The others were Earl Smith (225) and Pat Duncan (208). (Courtesy of Hennepin County Library Special Collections.)

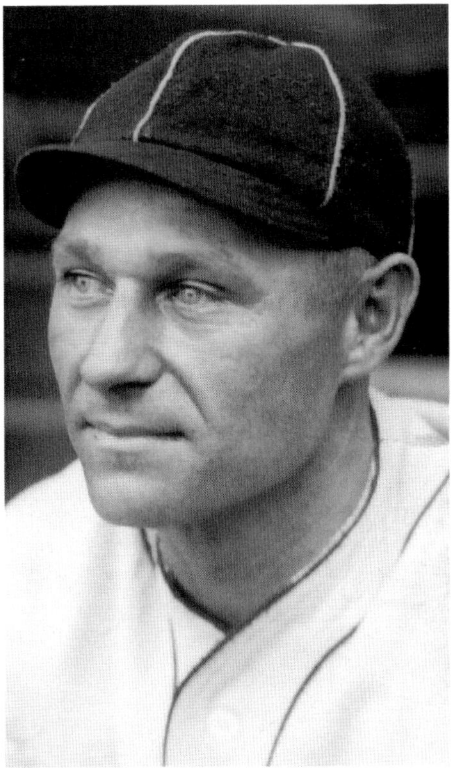

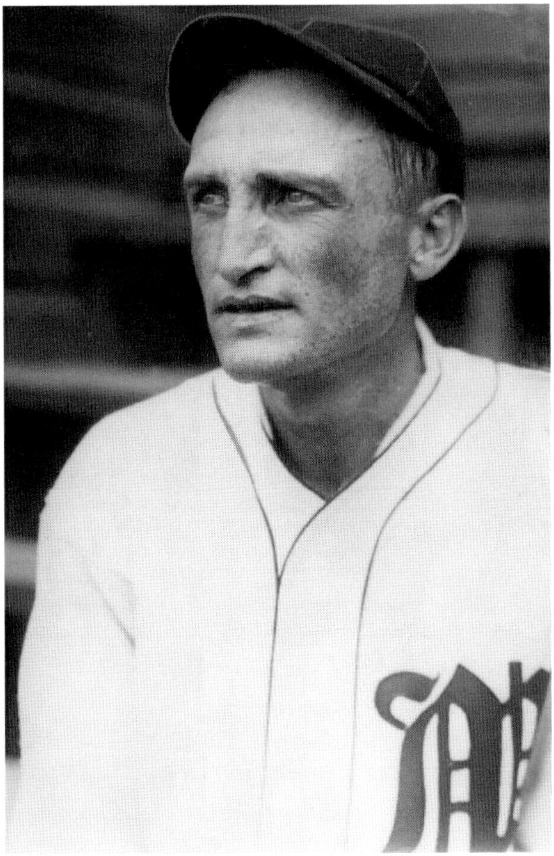

Johnny "Red" Rawlings (1927–1929). Becoming a Miller after his 12-season major league career was complete (1914–1926), the second baseman/shortstop spent the 1927 season with the Columbus Senators and Minneapolis in a combined 81 games, batting .290 with 11 doubles. The following season, he split his time between the Toledo Mud Hens and the Millers, batting .293 with 31 two-baggers in 141 games at the age of 35. Having earned some stability, he played the entire next season at second base for Minneapolis (with a fine .968 fielding average), batting .268 with 28 doubles. (Courtesy of Hennepin County Library Special Collections.)

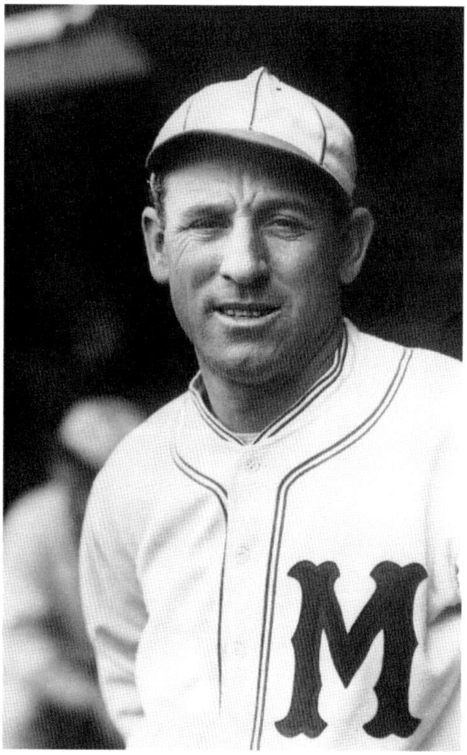

Sam Bohne (1927–1929). Born Samuel Arthur Cohen, the five-foot-eight, 175-pound San Franciscan came to Minneapolis with seven seasons of major league experience. Playing third base in nearly 100 games and second base in nearly 40, Bohne's versatility, solid fielding, and speed were his strengths in 1927. The club leader in stolen bases (with 23), Bohne batted .279 with 26 doubles that year. While appearing in only 101 games the next season, Bohne's .294 average was the second best of his career but still several points off the stunning .333 he mustered with the Seattle Rainiers in 177 games during the 1920 season. (Courtesy of Hennepin County Library Special Collections.)

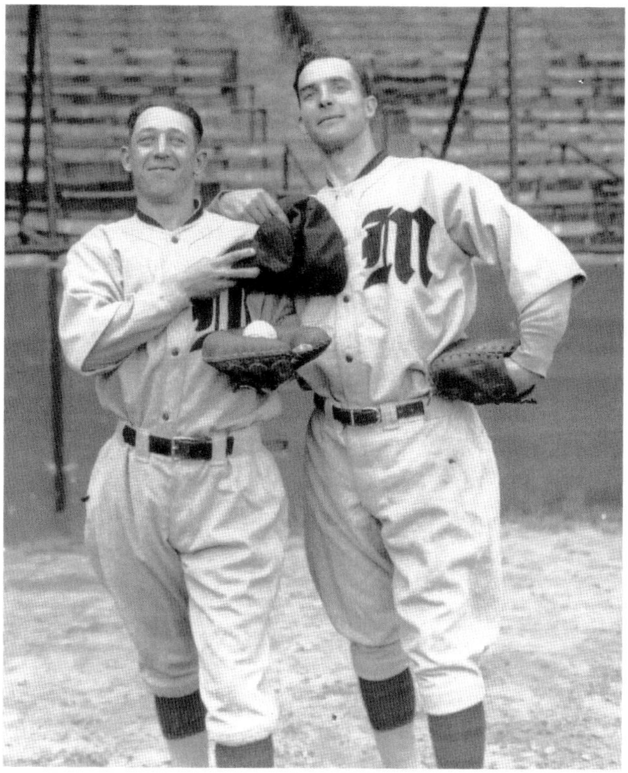

The 1928 Backstop Boys. Casting a vaudevillian aura, catchers Eddie "Scrap Iron" Kenna (left; 1926–1929), 30, and Hugh McMullen (1928–1932), 26, engage in some pregame antics at Kansas City's Muehlebach Field. The five-foot-seven Kenna, a native of San Francisco, weighed in at just 150 pounds; he batted .295 in 41 games in 1928 with four home runs. This represented a considerable dip from his outstanding 1927 season, when he batted .340 with 10 home runs in 93 games. The switch-hitting McMullen, from La Cygne, Kansas, batted .313 in 76 games with nine doubles in 1928. (Courtesy of the Kansas City Public Library.)

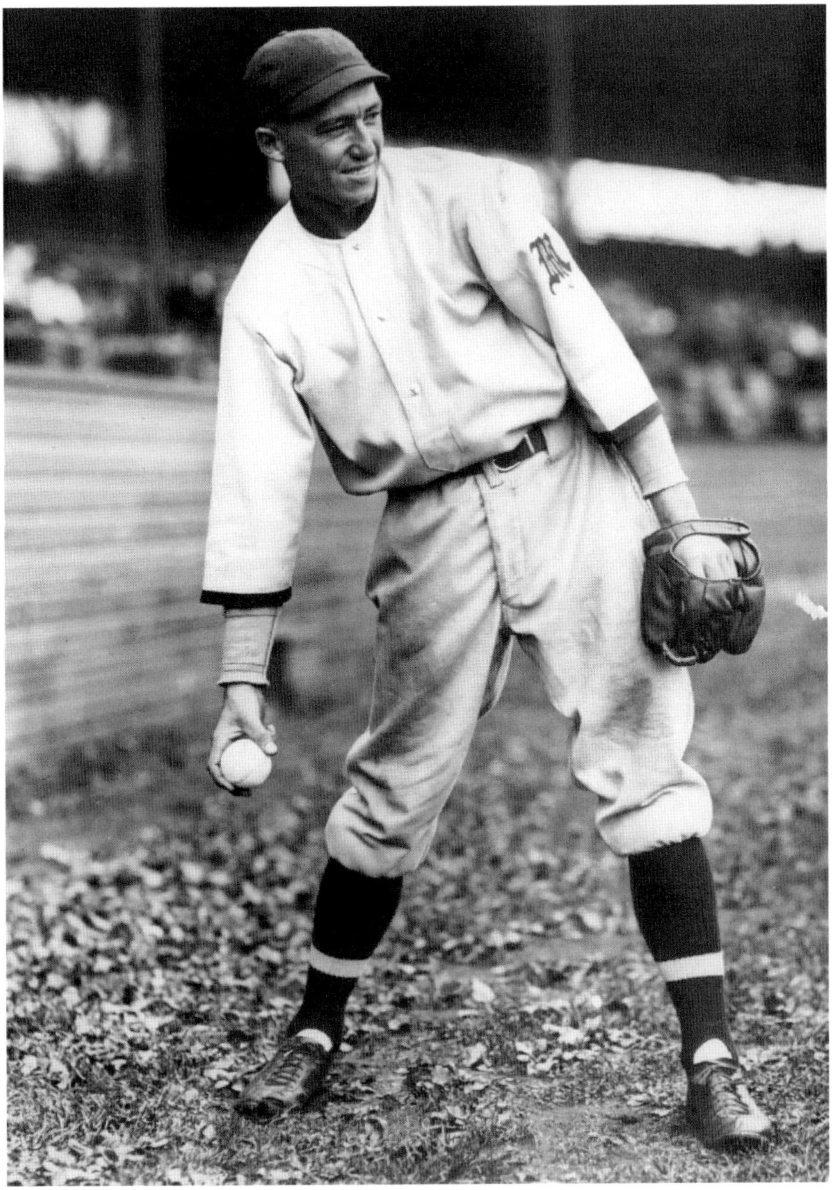

AD LISKA (1928, 1932). The five-foot-eleven, 160-pound Adolph James Liska first came to the Millers at the age of 21 and was quick to impress, owning one of the finest single-season records for a Miller pitcher in club history. With 20 wins against only four losses (.833), his winning percentage led the circuit as he paved the way for one of the best Miller seasons in years. Striking out 82 batters while walking 61 in 225 innings of work showed he was not a dominating pitcher, but his 3.68 ERA indicated he was tough to score against. The native of east-central Nebraska moved up to the majors the following season, winning three and losing nine as a Washington Senator. His subsequent career was highlighted by 14 straight seasons with the Portland Beavers of the Pacific Coast League (1936–1949). He married a Minneapolis woman, the former Lorrayne O'Brien, in 1929. (Courtesy of Hennepin County Library Special Collections.)

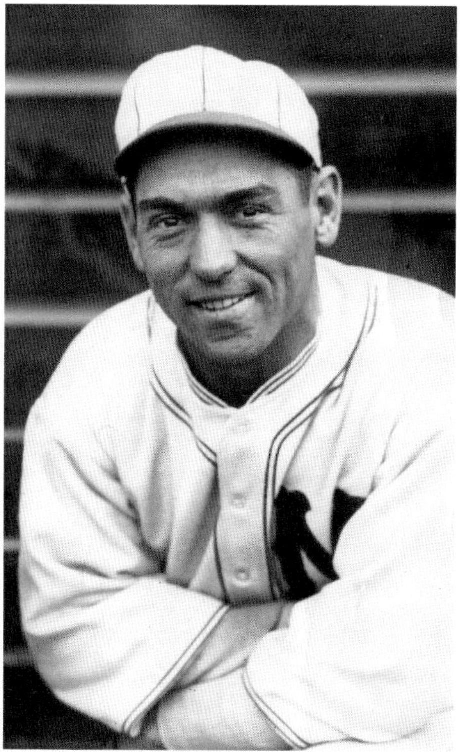

Elmer Yoter (1928–1930). In his first double-A season with the Indianapolis Indians, the Pennsylvania-born outfielder batted .306 in 1925 at the age of 25. In 1928, he became a Miller, batting .322 with 32 doubles and 13 triples (a club high). Predominantly a third baseman, his 50 doubles in 1929 tied for all-time fifth-best (with Carl Sawyer in 1920) among the Millers' single-season stars. His 294 total bases that year was a career high. Yoter's extensive résumé as a minor league manager spanned the years 1933 to 1961 and included 21 seasons. (Courtesy of Hennepin County Library Special Collections.)

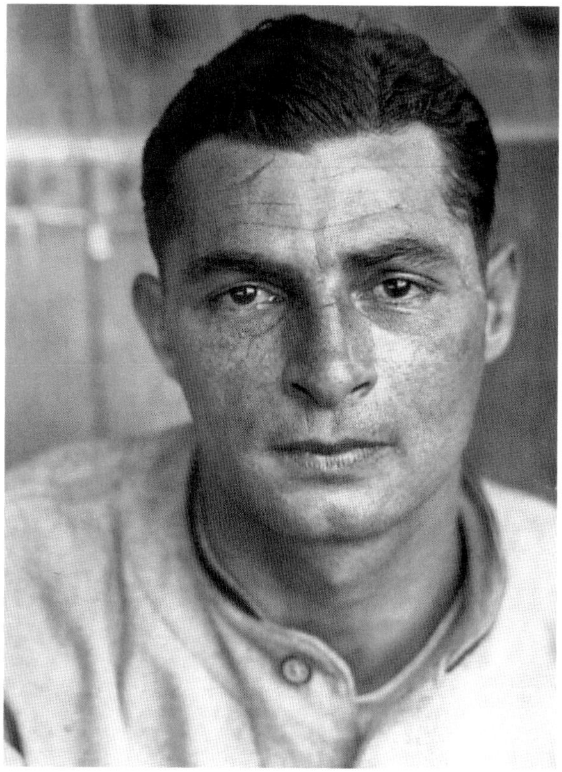

Ernie Orsatti (1928). Another key figure in the Millers' 1928 pennant run, the left-handed Californian came to Minneapolis after a successful trial by the St. Louis Cardinals in 1927. At five foot, seven inches tall and 154 pounds, the first baseman/outfielder was not the prototypical slugger. Still, he tore the cover off the ball for Mike Kelley in 1928, batting .381 in 123 games, including 15 home runs, 15 triples, and 32 doubles, and was actually the American Association's slugging leader with a .619 average (among qualifiers). The 25-year-old Orsatti held down the first sack with a .980 fielding percentage. (Courtesy of Hennepin County Library Special Collections.)

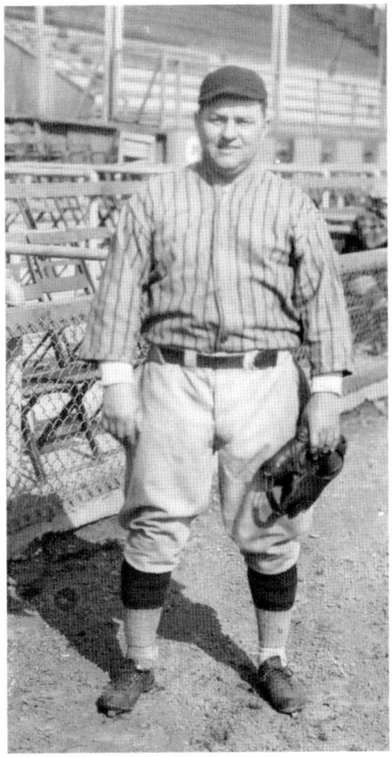

HACK MILLER (1928–1930). Not to be confused with Laurence H. Miller, the former Oakland Oaks slugger from the same period, Charles F. "Hack" Miller came to Minneapolis to aid the Millers' pennant drive down the stretch. When he was acquired from the Dallas Steers, Miller's reputation as a strong hitter preceded him, but the outfielder's fielding immediately impressed Millers fans. His 1928 numbers were strong indeed, with a .311 average, four home runs, and 10 doubles in just over 100 at-bats (28 games), but Minneapolis faltered late and yielded the top spot to Indianapolis. (Courtesy of Hennepin County Library Special Collections.)

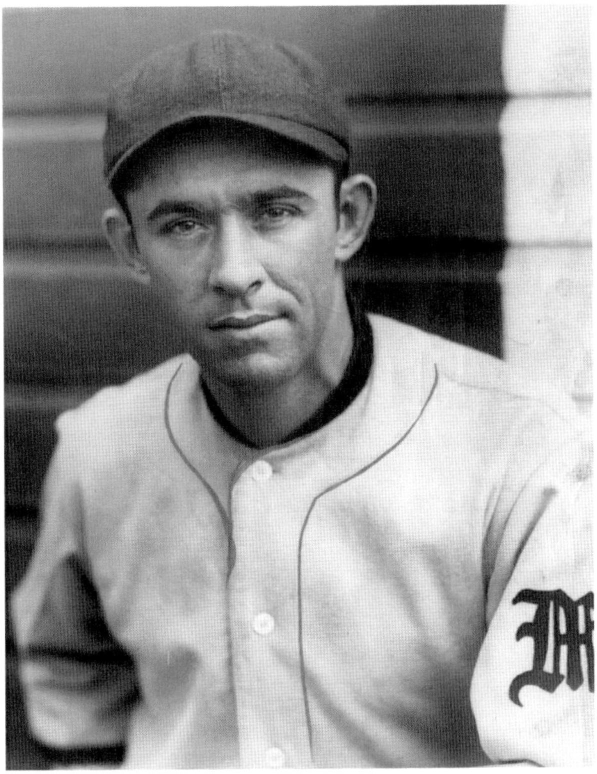

HOD LISENBEE (1928). A right-handed pitcher from Clarksville, Tennessee, Lisenbee was 29 in his only season wearing the Miller flannel. Winning eight and losing six in 26 games, Horace Milton Lisenbee was integral to Mike Kelley's rotation that year. Along with fellow hurlers Ad Liska, John Brillheart, and Rube Benton, Lisenbee helped the Millers achieve one of the best seasons in Minneapolis history. Thanks to some heavy hitting by such swatters as Spencer Harris, Ernie Orsatti, Earl "Sheriff" Smith, and Elmer Yoter, the "Kels," as the Millers were known under Mike Kelley, finished with a record of 97-71, just two and a half games behind Bruno Betzel's Indianapolis Indians. (Courtesy of Hennepin County Library Special Collections.)

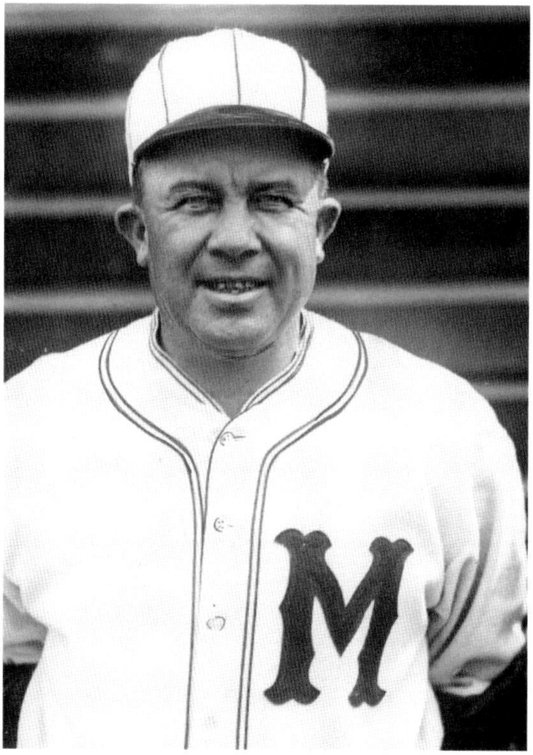

Joe Pate (1928–1929). In his second season with Minneapolis, Pate put up solid numbers, winning 11 games and losing five at the age of 37. Born in Alice, Texas, in 1892, Pate entered professional ball with the Corpus Christi Pelicans in 1911. His career reflected not only his competence but also a remarkable longevity. By the time his 20-year career wrapped up in 1932, he had won 257 games and lost 134 (.657) with over 3,300 innings pitched. Included in that record was the two-year period he spent in the majors pitching for the Philadelphia Athletics under Connie Mack (he went 9-0 in 1926). (Courtesy of Hennepin County Library Special Collections.)

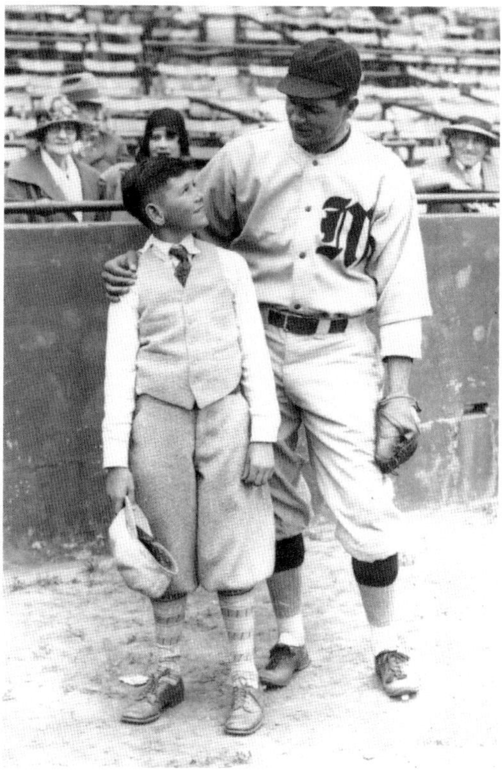

Zack "Buck" Wheat (1928). The Hall-of-Fame left fielder spent 18 seasons with the Brooklyn National League club (1909–1926). He appears in this photograph not far from his birthplace of Hamilton, Missouri, giving a youngster a few pointers at Kansas City's Muehlebach Field in 1928. Inducted into the National Baseball Hall of Fame in 1959, he became a Miller in 1928 at the age of 40, ending his professional years by hitting .309 in 82 games with five home runs. That is quite a swan song. (Missouri Valley Special Collections, Kansas City Public Library, Kansas City, Missouri.)

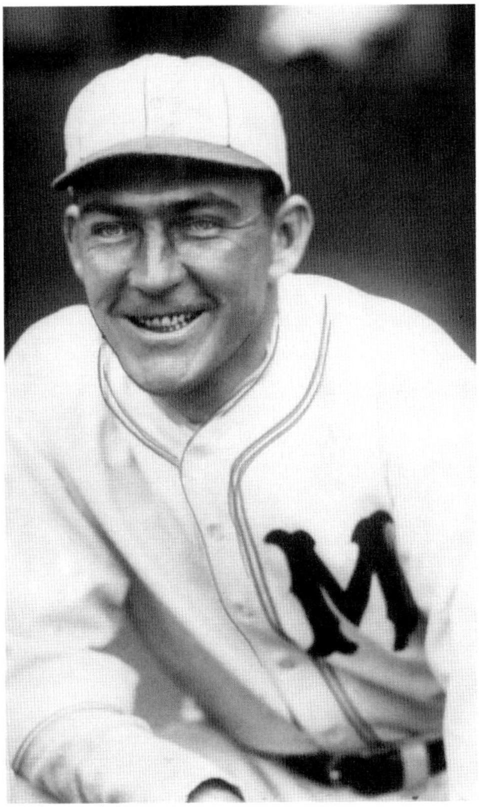

Flint "Shad" Rhem (1929). The 28-year-old pitcher from Rhems, South Carolina, came to the Millers after five seasons with the St. Louis Cardinals, posting a record of 5-11 in 23 games. Rhem returned to the Cardinals the following year and promptly elevated his standing with 12 wins against eight losses. (Courtesy of Hennepin County Library Special Collections.)

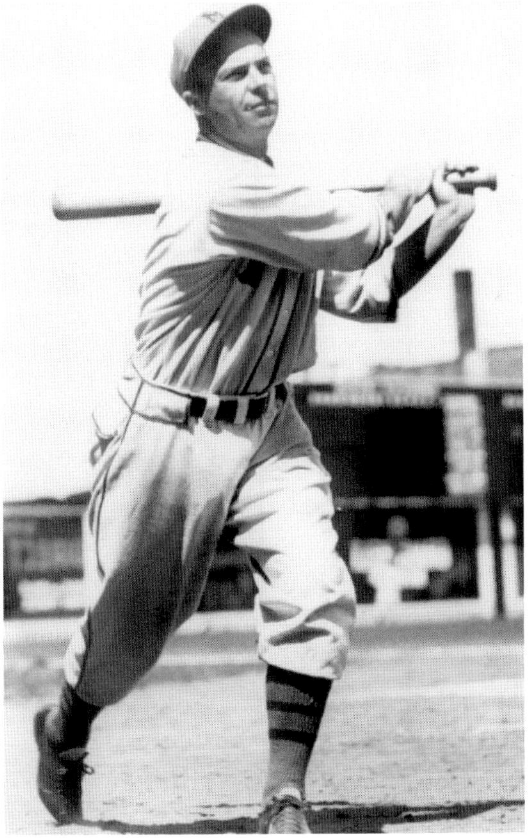

Spencer "Spence" Harris (1928–1937). Harris, a native of Duluth, Minnesota, joined the Millers at the age of 27 after four years in the low minors and two major league seasons (1925 and 1926) spent with the Chicago White Sox. In his first season with Minneapolis, Harris had a career year. A fleet-footed flychaser with a sizzling bat, he stole 25 bases while posting a league-high 32 circuit clouts and amassing 364 total bases. He led the league in at-bats (669), runs (133), doubles (41), bases on balls (87), and home runs. (Courtesy of Hennepin County Library Special Collections.)

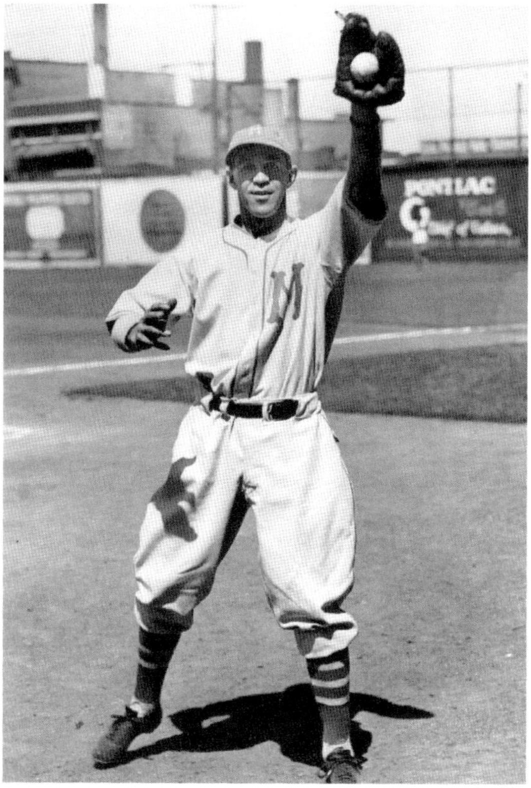

Ernie Smith (1930–1934). Smith's moniker, the "Kansas City Kid," was possibly in reference to his playing days with the Kansas City Blues during the 1920s. The New Jersey native came to Minneapolis just after spending 24 games in his major league debut with the Chicago White Sox in 1930. At five feet, eight inches, and 155 pounds, Smith was a versatile infielder and contact hitter whose offensive momentum lifted the Millers to the flag in 1932. That year, he joined the vaunted 200-hit club (202), while his 56 doubles put him second all-time on the Millers' single-season ledger. (Courtesy of Hennepin County Library Special Collections.)

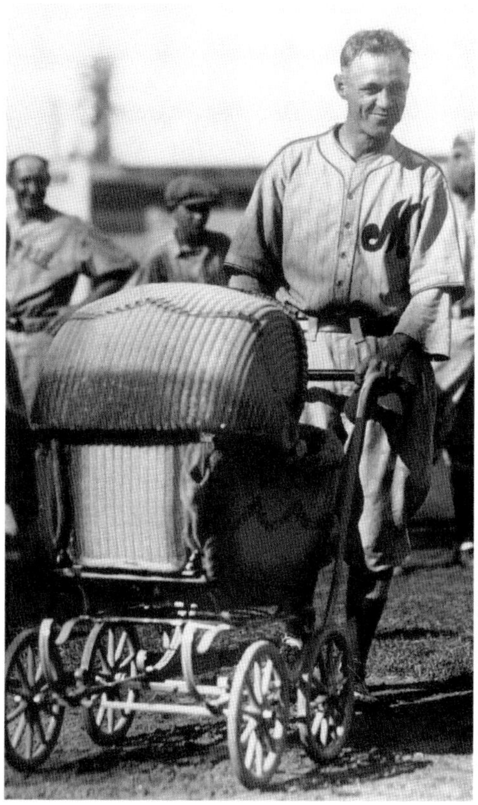

Eddie Sicking (1930–1932). The southern Ohio native spent three seasons as a Miller. Among the best in his 15-year minor league career was the 1931 season, when he played in 125 games as the Minneapolis second baseman, batting .323 with 28 doubles. The 34-year-old looks as though he is having a good time entertaining a new addition to the family in this 1930 photograph. He later operated a bowling alley near Cincinnati. (Courtesy of Hennepin County Library Special Collections.)

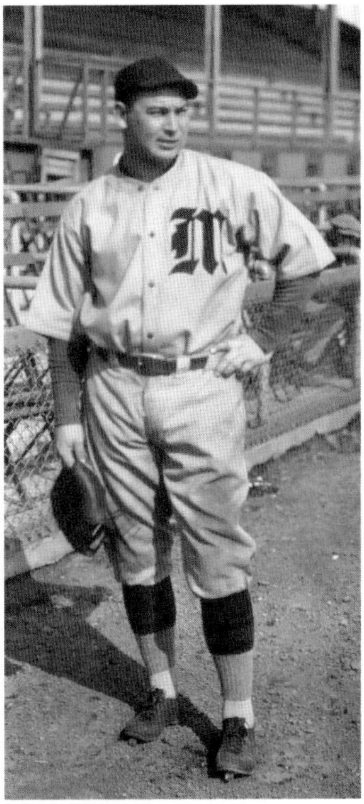

Mule Shirley (1929). With a pair of brief seasons at the major league level under his belt, Ernest Raeford Shirley came to Minneapolis at the age of 28, appearing in 47 games (20 as outfielder, 13 at first base, and 14 games on offense), batting .331 with seven home runs for Mike Kelley's third-place Millers. Shirley spent 13 seasons as an active player in the minors, managing in four of them. (Courtesy of Hennepin County Library Special Collections.)

George "High Pockets" Kelly (1930–1931). After playing with the Cincinnati Reds and Chicago Cubs during the 1930 season, the 34-year-old Kelly became a Miller the same year, appearing in 34 games and hitting .361 under Mike Kelley. At six feet, four inches, and 190 pounds, Kelly was ideal as their everyday first baseman, a role he assumed the following year. Combining with Spencer Harris and Ernie Smith to provide the "tip of the spear," Kelly led the team with 20 home runs, batting .320. Despite their firepower and 23-game winner Frank "Dutch" Henry, the Millers finished in sixth place at 80-88. San Francisco native Kelly was inducted into the National Baseball Hall of Fame in 1973 after 16 years in the majors (1915–1932). (Author's collection.)

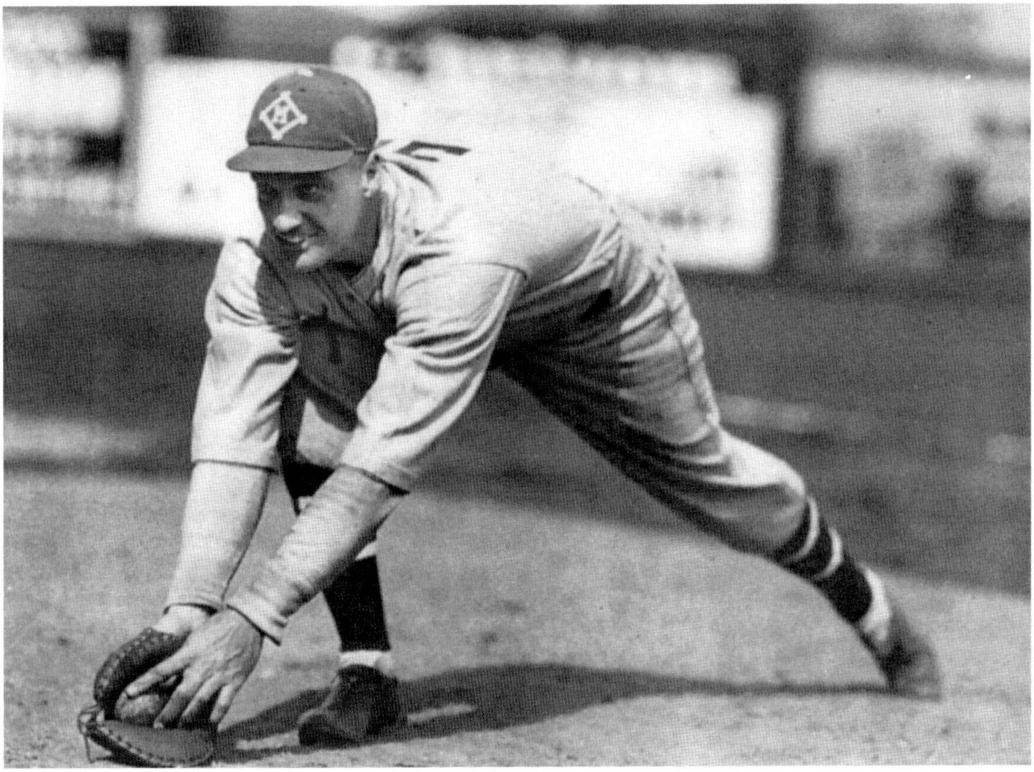

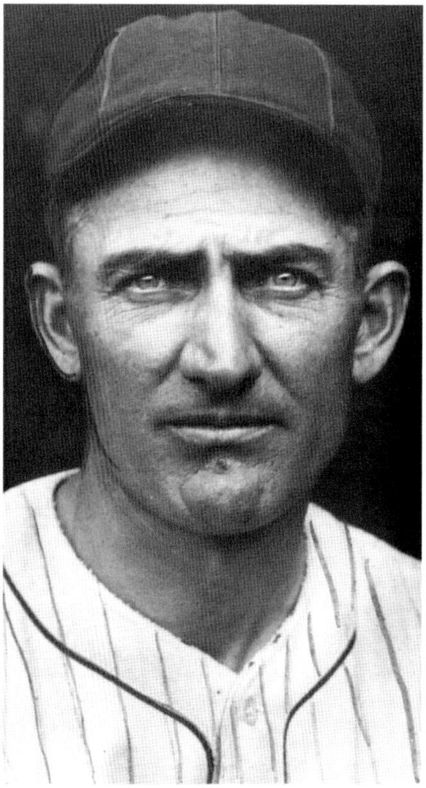

ELMER SMITH (1930). One of four players named Smith on the 1930 Millers (the others being Earl, Ernie, and Hal), 37-year-old Elmer showed Minneapolis fans he still had plenty of life in his bat by hitting 16 home runs in 84 games and batting .332 while roaming the outfield in 60. Smith, from Erie County, Ohio, began his professional career at the age of 18 playing for the Adrian (Michigan) Yeggs. In addition to 10 years spent in the minors, during which he batted .307, Smith's record included 10 seasons in the majors with a career batting average of .276. (Courtesy of Hennepin County Library Special Collections.)

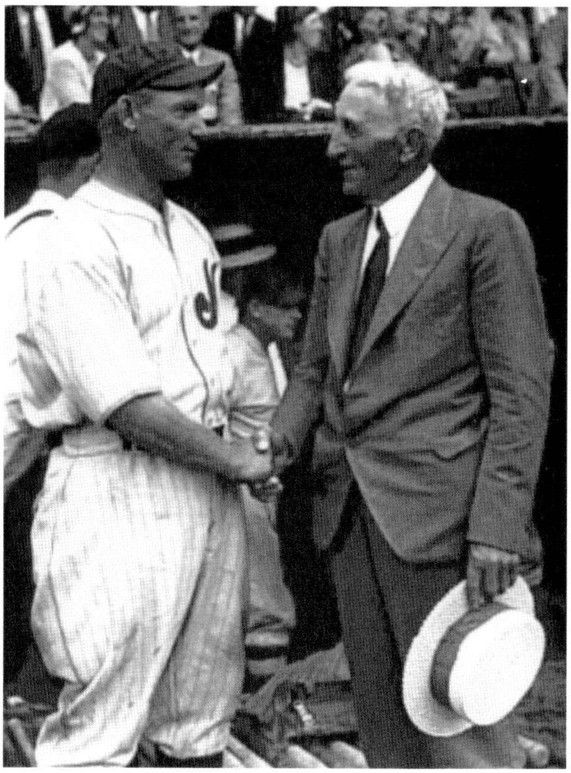

NICK "TOMATO FACE" CULLOP (1920, 1930). In 1930, the St. Louis–born swatter lit up the Minneapolis sky. In 139 games, the 29-year-old outfielder established new Minneapolis records in several areas while leading the league in runs (150), hits (152), home runs (54), total bases (393), and strikeouts (110). His outstanding .359 batting average, while not the club's declared leader that year, was officially the league's fourth-ranked mark. Here, he is shaking hands with Elmer Foster, the Minneapolis-born former major league southpaw who pitched and played various positions for a number of early Minneapolis and St. Paul teams in the late 19th century. (Author's collection.)

HY VANDENBERG (1931–1934). A graduate of Washburn High School in Minneapolis, big Hy Vandenberg, born at Abilene, Kansas, showed promise as a right-handed pitcher during his first season as a Miller, winning two games and losing none in 16 appearances at the age of 25. The following season, his promising career took off with 11 wins and six losses in 36 games with Minneapolis, but in 1934, he suffered a bit of a setback and was demoted to Class A. Vandenberg made his major league debut the following season with the Boston Red Sox. He is buried at Lakewood Cemetery on the south side of Minneapolis. (Courtesy of Hennepin County Library Special Collections.)

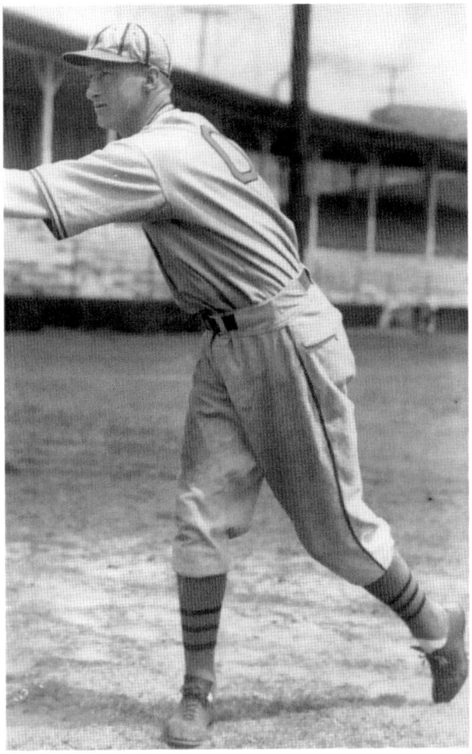

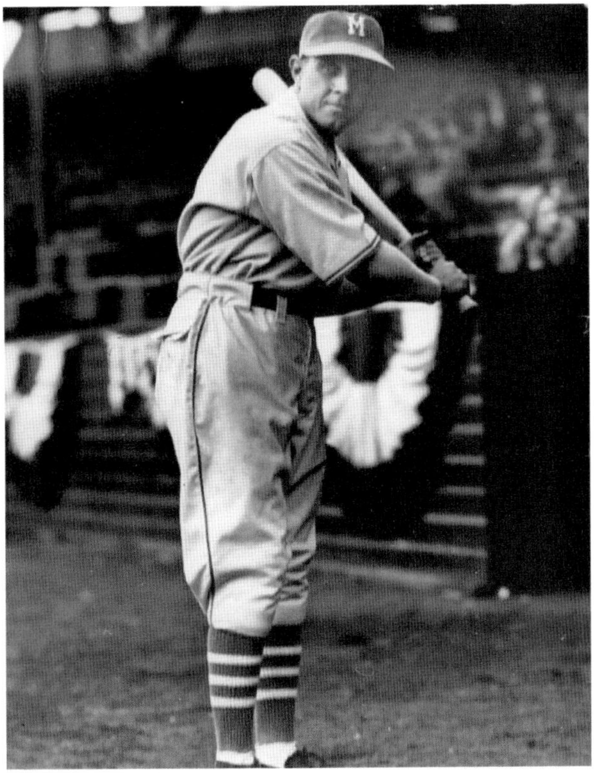

ART "SPEEDY" RUBLE (1931–1933). Coming off a 100-hit season with the Toronto Maple Leafs, Ruble endeared himself to Millers fans by erupting at the plate. After playing a subpar start with Toledo for 20 games to kick off the 1931 season, Ruble came north for 73 games, ripping into pitchers for 95 hits, belting 17 home runs, and batting .343 with 21 doubles. But the five-foot-ten Tennessean was just warming up. The next year, he went beyond his previous totals, compiling 345 total bases with 29 home runs, 25 doubles, and 11 triples, all under the umbrella of a .376 batting average. (Courtesy of Hennepin County Library Special Collections.)

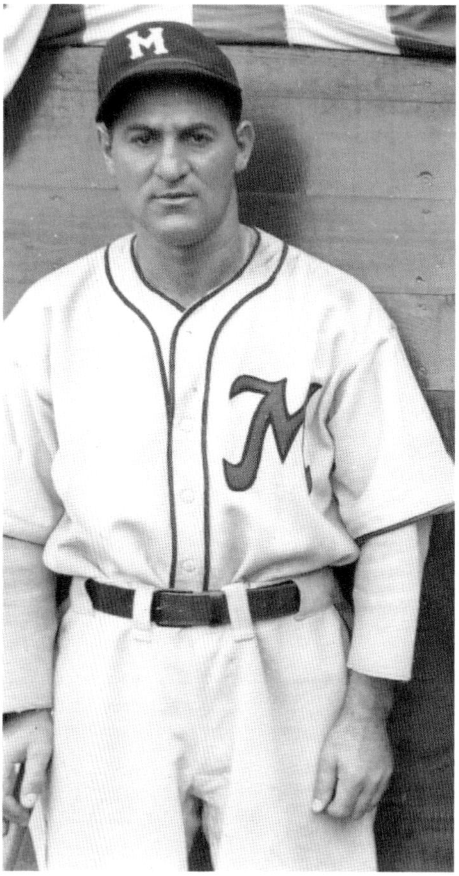

Andy Cohen (1932–1939). Cohen had some top-flight seasons with Minneapolis, but his 248 total bases in 1934 at the age of 29 topped the list. Batting .311 and ripping 33 doubles, he helped the Millers claim first place in 1934. Cohen's 207 hits, the most in any of his 18 seasons in professional ball, was his ticket to the Millers' all-time 200-hit list. Cohen managed Minneapolis for the early part of 1937 before Donie Bush returned to his job later in the year after being hospitalized. Cohen was an American Association All-Star in 1937. (Courtesy of Hennepin County Library Special Collections.)

Jess "The Silver Fox" Petty (1932–1935). World War I veteran Petty, shown here with manager Dave Bancroft (right) in 1933, had a career high 29-8 record (.784) in 1924 under Donie Bush at Indianapolis. Coming to Minneapolis in 1932, again to pitch for Bush, Petty, 37, won 16 games, losing only 10. Two exceptional seasons followed. Under Bancroft in 1933, he won 18 games, losing eight. In his final full season with the Millers, he excelled during their push to the pennant, winning 19 and losing seven (.731). His only home run in a 456-game minor league career came as a Miller in 1933. (Courtesy of Hennepin County Library Special Collections.)

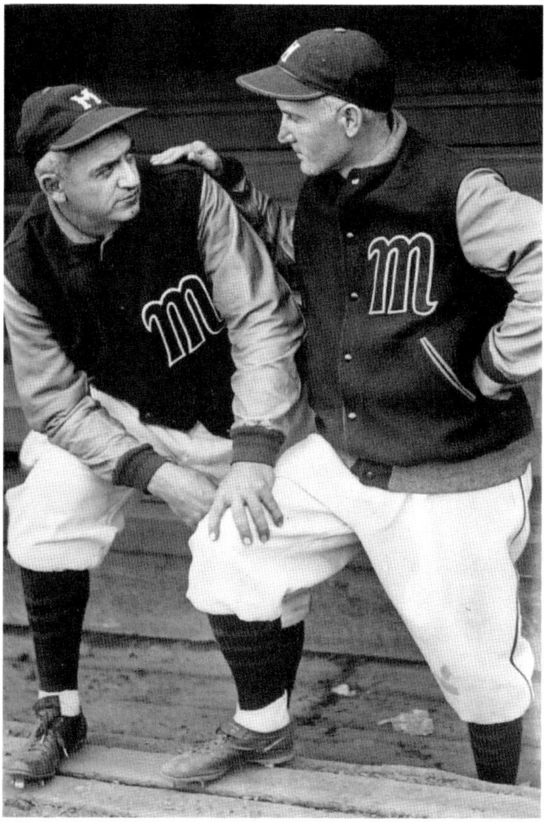

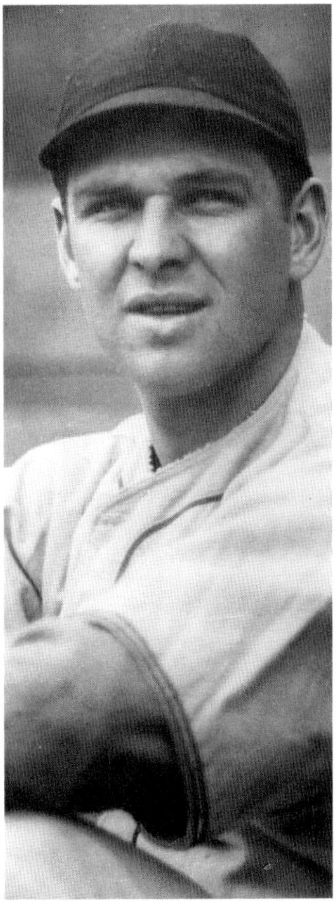

Babe Ganzel (1932–1935). In Ganzel's first year as the Millers' regular third sacker, the team captured its first league championship since 1915. Ganzel was at his best defensively at third base that year, and at the plate he approached a similar level of success to that achieved by his uncle John Ganzel, who earned the American Association batting title in 1902, hitting .311 with 23 home runs and 46 doubles while appearing in 163 games. In fact, Babe slugged .502 that year, his best full-season mark, compared with John's .532 (.366 batting in 136 games). The Massachusetts-born Babe later served as manager for the St. Paul Saints. (Courtesy of Hennepin County Library Special Collections.)

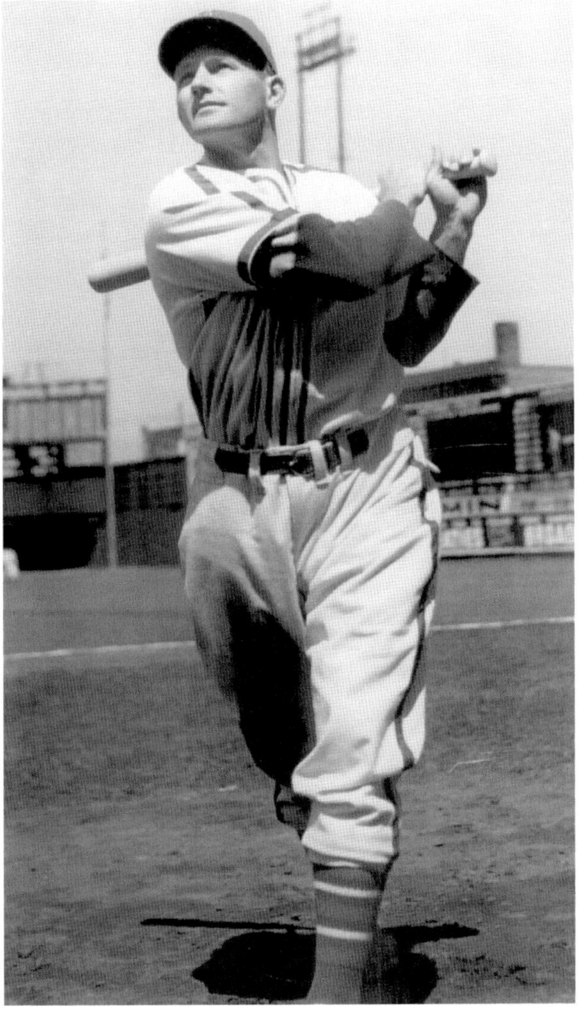

Ab Wright (1931–1934, 1939–1944). In 1934, the big 27-year-old Wright went full throttle, leading the club in two key categories: hits (with 214, a 17th all-time Minneapolis single-season high), and doubles (with 47). Wright's 29 home runs were ranked third on the club that year, but, being mentored by Buzz Arlett and Joe Hauser, he may not have minded his "secondary" standing—he made up for it by leading the Association with 366 total bases. On the season, he batted .353, fifth in the league. He was a two-time Minneapolis representative to the American Association All-Star squad (1939–1940). (Courtesy of Hennepin County Library Special Collections.)

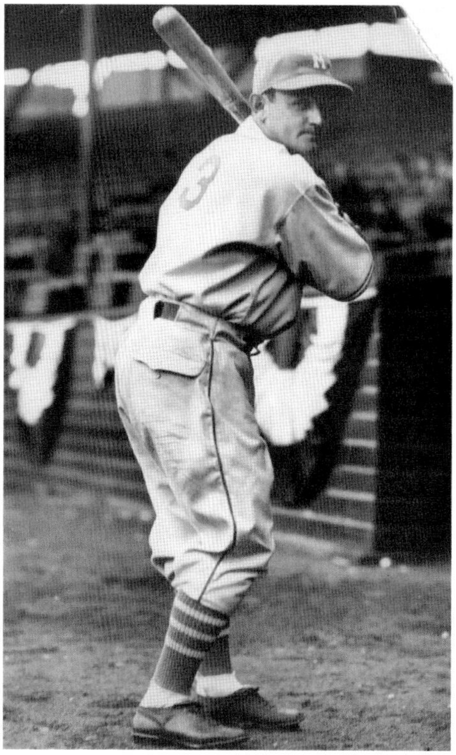

Harry Rice (1932). Raising his professional stature by batting .345 in his only year as a Miller, Rice spiced up the dish with 11 home runs and 15 doubles. The lefty-batting, righty-throwing Illinoisan played outfield in 98 of his 117 games, batting in 55 runs at the age of 30. Rice batted .329 during his 11-year minor league career, .299 during his 10 seasons in the majors. (Courtesy of Hennepin County Library Special Collections.)

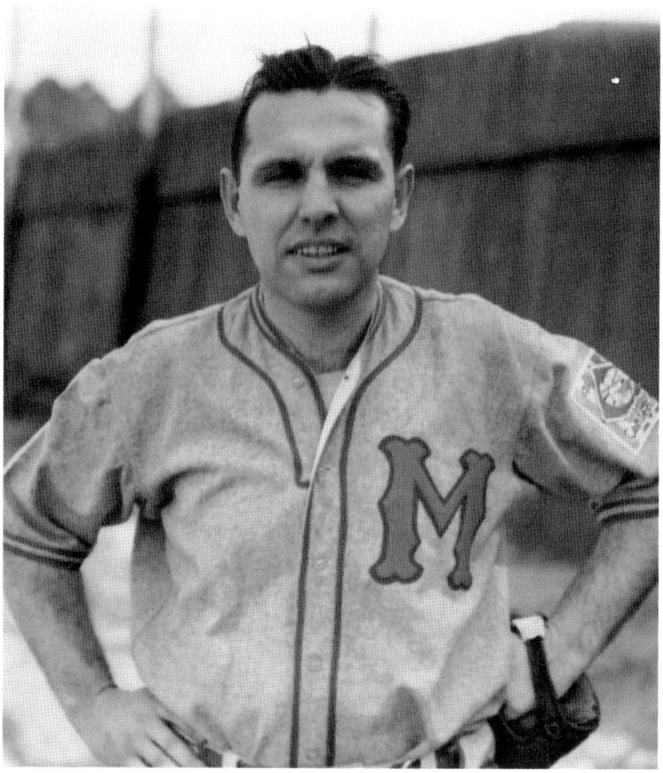

Joe Mowry (1931–1933). One of the Millers' shining stars of the 1930s, St. Louis, Missouri–born batsman Mowry collected 257 hits, the highest single-season total in Millers history, in 1933. He batted an eye-popping .348 while appearing in all 168 games, the only Miller to perform in every game that year. A major factor in the Minneapolis pennant run, Mowry led the league in games (168), at-bats (739), runs (175), and hits. In addition to his club record for hits, he owned the highest average of hits per game in Minneapolis history, with a mark of 1.53. (Courtesy of Hennepin County Library Special Collections.)

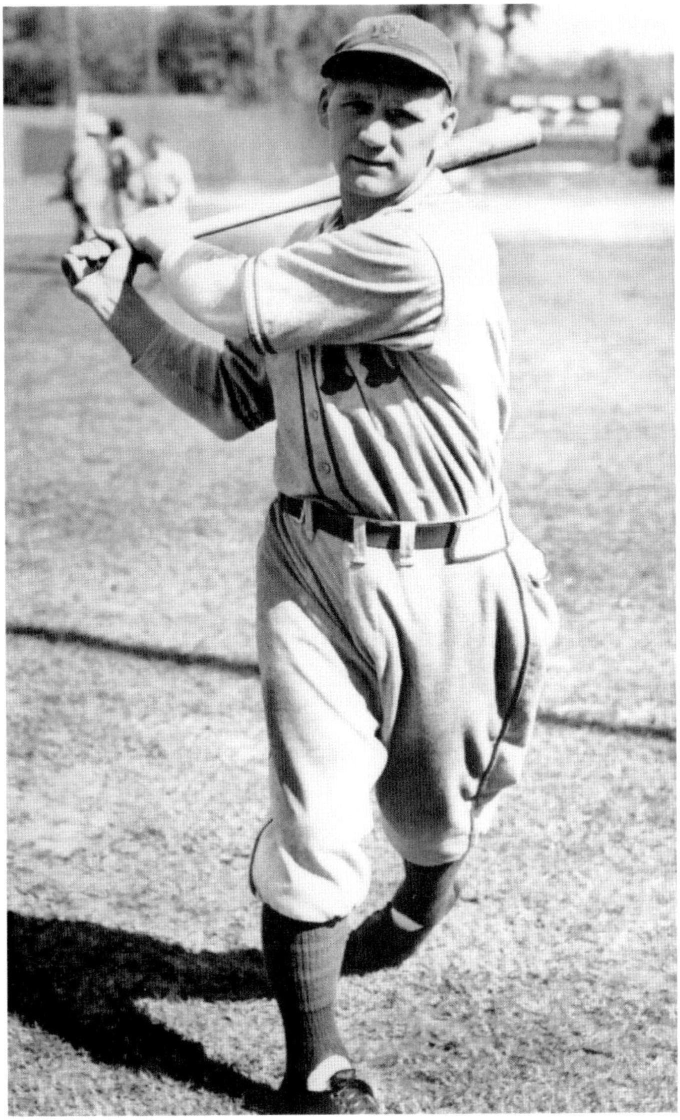

Joe "Unser Choe" Hauser (1932–1936). Milwaukee-born Joe Hauser (whose nickname, "Unser Choe," is "Our Joe" in German) stood out as one of the most prolific sluggers in American Association history. Beset by injuries throughout his career, he landed in Minneapolis in 1932 after an off year with the Baltimore Orioles of the International League. At the age of 33, he resurrected his career in hitter-friendly Nicollet Park, swatting 49 home runs his first year. In 1933, Hauser hit his stride, banging out 69 home runs—a new Association record by a considerable margin and one that stood in the annals of minor league ball for another two decades. Hauser's complete minor league tab included 379 home runs and a 15-season batting average of .294. Hauser operated a sporting goods shop in Sheboygan, where the great left-handed slugger spent his life after playing ball. The shop closed in 1984. Joe joined the "Great Majority" on July 11, 1997, at the age of 98. Hauser is buried next to his wife, Irene (née Kaye), to whom he was married for 62 years. They are buried at Calvary Cemetery in Sheboygan, Wisconsin. (Author's collection.)

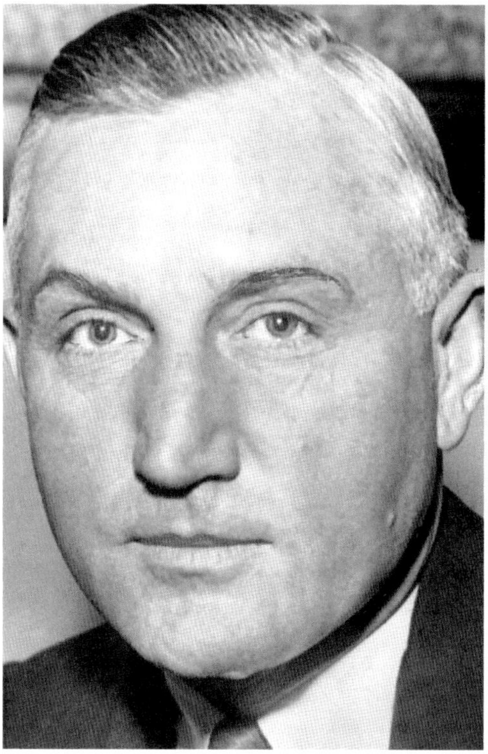

DAVE "BEAUTY" BANCROFT (1933). Inducted into the Hall of Fame in 1971, Bancroft, a native of Sioux City, Iowa, took on the managerial duties of the Millers at age 42. With four lackluster seasons managing the Boston Braves under his belt as a player-manager, he was prepared to lead Minneapolis, which finished second with a record of 86-67 in 1933. The former shortstop, who spent the first five of his 16 major league seasons with the Philadelphia Phillies, was making his debut in the American Association when he came to Minneapolis. (Courtesy of Hennepin County Library Special Collections.)

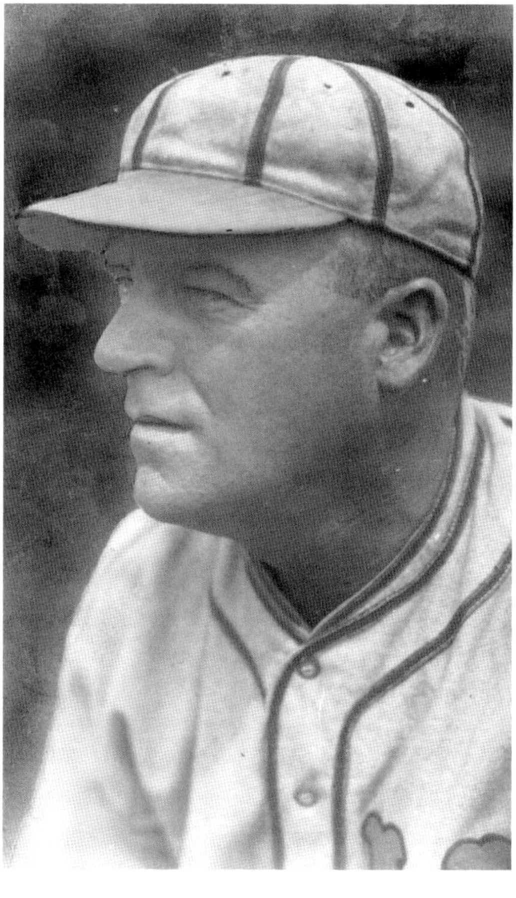

ROSY RYAN (1932, 1934–1936, 1944–1946). Wilfred (Bill) "Rosy" Ryan came up through the ranks as a pitcher, coach, and manager of the club. The native of Worcester, Massachusetts, entered professional ball in 1919 at the age of 21 with the Buffalo Bisons before embarking on an eight-year major league career spent mainly with the New York Giants. In 1932, his first season with the Millers, Ryan won 22 games to lead the Association, losing 13, with a circuit-high 60 games. Ryan managed the Millers from 1944 to 1946 before becoming their general manager. (Courtesy of Hennepin County Library Special Collections.)

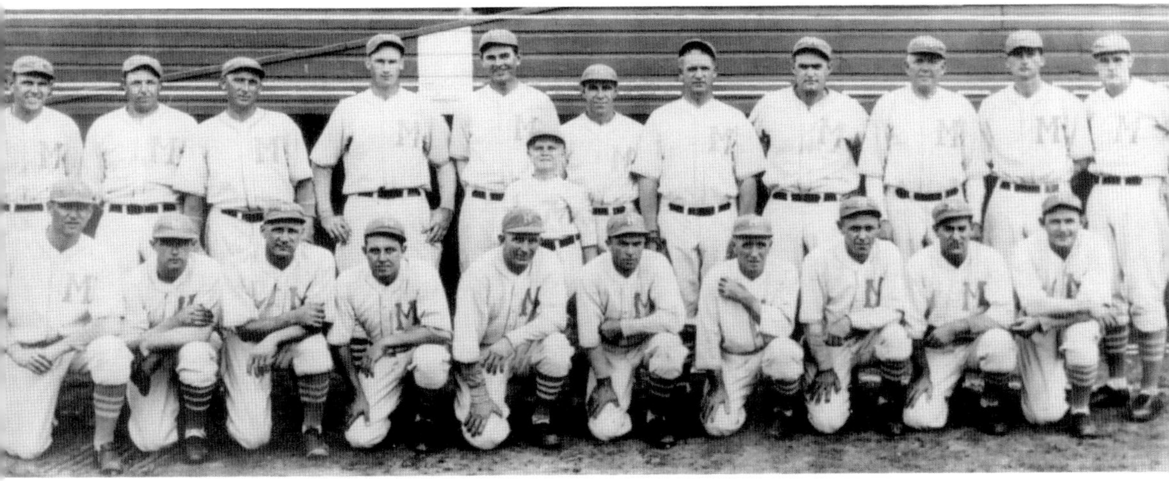

THE 1932 MINNEAPOLIS MILLERS. Minneapolis finished in first place for the first time since 1915. Donie Bush capitalized on an abundance of hitting during his first year as manager. Strong pitching gave them the balance they needed to win 100 games, as the club featured several league leaders, including outfielder Joe Mowry, with 175 runs and 257 hits, and fellow outfielder Art Ruble, who nailed down the batting championship with a .376 average. Joe Hauser was the Association's home run king with 49. Rosy Ryan won 22 games in 60 appearances, also a league best. Minneapolis won 100 games, lost 68, and finished 10 1/2 games ahead of the second-place Columbus Red Birds. In this photograph, from left to right, are (first row) Babe Ganzel (third baseman), Ray Fitzgerald (outfield), Joe Hauser (first baseman), Art Ruble (outfielder), Wes Griffin (catcher), Spencer Harris (outfielder), Donie Bush (manager), Eddie Sicking (second baseman), Andy Cohen (shortstop), and Harry Rice (outfielder); (second row) Joe Mowry (outfielder), Elam Vangilder (right-handed pitcher), Pea Ridge Day (right-handed pitcher), Hy Vandenberg (right-handed pitcher), Pete Donohue (right-handed pitcher), Ernie Smith (shortstop), Jess Petty (left-handed pitcher), Frank "Dutch" Henry (left-handed pitcher), Rube Benton (left-handed pitcher), Paul Richards (catcher), and Carmen Hill (right-handed pitcher). (Author's collection.)

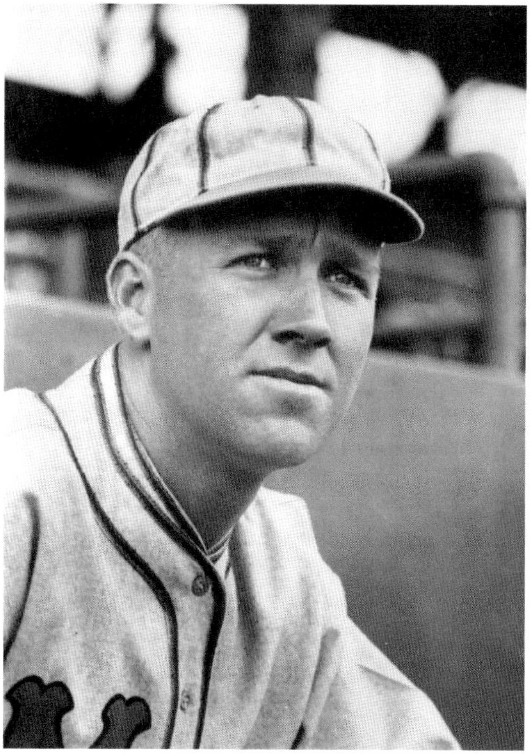

Whitey Hilcher (1933). Burdened by a portly ERA of 6.29, the Chicago-born righty's one season in Miller garb was otherwise successful. Posting a 12-8 record in 43 games under Dave Bancroft, the 24-year-old former Cincinnati Red was sharpening his skills. As a Toronto Maple Leaf the following year, he continued to show improvement, and by 1935, Hilcher was ready for his second, and final, call-up to the majors. He died in Minneapolis in 1962 at the age of 53 and is buried at Fort Snelling National Cemetery there. (Courtesy of Hennepin County Library Special Collections.)

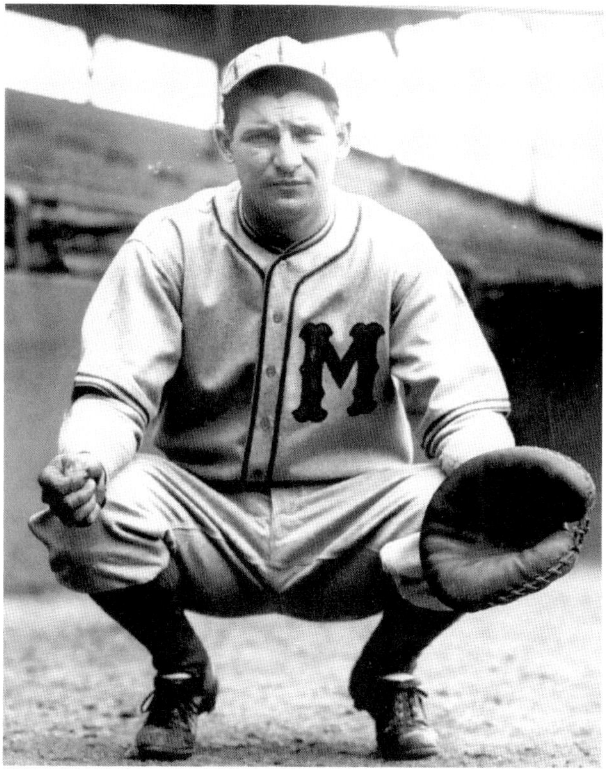

Joe "Gabby" Glenn (1933). Joe Glenn made his one season with the Millers a good one. The former New York Yankee catcher appeared in 137 games for Dave Bancroft's second-place Millers in 1933, catching in 125. Glenn hit over .300 with Class-B Hazleton (Pennsylvania) in 1930 but in only 59 games; Minneapolis fans may have been surprised when his bat caught fire like a summertime sparkler, bringing with it a .333 average, including 36 doubles and 17 home runs. Glenn played for Newark (AA) the next year, but he could not replicate the success he had enjoyed in Minneapolis. (Courtesy of Hennepin County Library Special Collections.)

JOHNNY EVERS AND JOE MOWRY (1933). The generations comingle as the up-and-coming Joe Mowry, one of the best players in Miller history, meets deadball-era hero Johnny Evers (with newspaper and cigar in hand) at the train. Both appear genuinely glad to see one another. According to the caption, the two are about to board the train to Boston, where Mowry will join the Braves, who purchased his contract from the Millers "for a large sum of money and two players." The photograph is dated May 12, 1933. (Courtesy of Hennepin County Library Special Collections.)

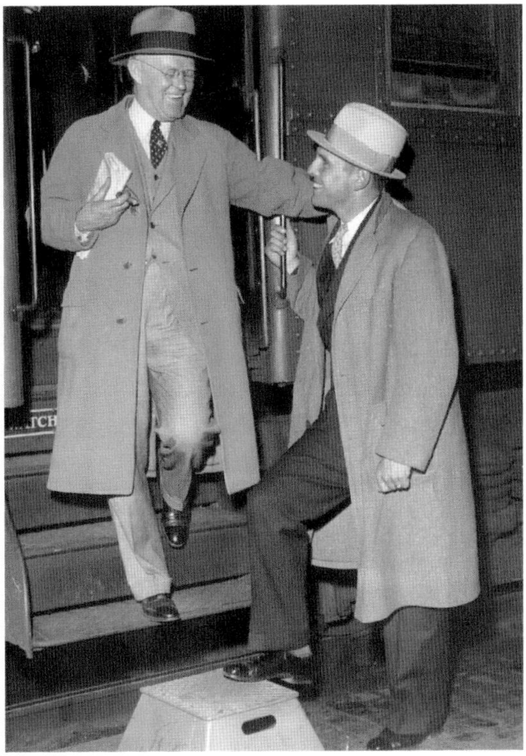

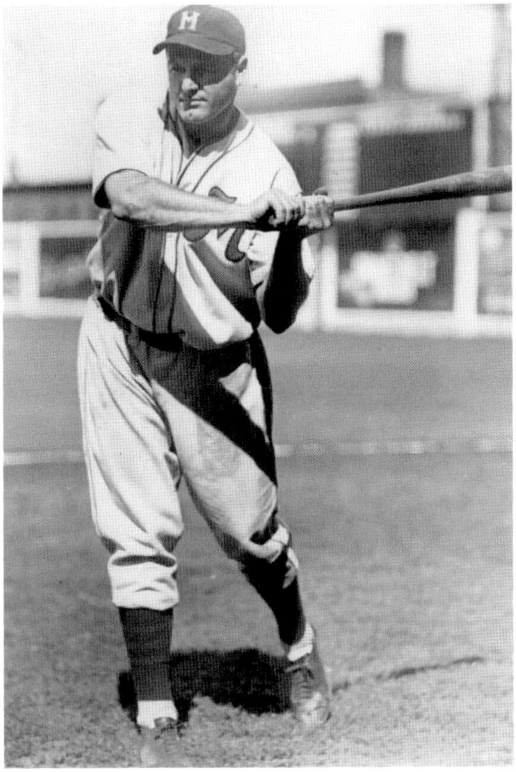

BUZZ ARLETT (1934–1936). Having made a solid case for himself as a legacy player with the Oakland Oaks in the Pacific Coast League, Arlett joined the Millers after stops in Baltimore (Class AA) and Birmingham (A) at the age of 35. He introduced himself to Minneapolitans by belting 41 home runs to capture the league's home run crown, hitting .319 with 32 doubles along the way. His numbers fell precipitously henceforth, and he played his last few games with Syracuse (AA) in 1937. He was a career .336 hitter in the minor leagues, with a total of 367 home runs in 17 seasons. Arlett died at age 65 in Minneapolis and is buried at Lakewood Cemetery there. (Courtesy of Hennepin County Library Special Collections.)

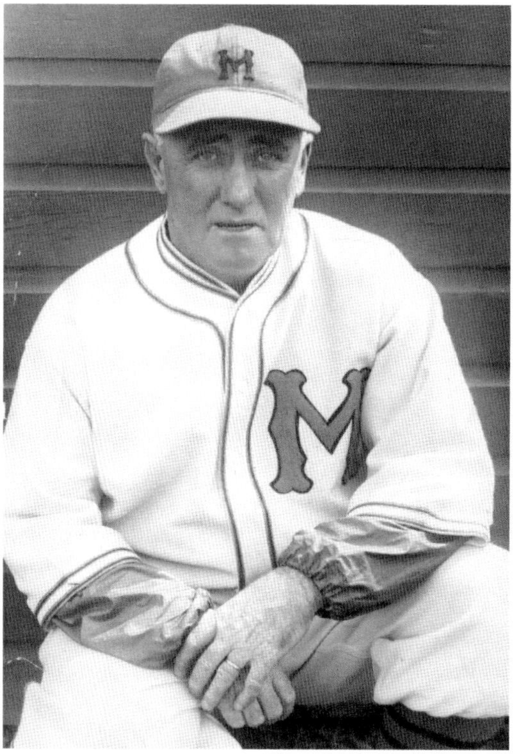

Owen "Donie" Bush (1932, 1934–1938). Born October 8, 1887, in Indianapolis, Bush was a baseball man from the get-go. After getting a look with the Detroit Tigers in 1908, he spent the next 13 seasons in a Tiger uniform, excelling as their regular shortstop. Getting his first taste of managing in 1923 with the American League's Washington Senators, Bush came home to pilot the American Association's Indianapolis Indians in 1924, bringing them to a second-place finish with a record of 92-73, just three games behind the St. Paul Saints. Bush first took the reins in Minneapolis in 1934 and remained with the club through the 1938 season. Under Bush, the Millers staged some of their most successful seasons. (Courtesy of Hennepin County Library Special Collections.)

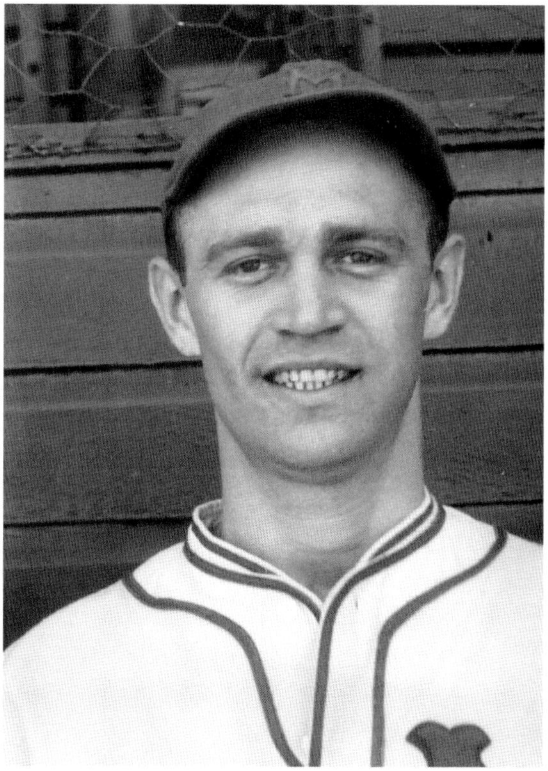

Bill "Lefty" Perrin (1935). In his only season with Minneapolis, Perrin was part of the charge to the top with his record of 14-13 in 32 starts. His tendency to walk batters was reflected by the 106 bases on balls he issued in 231 innings, most on the club, but he struck out 119 in 47 appearances. His long career in baseball culminated with a five-year stretch managing in Florida. (Courtesy of Hennepin County Library Special Collections.)

BUCK MARROW (1934–1935). The big righty from Tarboro, North Carolina, graduated from nearby Davidson College, where he played all three main team sports. Marrow appeared in 18 games for the Detroit Tigers in 1932. Coming to Minneapolis in 1934, he posted a 9-10 record en route to the Millers' sixth championship season, appearing in 43 games with 78 strikeouts. The following year, he left the club midseason to pitch for the Louisville Colonels in 1935. (Courtesy of Hennepin County Library Special Collections.)

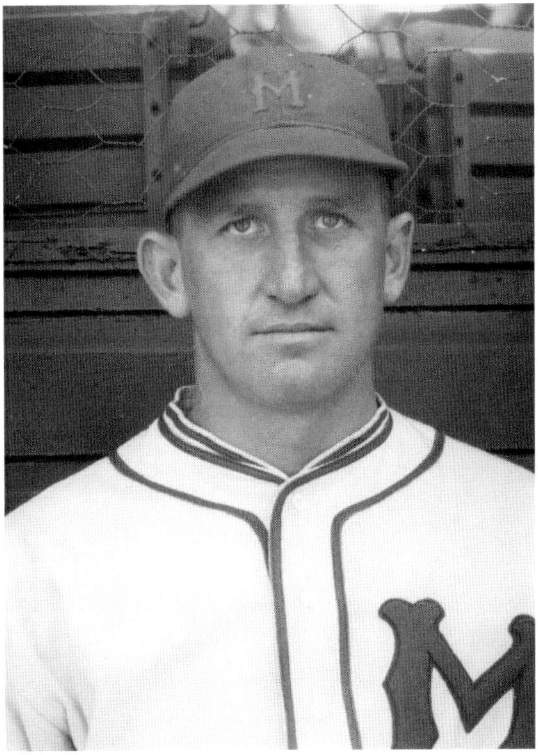

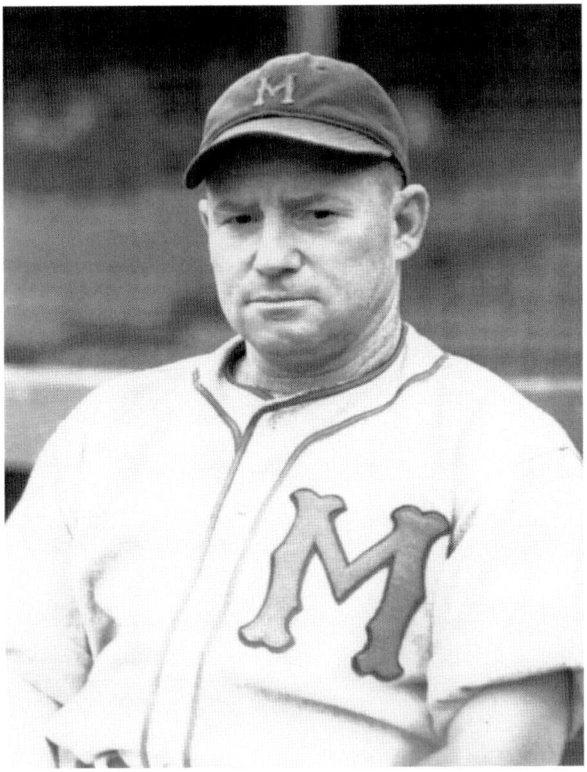

PINKY HARGRAVE (1934–1936). Younger brother of former Millers and St. Paul Saints star backstop Eugene "Bubbles" Hargrave, catcher William McKinley "Pinky" Hargrave spent a decade in the major leagues before joining Minneapolis. During his first season as a Miller, the 38-year-old Hargrave had a career year, batting .356 in 147 games with 29 doubles, an exceptional accomplishment at his age. In addition, Hargrave pounded out 16 home runs and produced 286 total bases, fifth-best on this offensive juggernaut. The Millers batted .308 to lead the Association on their way to capturing the top spot in the standings. They were denied the championship in a seven-game playoff against the Columbus Red Birds in 1934. (Author's collection.)

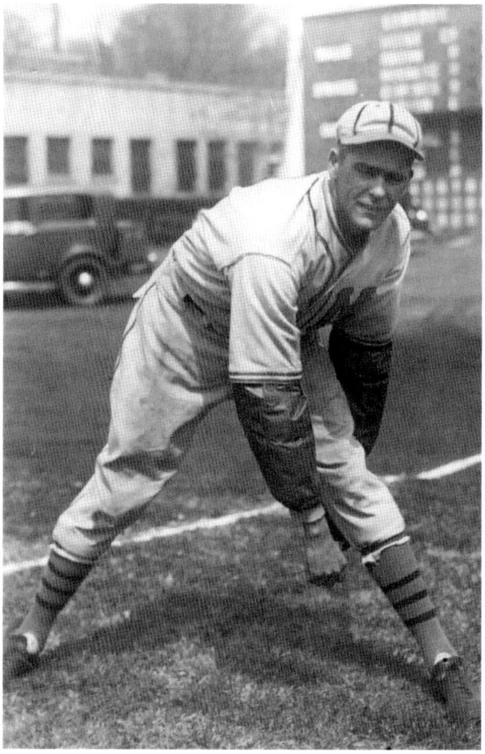

Ray "Iron Man" Star (1934–1935). A future National League All-Star right-hander, Starr joined the Millers in 1934 and contributed 260 innings to their championship season that year, going 16-17 but leading the league with 123 bases on balls. Balancing the equation, however, he struck out a club-high 110 batters; behind the bat, the 28-year-old Oklahoman also contributed a home run, adding some gloss to his anemic .167 batting average that year. (Courtesy of Hennepin County Library Special Collections.)

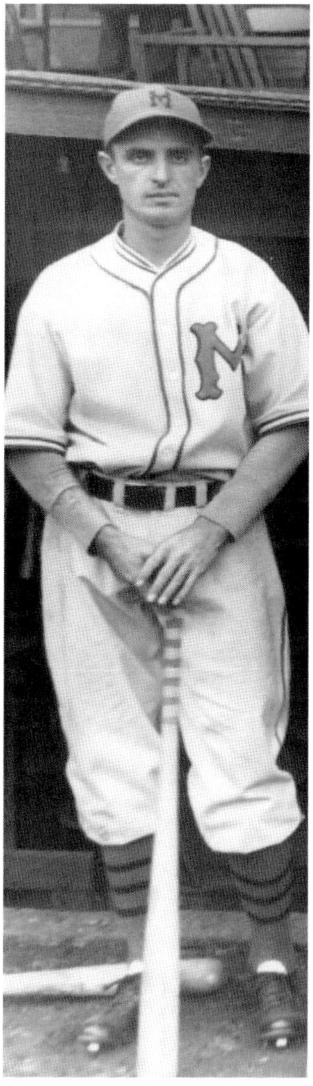

Leo Norris (1930–1935). Norris was just 22 when he joined the Millers, appearing in only two games in 1930. The following year, he set a precedent for what fans could expect: a .292 batting average with 17 homers, 20 doubles, and nine triples. Splitting his time evenly between third base and second base that year, the native of Bay St. Louis, Mississippi, eventually specialized at shortstop. His best year as a Miller came in 1935, when he batted .290 with 22 long balls, 39 doubles, and 11 triples as one of only seven players in the league to appear in all 154 games. (Courtesy of Hennepin County Library Special Collections.)

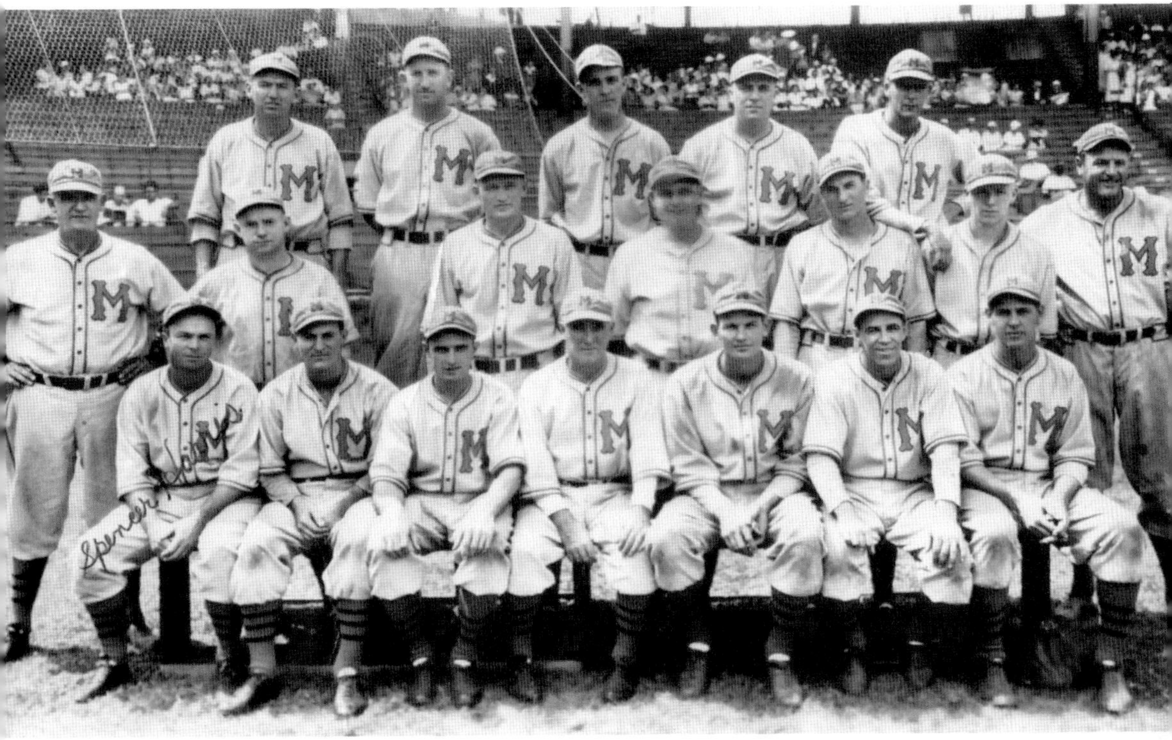

THE 1934 MINNEAPOLIS MILLERS. In 1934, the Millers finished in first place for the second time in three years, narrowly escaping the clutches of the Columbus Red Birds, who finished just two games behind. With 85 wins in the Association and 64 losses (.570), the Millers had the fewest wins of any previous first-place team and the poorest first-place record since the 1909 Louisville Colonels posted a winning percentage of .554 (93-75). Each of the nine Miller position players appearing in at least 80 games batted over .300, including utility man Ernie Smith (.325 in 95 games). Pictured here, from left to right, are (first row) Spencer Harris (outfielder), Andy Cohen (second baseman), Leo Norris (shortstop), Donie Bush (manager), Ab Wright (outfielder), Ernie Smith (third baseman), and Russ Young (catcher); (second row) Jess Petty (left-handed pitcher), Pinky Hargrave (catcher), Johnny Butler (coach), Babe Ganzel (third baseman), Syd Cohen (left-handed pitcher), Charles "Lefty" Johnson (left-handed pitcher), and Buzz Arlett (outfielder); (third row) Tiny Chaplin (right-handed pitcher), Buck Marrow (right-handed pitcher), Walt Tauscher (right-handed pitcher), Rosy Ryan (right-handed pitcher), and an unidentified player. (Author's collection.)

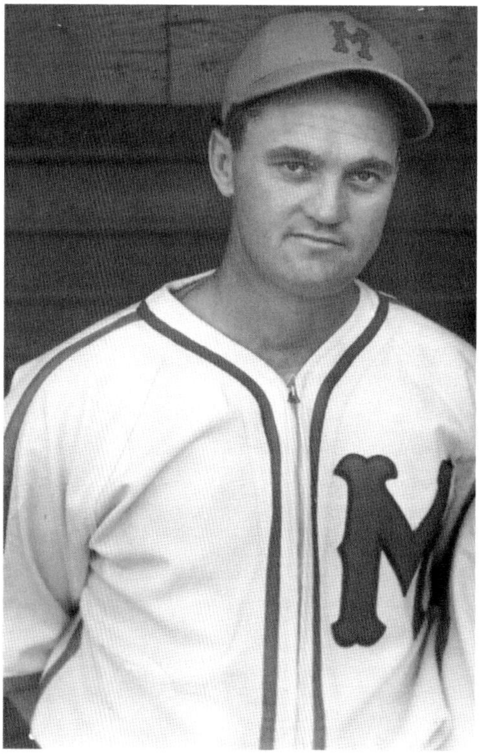

Belve Bean (1935–1940). When Minneapolis baseball fans got a taste of the well-built Texas hurler in six games during the 1935 season, they probably wondered how to say the name of Beveric Benton "Bill" Bean. Belve rhymes with "twelve," according to one official source. Bean became a fixture on the Miller club until the 1940 season after compiling a record of 51-38 in over 140 games, most of which were starts. In 1937, Bean's bat complemented his arm, providing support to the tune of a .309 batting average (with four home runs) while he posted a record of 16-11 from the hill. (Courtesy of Hennepin County Library Special Collections.)

Denny Galehouse (1935). Growing up near Barberton, Ohio, Galehouse was in his sixth year of professional ball when he reached the Double-A level. Under Donie Bush, the six-foot-one righty made 27 starts in 35 games with an unflattering 5.39 ERA, winning 15 and losing eight. He led the Millers with 140 strikeouts, second in the league, doubling up on his 71 bases on balls. For most of his remaining career, he pitched in the majors. Galehouse spent the 1945 season in service to his country as a member of the US Navy. (Courtesy of Hennepin County Library Special Collections.)

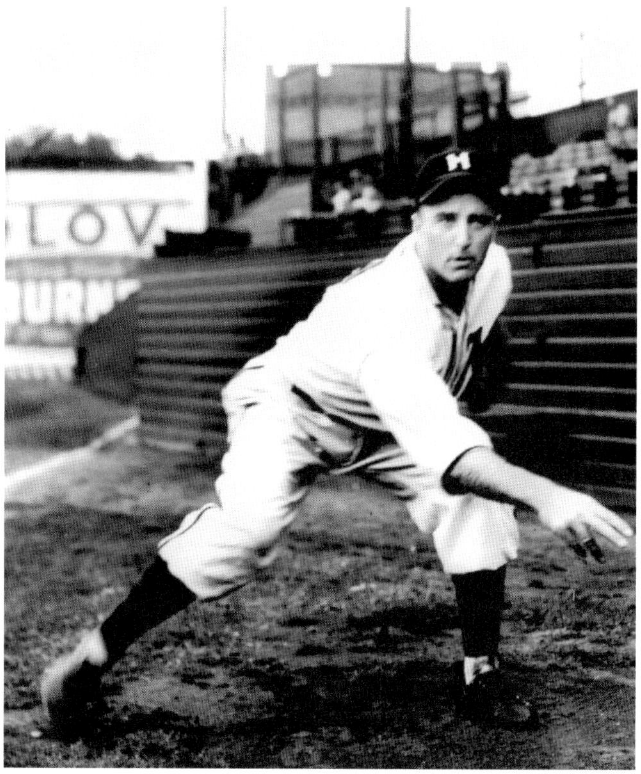

JOHNNY "PATCHEYE" GILL (1934–1935). The slugger from Nashville, Tennessee, got a lot of attention in American Association circles with his potent bat in 1935. Property of the Cleveland Indians, Gill balanced his outfield finesse (only 13 errors in 148 games) with a bulging bat while playing a major role in igniting Minneapolis to the league's 1935 championship. He led the circuit in runs (148), RBIs (154), home runs (43), and total bases (400), with a remarkable .361 average. He joined the Chicago Cubs in 1936. Gill spent 21 seasons in professional ball, managing in the Kentucky-Illinois-Tennessee (KITTY) League as a player-manager during the 1940s. (Courtesy of Hennepin County Library Special Collections.)

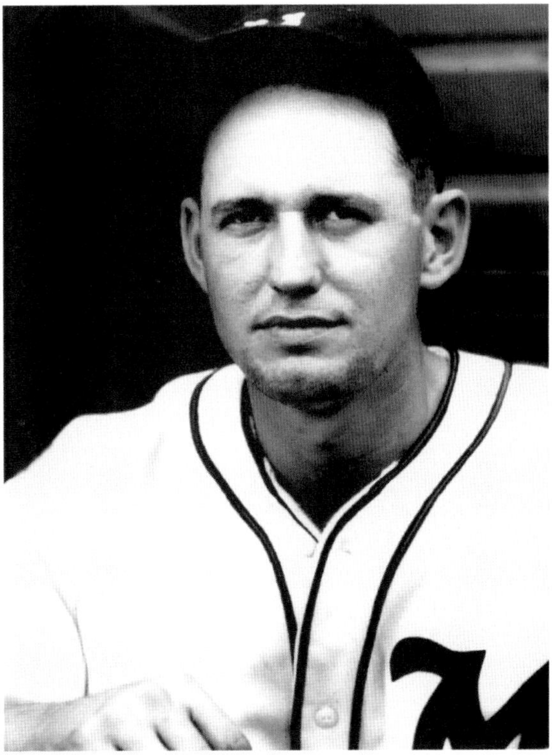

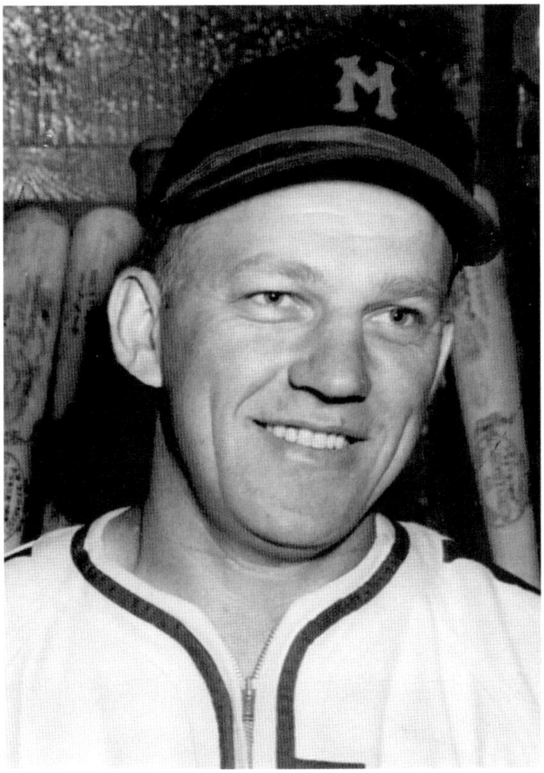

FABIAN GAFFKE (1935–1938, 1940–1941, 1946). Milwaukee native Gaffke showed exceptional talent as a 21-year-old, batting .302 with 19 home runs and 29 doubles during the Millers' 1935 pennant drive. In 1936, he blossomed, batting a team-leading .342 with 25 home runs and 37 doubles and becoming a member of the Millers' 200-hit club with 213, also a team high that year. Gaffke was the lone Minneapolis representative to the American Association All-Star squad in 1936. He is buried at St. Adalbert's Cemetery in Milwaukee, where his baseball-themed headstone leaves a lasting reminder of his passion for the game. (Courtesy of Hennepin County Library Special Collections.)

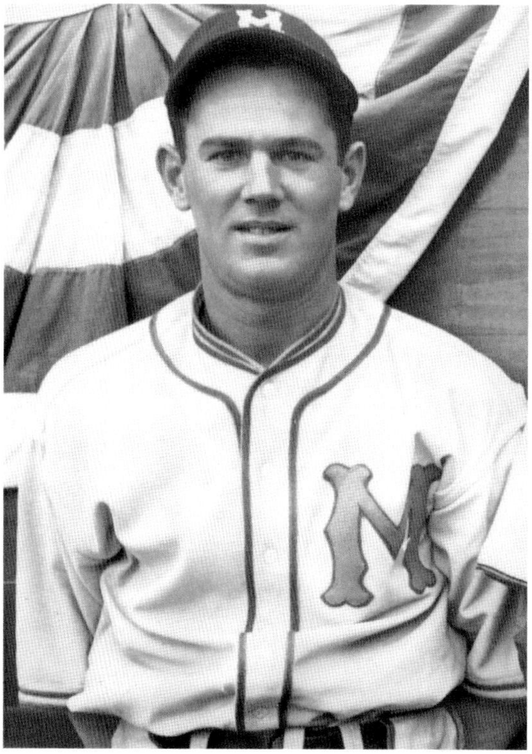

Al Leitz (1935–1936). Starting off a career in professional ball at the Double-A level is an uncommon occurrence, yet that is what Leitz did when he broke in with the Millers in 1935 at the age of 25, backing up Miller mainstay Pinky Hargrave. With three home runs, Leitz batted .249 in 69 games. Although he returned to Minneapolis in 1936 for seven games, he spent the rest of his baseball career at Single-A or below. He began a seven-year managerial career with the Waycross (Georgia) Bears (Class D) in 1939 at the age of 29. (Courtesy of Hennepin County Library Special Collections.)

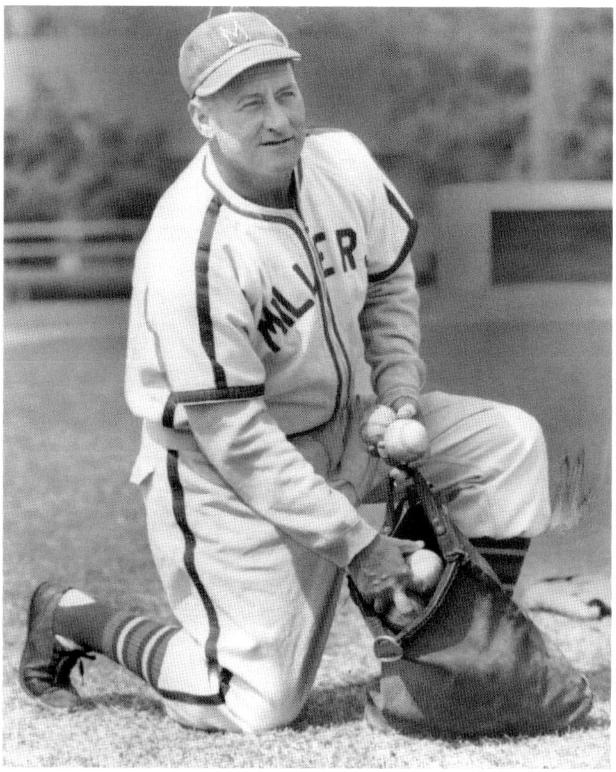

Ray Kolp (1935–1936). A decade after winning 22 games for the Millers' archrival, the St. Paul Saints, in 1925, Kolp joined Minneapolis at the age of 40, making 28 starts and nailing down 11 wins against nine losses. It was not a bad showing for a quadragenarian. He would later coach Millers pitchers, adding to his already lengthy professional baseball vita. (Courtesy of Hennepin County Library Special Collections.)

EARL "SNITZ" BROWNE (1936). After four mixed seasons with the Little Rock Travelers, Browne came north to ply his trade as a left-handed first baseman and outfielder. Born in Louisville, Kentucky, the left-handed swinging Browne thrived at Nicollet Park, belting a club-high 35 home runs in 1936 with a .328 batting average. He was the clear club leader in total bases with 372, among the leaders since 1930. In addition to playing first base, Browne pitched in 128 games during his six minor league seasons, but none for Minneapolis. The Millers wound up fifth in the league with a record of 78-76 in Browne's only season with the club. (Courtesy of Hennepin County Library Special Collections.)

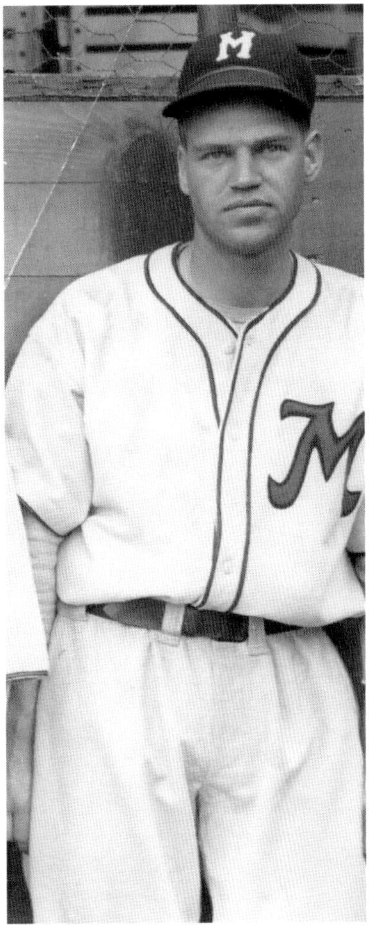

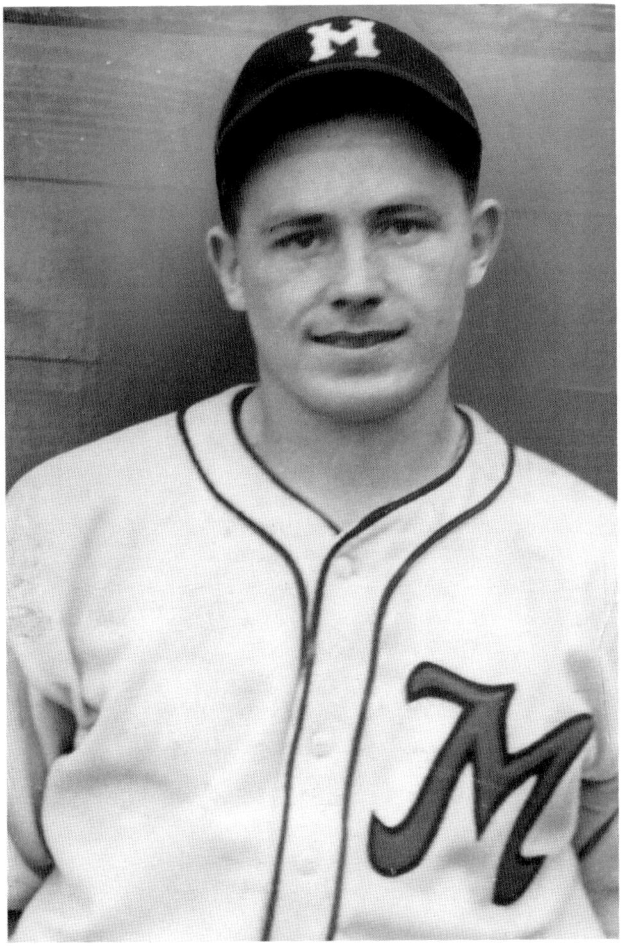

JIM WASDELL (1936, 1939). After a cup of coffee with Minneapolis in 1936, outfielder Wasdell came back to the Millers after spending two seasons playing for the Washington Senators. The experience proved beneficial for the 25-year-old Cleveland, Ohio, native, as reflected by his 29 home runs, 23 doubles, and .323 batting average for Tom Sheehan's third-place Millers in 1939. (Courtesy of Hennepin County Library Special Collections.)

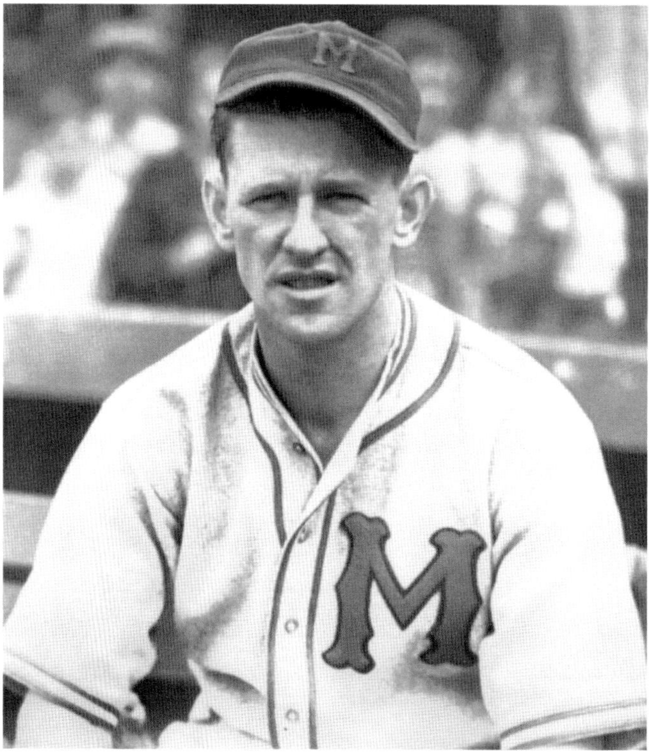

Reggie Grabowski (1936–1938). Grabowski, a lean righty from Syracuse, New York, won a combined 20 games with Minneapolis during his only Association seasons. He was not directly related to Johnny Grabowski, a Miller catcher from 1923 to 1924, but they shared an unfortunate fate: both died young. Reggie Grabowski, a local top bowler after his baseball career, died of a heart attack at the age of 47; Johnny "Nig" Grabowski passed away at the age of 46 as the result of burns sustained in a fire that consumed his home in Guilderland, New York. (Author's collection.)

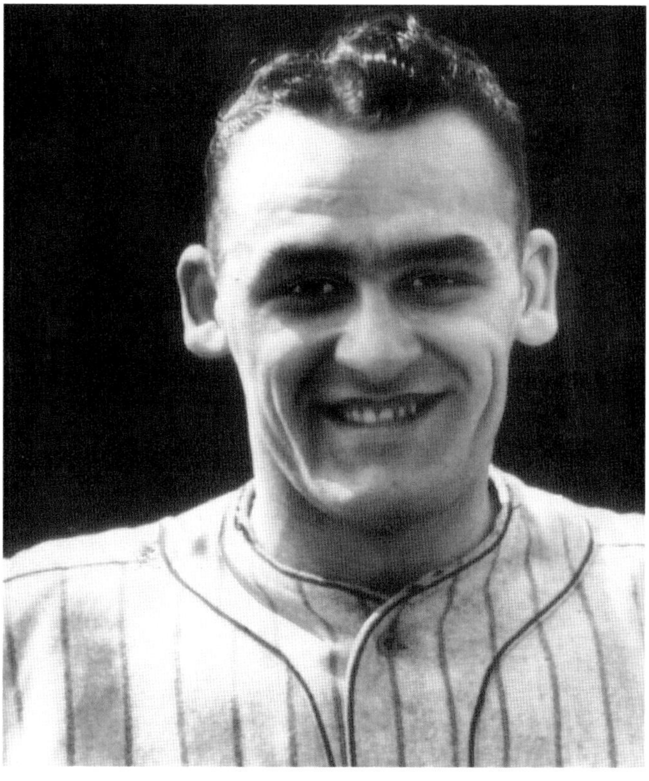

Al "Happy" Milnar (1936). After a cup of coffee with the Cleveland Indians, Cleveland native Milnar entered the American Association fray at the age of 22, finishing with an 8-15 record with 31 appearances. Miller pitchers were led by Archie McKain's 19 wins, 12 losses, and 127 strikeouts. With 118 strikeouts, Milnar was the club's runner-up, but the southpaw's record was offset by a propensity to walk batters. He was a member of the American League All-Star team in 1940 and entered the military in 1944. (Courtesy of Hennepin County Library Special Collections.)

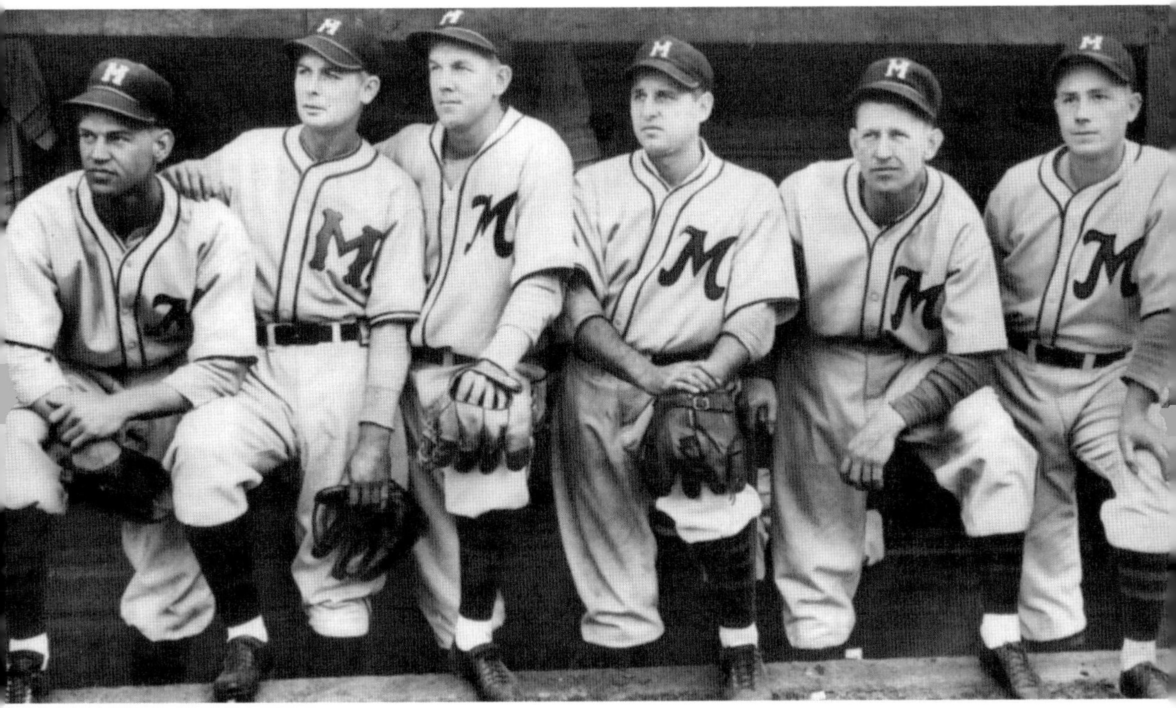

VISIONS OF PENNANT. The newest members of the 1936 Minneapolis Millers gather upon the dugout steps at Nicollet Park in hopeful anticipation as they contemplate their pennant chances. Pictured in this May 10, 1936, *Minneapolis Tribune* photograph taken by George M. Ryan, are, from left to right, Earl Browne (outfielder/first baseman), Jake Baker (left-handed pitcher), Blondy Ryan (shortstop), Roy Pfleger (infielder), Reggie Grabowski (right-handed pitcher), and Jim Wasdell (first baseman/outfielder). (Author's collection.)

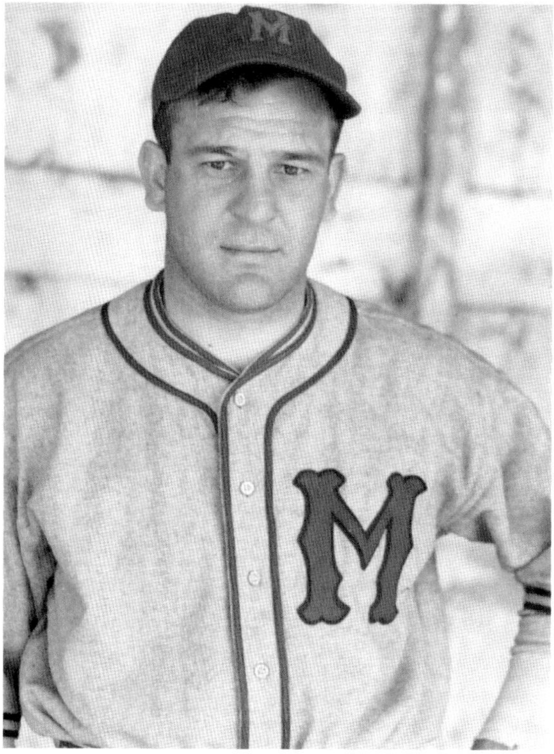

DUSTY COOKE (1937). Hitting from the left side, the big North Carolinian batted .345 with 47 doubles, second only to teammate Carl Reynolds's .355 and 49 two-baggers; the pair led the circuit in doubles. Appearing in 151 contests, Cooke blasted 18 home runs and laced eight triples on this potent Miller team. He came to Minneapolis with eight years of major league experience in the American League, including two exceptional seasons with the Boston Red Sox. Cooke, 30, led the club's outfield with an unusually high 18 errors but was an American Association All-Star in a Miller uniform. (Courtesy of Hennepin County Library Special Collections.)

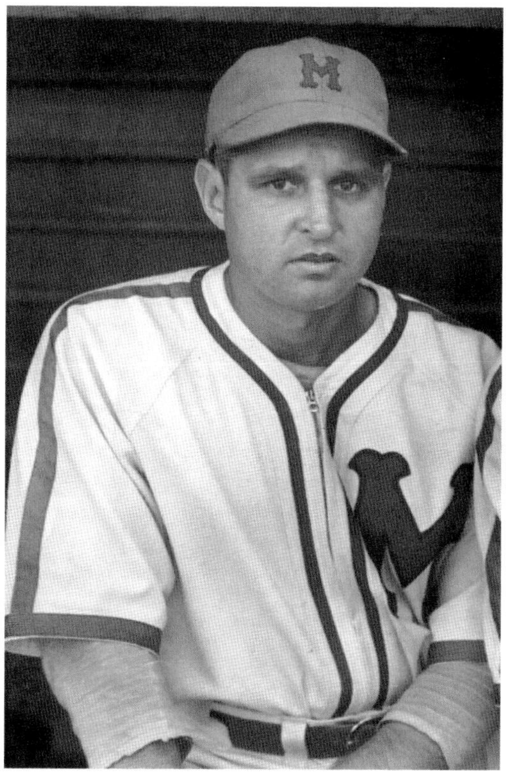

ROY PFLEGER (1936–1939). A utility infielder, the Millers took advantage of the 27-year-old's versatility by playing him predominantly at second base (58 games), and also at third base and shortstop in his first year, platooning with Minneapolis's perennial keystone sacker Andy Cohen. The lefty-batting, righty-throwing Ohioan showed some shine with his bat his first two seasons with a combined 54 circuit clouts, 25 in 1936 and a league-high 29 in 1937, when he batted a career-high .326 with a .565 slugging average. (Courtesy of Hennepin County Library Special Collections.)

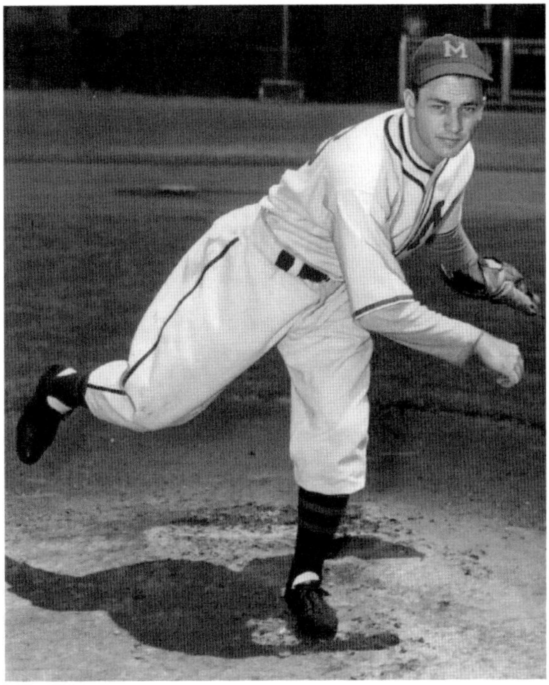

CHARLIE "BROADWAY" WAGNER (1937–1938). During his two seasons with Minneapolis, Wagner was preparing for a successful six-year career, interrupted by military service, with the Boston Red Sox (1938–1942, 1946). He opened his American Association term with a 20-win season. The Millers finished third in the race in 1937, as Wagner led the club in wins, topping the league with 20 complete games. He opened the 1938 season with Boston, returning to Minneapolis later that year and posting a record of 8-3. Wagner was a Minneapolis representative to the American Association All-Star squad in 1937. (Courtesy of Hennepin County Library Special Collections.)

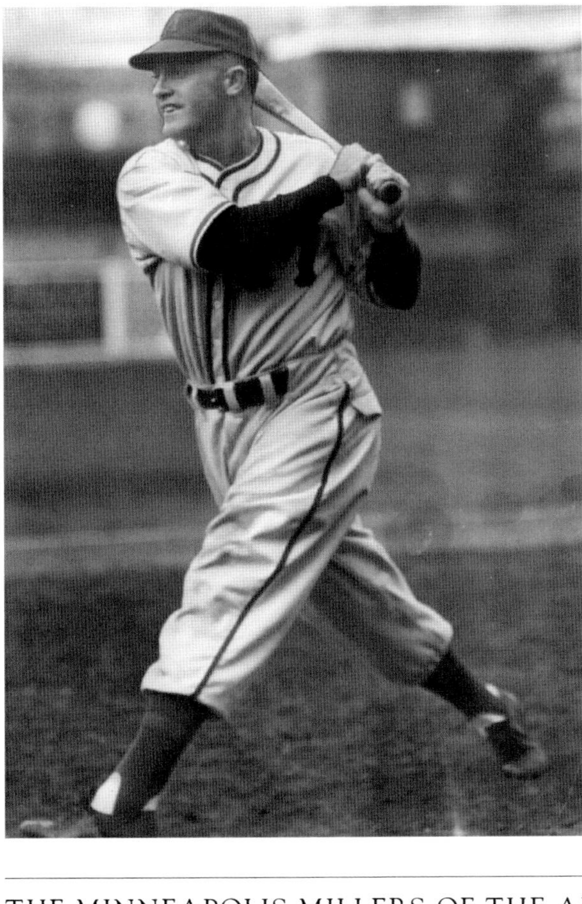

RED KRESS (1937). Kress, the Minneapolis shortstop, was the league's only player appearing in 158 games (in a 154-game schedule). The 32-year-old from Columbia, California, collected 217 hits (placing him 14th in the Millers' all-time 200-hit club among single-season leaders), hitting .334 with a league-high 157 RBI—nearly one per game! Having honed his eye with 10 previous seasons of major league experience, Kress squared up for 29 home runs, the best in the Association. He was a career .286 hitter in the majors and had a .301 mark in nine minor league seasons. He represented Minneapolis in the American Association All-Star game. (Courtesy of Hennepin County Library Special Collections.)

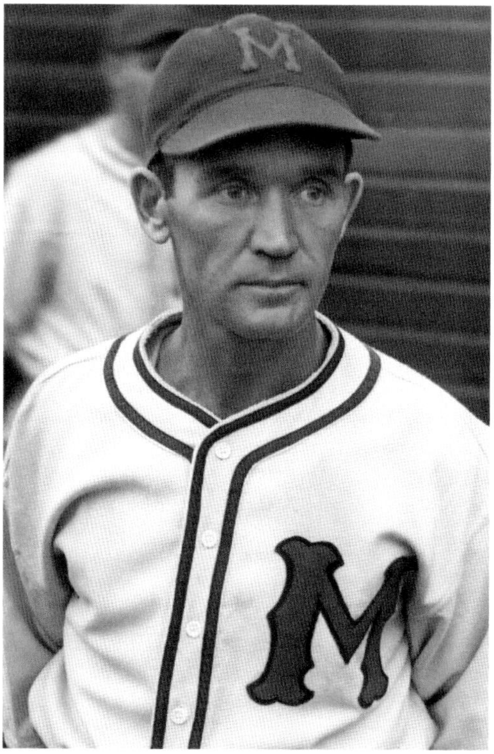

LEON "LEFTY" PETTIT (1937). The sturdy southpaw flourished with the Class-A Chattanooga Lookouts before his first taste of Double-A ball with the Albany Senators when he went 9-22 in 1936. With Minneapolis the following year, he was used largely in relief, winning four games and losing six in 28 appearances. (Courtesy of Hennepin County Library Special Collections.)

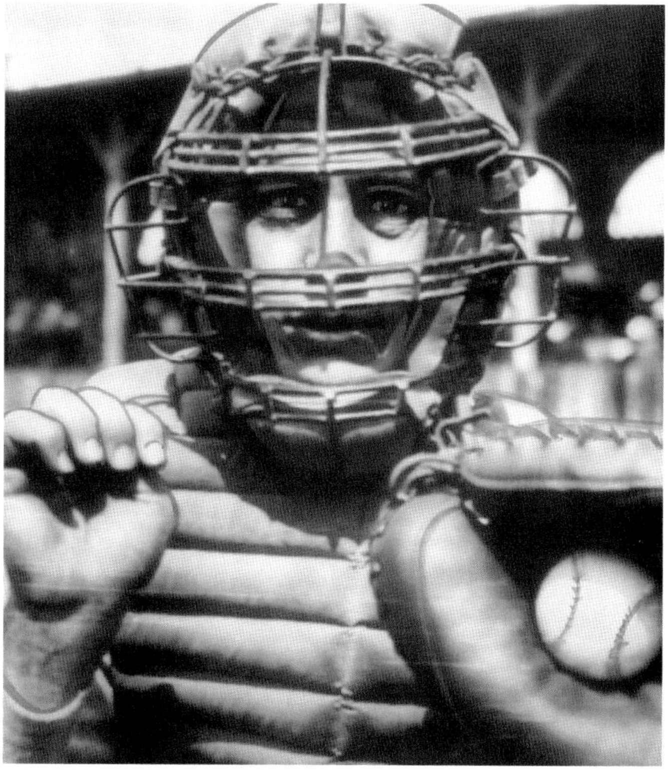

JOHNNY PEACOCK (1937). As the lead catcher for the third-place Millers in 1937, Peacock strutted his stuff with a .311 batting average and seven home runs in 109 games. He'd had a career year with the Nashville Volunteers the season before, batting .334 in 112 games. These accomplishments helped him develop his skills for catching with the Boston Red Sox, among other teams. He went on to manage the New Orleans Pelicans (AA) in 1946. Peacock was a Minneapolis representative to the American Association All-Star squad in 1937. (Courtesy of Hennepin County Library Special Collections.)

Stan Spence (1937–1938). Spence, a future four-time American League All-Star outfielder, was applauded for the strength and consistency of his hitting. In his first season with sixth-place Minneapolis, the Kentucky native batted .321 in 117 games; in 1938, he sported a .322 mark in 136 tilts while accompanying teammate Ted Williams in the outfield in 130. (Courtesy of Hennepin County Library Special Collections.)

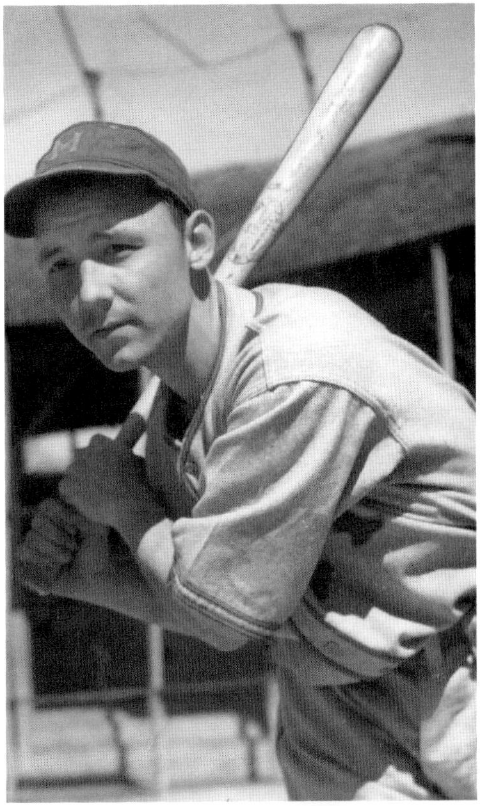

Harry Taylor (1937–1939). Timing his arrival in Minneapolis with the twilight of his career, the Pennsylvania-born, left-handed first baseman batted .284 in 16 minor league seasons. In 1937, the Red Sox prospect covered the initial sack in 153 games, committing just 13 errors for a fielding percentage of .992; it was the spitting image of the mark he posted in 157 games for Chattanooga the year prior, and it was also identical to his average in 1938! He was a Minneapolis representative to the American Association All-Star squad in 1937. (Courtesy of Hennepin County Library Special Collections.)

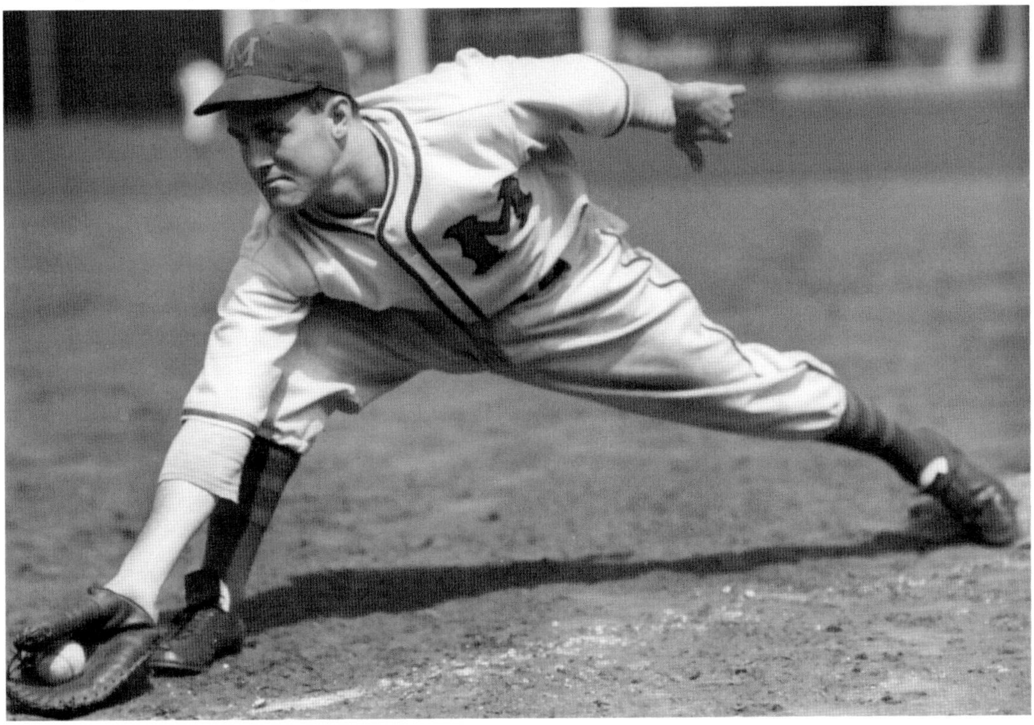

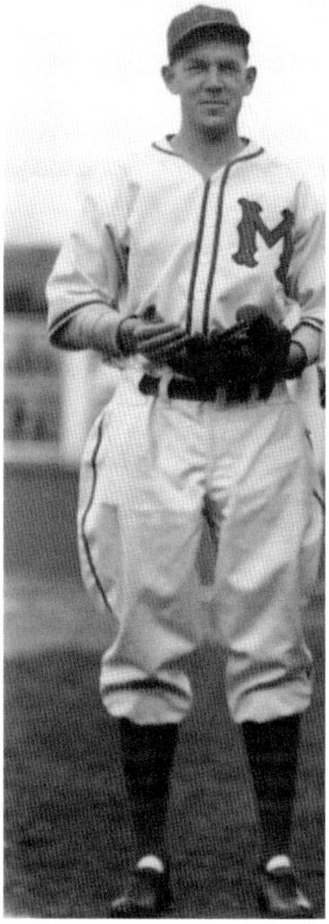

BLONDY RYAN (1936–1937). After joining Minneapolis in 1936 and having completed the majority of a six-year major league career, infielder Ryan became property of the Cleveland Indians, then the parent club of the Millers. During that first year, he hit a solid .283 in 77 games. He later managed the Clinton (Iowa) Giants (Class B). (Courtesy of Hennepin County Library Special Collections.)

DYNAMIC DUO. Perched upon the steps of their Pullman, Red Kress (left) and Roy Pfleger were one hot infield combo for the third-place Millers (87-67, three games back of Columbus) in 1937. With Kress at shortstop (easily remembered with the ss in Kress), and Pfleger at third, the pair proved powerful, with a combined batting average of .331, including 64 doubles and 56 home runs. The duo accounted for 219 runs, nearly 21 percent of the Minneapolis total of 1,058 that year. Here, their broad smiles indicate there may have been a win on the day of this photograph. (Courtesy of Hennepin County Library Special Collections.)

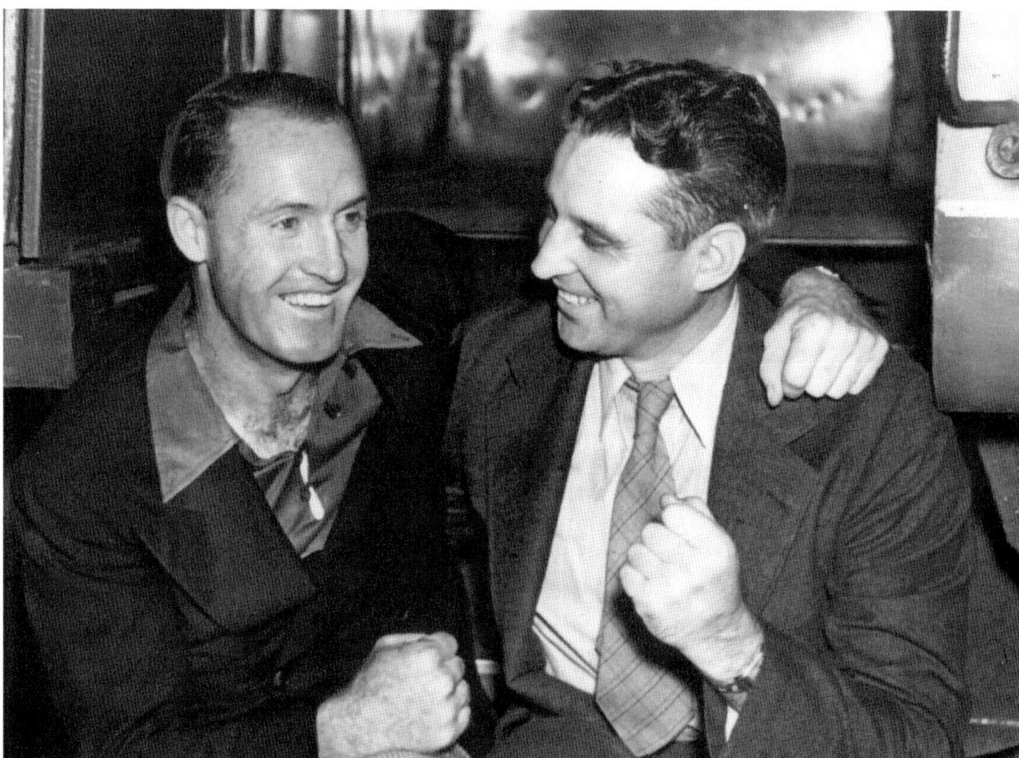

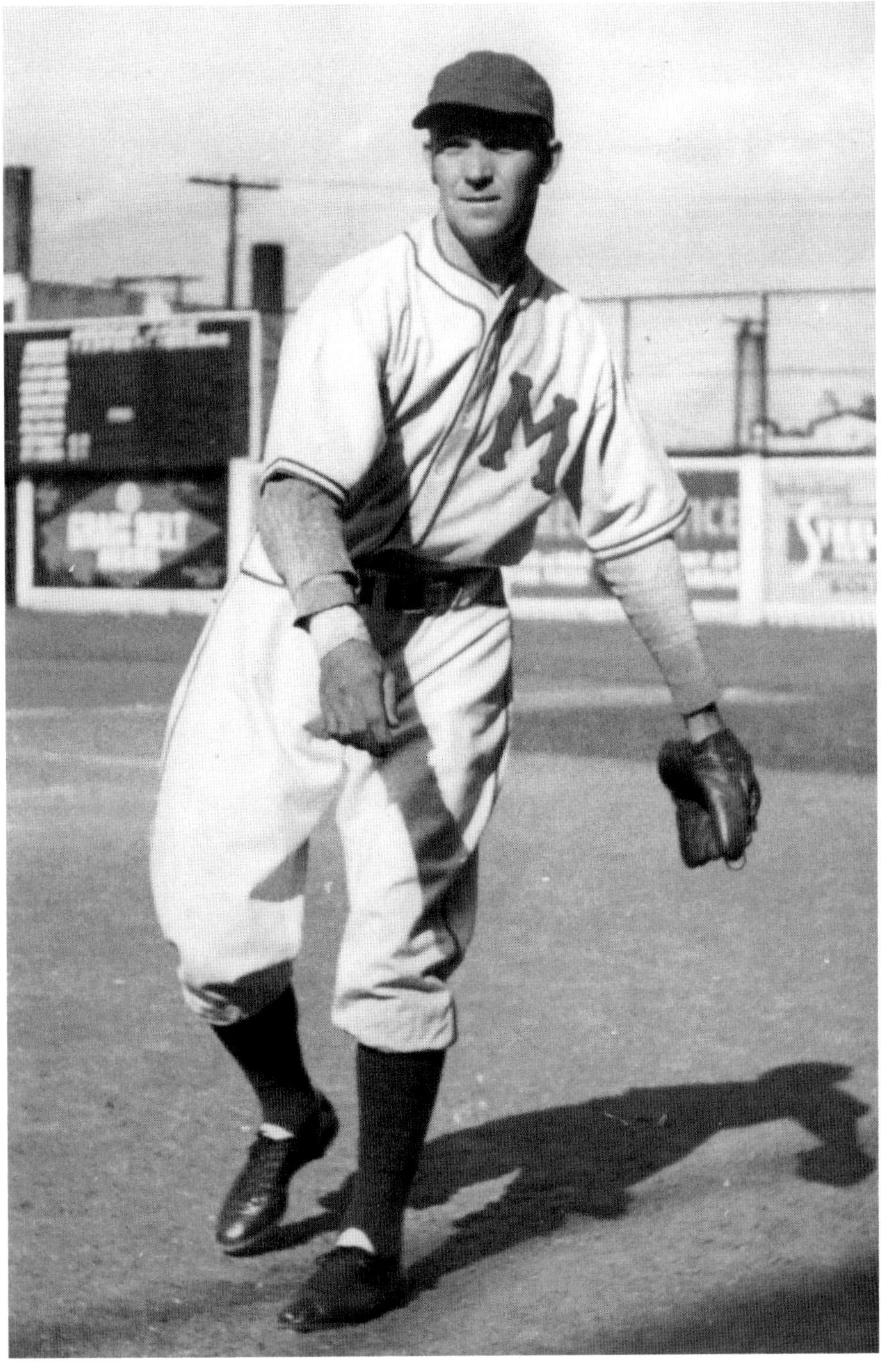

WALTER TAUSCHER (1933–1941). Tauscher embarked upon an extended journey with the Millers at the age of 31. A right-hander with plenty of gumption, he was a perennial member of the Millers' pitching staff during the 1930s, compiling an aggregate record 133-79, a .627 winning percentage. During his nine seasons sporting the Millers' orange and black, the Illinois native suffered just one losing season. (Courtesy of Hennepin County Library Special Collections.)

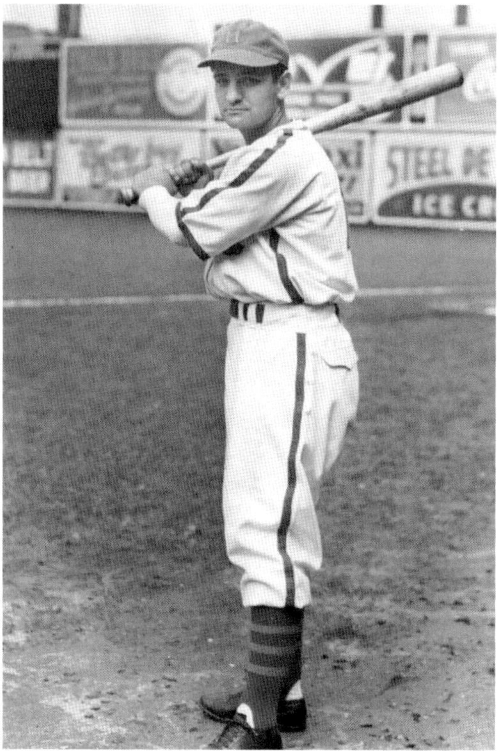

JOHNNY MIHALIC (1938). After three years in the majors spent as a Washington Senator, Johnny Mihalic played one season in the Miller infield—primarily as their shortstop—appearing in 78 games and batting .293 with three home runs. He was a career .300 hitter in 13 seasons, most of which were spent in Class A or above. (Courtesy of Hennepin County Library Special Collections.)

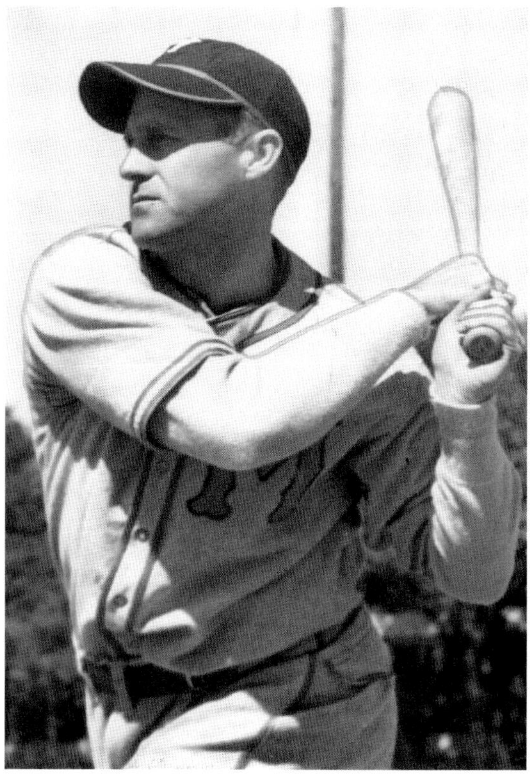

CARL REYNOLDS (1937). After a decade with American League teams, 34-year-old outfielder Carl Reynolds arrived in Minneapolis with a slew of strong stats, especially from his days with the Chicago White Sox. Under managers Donie Bush and Andy Cohen in 1937, the big Texan was quick to reinforce his reputation among American Association pitchers, racking up a league-high 49 doubles. His colossal .355 batting average was garnished by 17 triples, 17 round-trippers, and 110 RBIs. With 218 hits all told, Reynolds ranked 11th, tied with Pat Duncan (1925) and Elmer Yoter (1929) among the most prolific single-season swatters in club history. With a stick as sharp as his, Reynolds was a shoo-in to become yet another Minneapolis representative on the American Association All-Star team in 1937. (Courtesy of Hennepin County Library Special Collections.)

JENNINGS "JINX" POINDEXTER (1938). After a cup of coffee with the Boston Red Sox in 1936, the five-foot, ten-inch southpaw from Pauls Valley, Oklahoma, put himself on display with the Little Rock Travelers before coming to Minneapolis in 1938. Winning nine and losing seven in 16 starts as a Miller, "Jinx" continued to post victories in sequential fashion, 10 and 11 for Atlanta, then combining for 12 in 1941 for Atlanta and Knoxville. (Courtesy of Hennepin County Library Special Collections.)

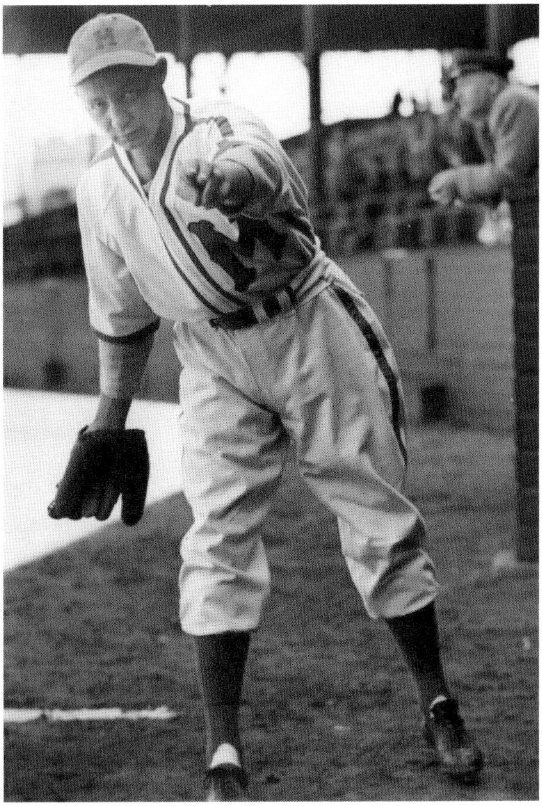

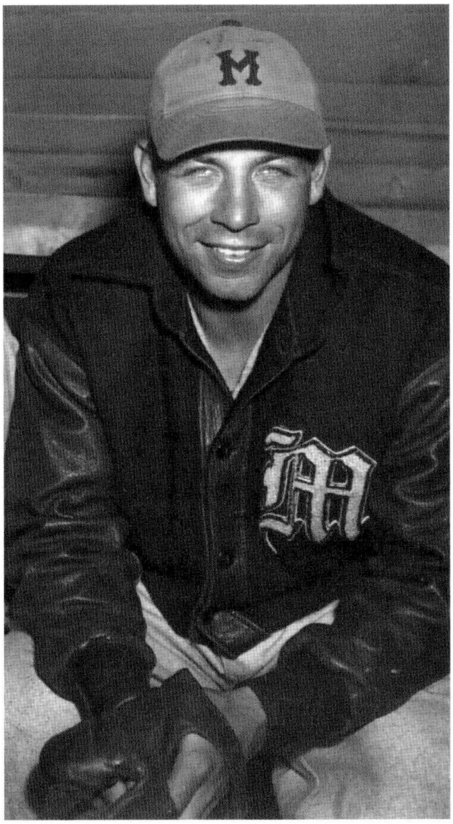

ROY "TARZAN" (BUD) PARMELEE (1938). As a 31-year-old with the Millers, by now an affiliate of the Boston Red Sox, Michigan native Parmelee gave his new team all he had, leading the league with 32 starts while compiling a record of 14-13. In Donie Bush's final season managing, the club finished four games over .500, in sixth place. Known for his wildness, Parmelee reluctantly etched a wary record in stone by walking 167 batters in 240 innings; it was not a league mark, but it came close. Nonetheless, he represented Minneapolis in the 1938 American Association All-Star game. (Courtesy of Hennepin County Library Special Collections.)

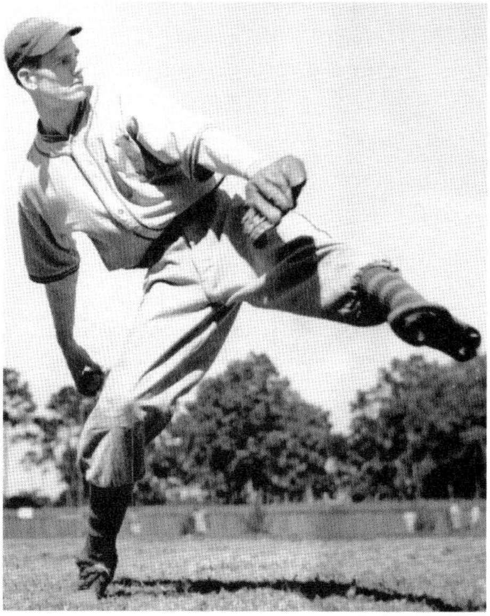

Bill Butland (1937, 1939). In 1939, Butland, 21, brought home 19 wins against 10 losses, helping propel the Millers into a second-place finish under Tom Sheehan. With 18 complete games in 29 starts, Butland ate up 218 innings, second to sterling mound mate Herb Hash, who led the league in that department with 256. Despite having the best record (by percentage) in franchise history with 99 wins and a .643 winning percentage, the Millers finished in second place and lost to fourth-place Louisville in the first round of the playoffs. Butland became an American Association All-Star in 1939. (Courtesy of Hennepin County Library Special Collections.)

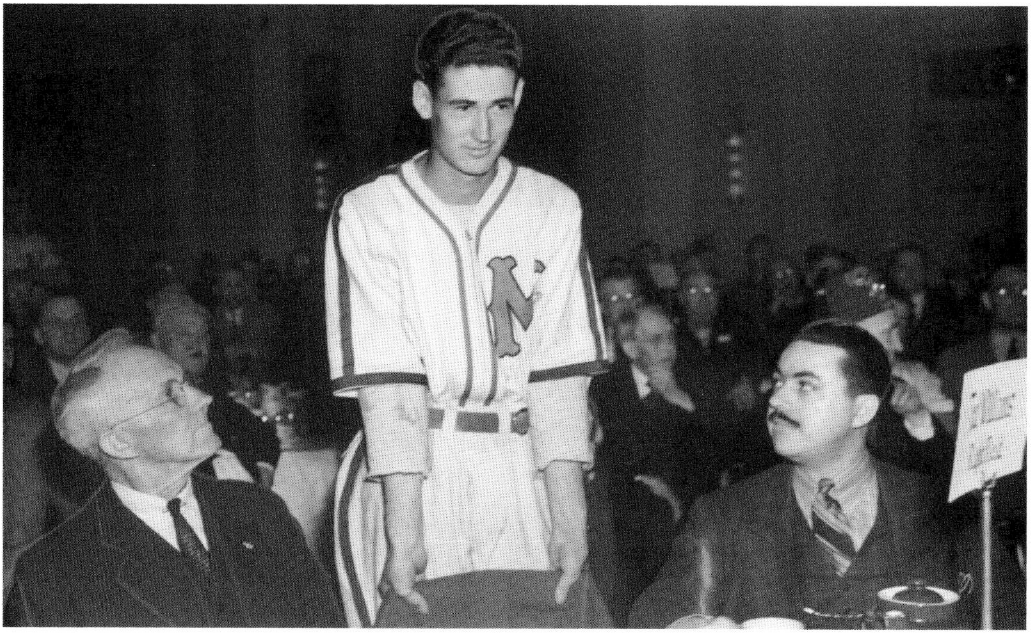

Ted Williams, Hall of Famer (1938). When "the Kid" from Southern California came north to play for the Millers, many of his Hall of Fame attributes were quickly put on display. Sporting uniform No. 19 (his age), the "Splendid Splinter" roamed the outfield for the 1938 Millers. In 148 games, Williams devoured Association pitching with a .366 batting average, 43 home runs, 30 doubles, and 142 runs batted in, topped off by a league-leading .701 slugging percentage. However, Minneapolis was unable to use the young stud to gain much momentum in the standings, and the club finished at 78-74 in fourth place under Donie Bush. Williams represented Minneapolis on the 1938 American Association All-Star team. (Courtesy of Hennepin County Library Special Collections.)

CHIEF HOGSETT (1939–1941, 1943–1944). With just a trace of Cherokee blood, Elon Chester "Chief" Hogsett was labeled "part Indian." But the label rang hollow to the Kansas-born lefty. Instead, he was "all-Tiger," playing in Detroit for eight seasons. Arriving in Minneapolis in 1939 at the age of 35, he racked up a record of 16-9, logging 199 innings with 25 starts for Tom Sheehan's second-place Millers. After going 16-11 the following year, the six-foot southpaw posted 18 wins and nine losses in 233 innings in 1941, with three shutouts in 30 starts, his best season with Minneapolis. (Courtesy of Hennepin County Library Special Collections.)

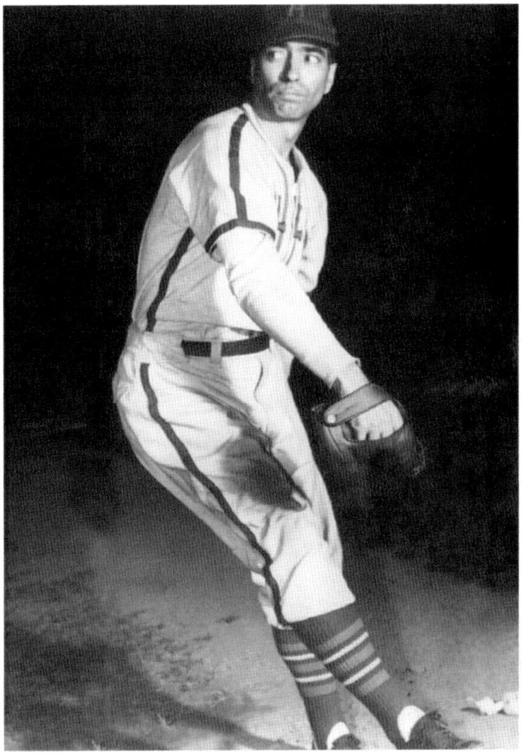

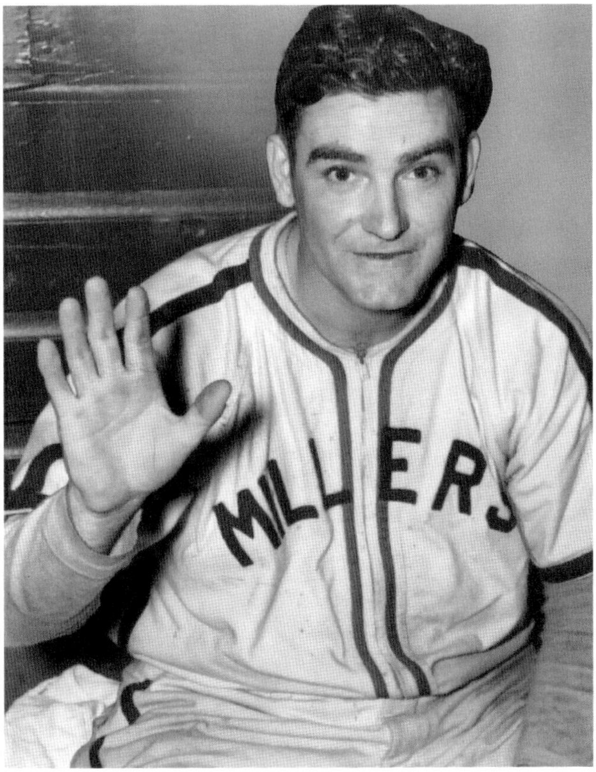

HARRY SMYTHE (1939–1941). In 22 minor league seasons, William Henry Smythe won 282 games against only 210 losses. During his time with Minneapolis, the Georgia-born southpaw went 12-12 and 13-9 in his first two seasons, respectively. Smythe was a remarkable hitter for a pitcher: in 1939, he hit .299 with a home run and three doubles. The next year, he batted .310 with a pair of long balls. He owned the best ERA of any of the Millers' six starters in 1940, with a 3.80 mark when Minneapolis finished third under Tom Sheehan. (Courtesy of Hennepin County Library Special Collections.)

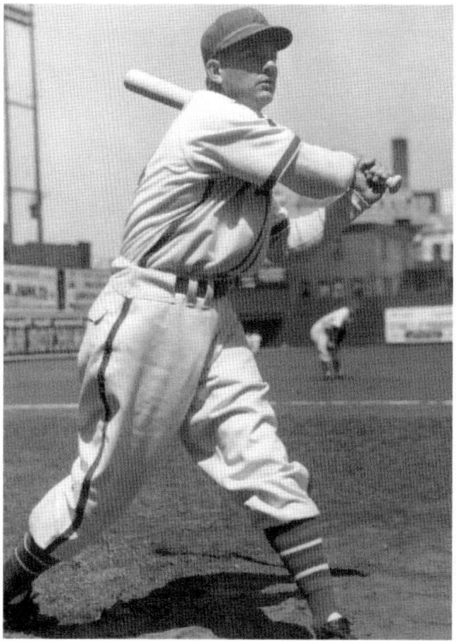

HUB WALKER (1939–1942). In four seasons with the Millers, Hub Walker, a 33-year-old Mississippi native, appeared in more than 500 games. Batting from the left side, Walker hit .318 with 25 home runs and compiled 285 total bases in 1940 at the age of 33, having the most productive season in his professional career. The former major leaguer slumped in 1941, hitting just .254, well below his 12-year average of .300. He earned honors as a two-time Minneapolis representative to the American Association All-Star squad (1939–1940). (Courtesy of Hennepin County Library Special Collections.)

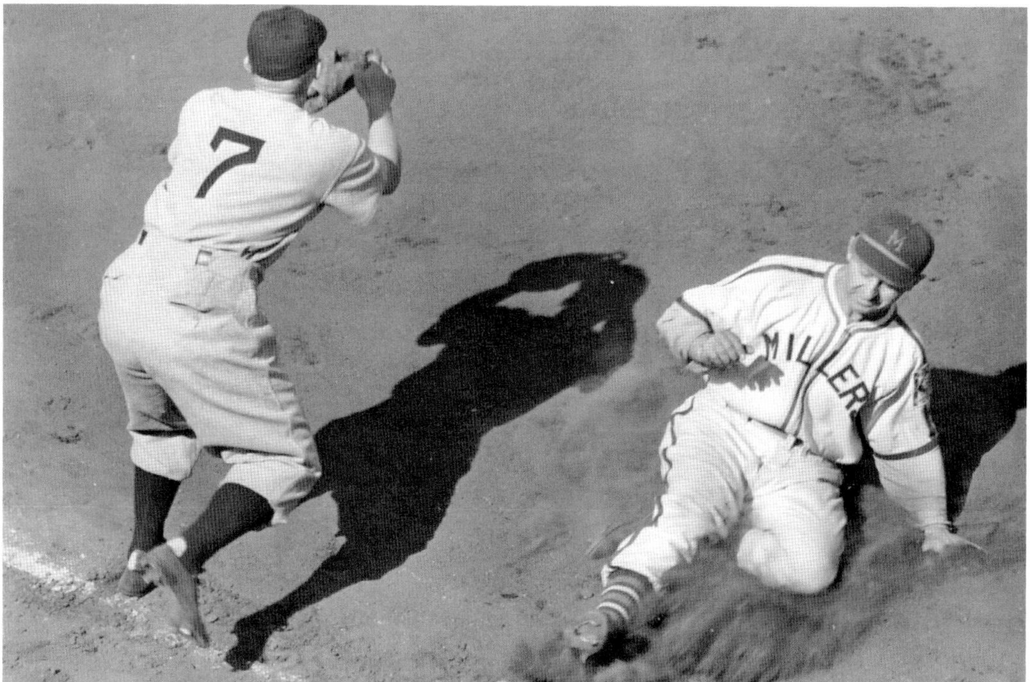

SLIDES IN A CLOUD OF DUST! During this 1939 game at Nicollet Park, Phil Weintraub (1939–1940) went into third base in a cloud of dust, obviously beating the tag by Indianapolis third baseman Don Lang. The element of tension posed by this extraordinary photograph retains its drama some 75 years later; note the 100th Anniversary of Baseball (1839–1939) commemorative patch on Weintraub's left sleeve. Weintraub was a two-time Minneapolis representative to the American Association All-Star squad (1939–1940). (Author's collection.)

PHIL "MICKEY" WEINTRAUB (1939–1940). Weintraub, a Chicago-born left-hander and exceptional hitter, came to the Millers to play first base at age 31 in 1939, posting superior batting numbers. He stole the show with 33 home runs that year, smacking 36 doubles and batting .331 while leading the club with 321 total bases (third in the league). His power numbers fell slightly the following season, but his average rose to .341 with 169 hits, exceeding his 1939 total by exactly one. (Courtesy of Hennepin County Library Special Collections.)

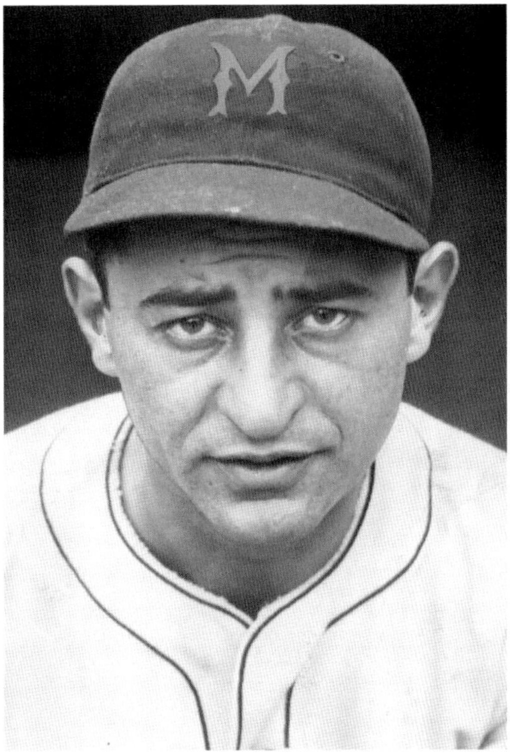

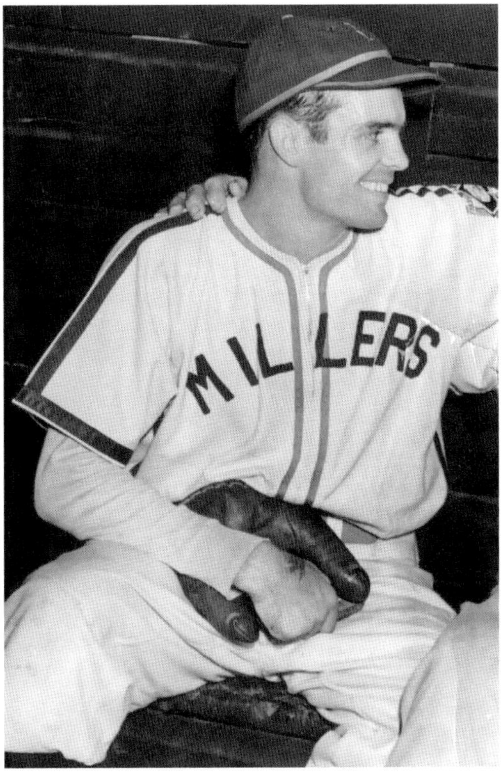

HERB HASH (1939, 1942). Hash, a 28-year-old right-hander from Woolwine, Virginia, made his mark on baseball with a career year in 1939, posting 22 wins for Minneapolis against just six losses, the .786 winning percentage fourth-best in Millers history (minimum 15 decisions). In a league-high 30 starts, he produced a well-earned ERA of 3.27 with 144 strikeouts, the Association's second-best mark. In addition, Hash led the league with 20 complete games. The Boston Red Sox called him up the following year. (Courtesy of Hennepin County Library Special Collections.)

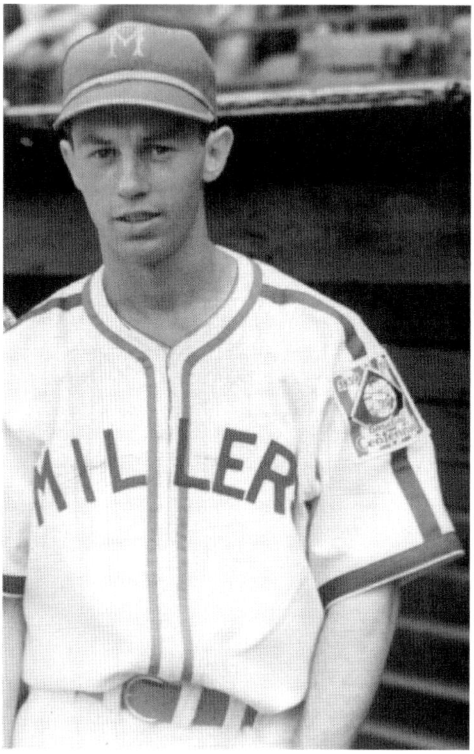

Jimmy Pofahl (1939, 1943). A native of Faribault, Minnesota, Jimmy Pofahl made headlines as a local favorite when he made the Millers' squad as the club's full-time shortstop at 22. After completing a Double-A internship with the Indianapolis Indians in 1938 (batting .244), Pofahl thrived in his home state, taking Association pitchers to task in 1939 with a .302 batting average and compiling 286 total bases, third on the club behind Phil Weintraub (321) and Ab Wright (307). Pofahl was a Minneapolis representative to the American Association All-Star squad in 1939. (Courtesy of Hennepin County Library Special Collections.)

Otto "Dutch" Denning (1938–1941). A catcher who filled in at first base for Minneapolis, Denning distinguished himself during his years as a Miller with prolific hitting and a workhorse record, appearing in a 327 contests as catcher from a total of 426 games combined. In 81 games his first year, he batted .342 with nine long balls and 18 doubles. His most productive season—the best of his professional career—came in 1941, with 261 total bases to his credit, when he batted .329 with 17 homers and 34 doubles. The Kansas native made his major league debut for the Cleveland Indians in 92 games the following year. He was a two-time Minneapolis representative to the American Association All-Star squad, first in 1939 and again in 1940 (both times as a Miller). (Courtesy of Hennepin County Library Special Collections.)

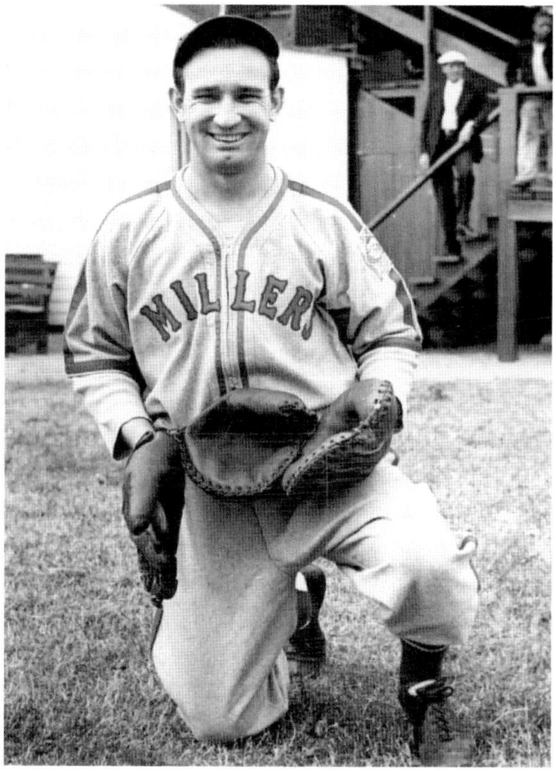

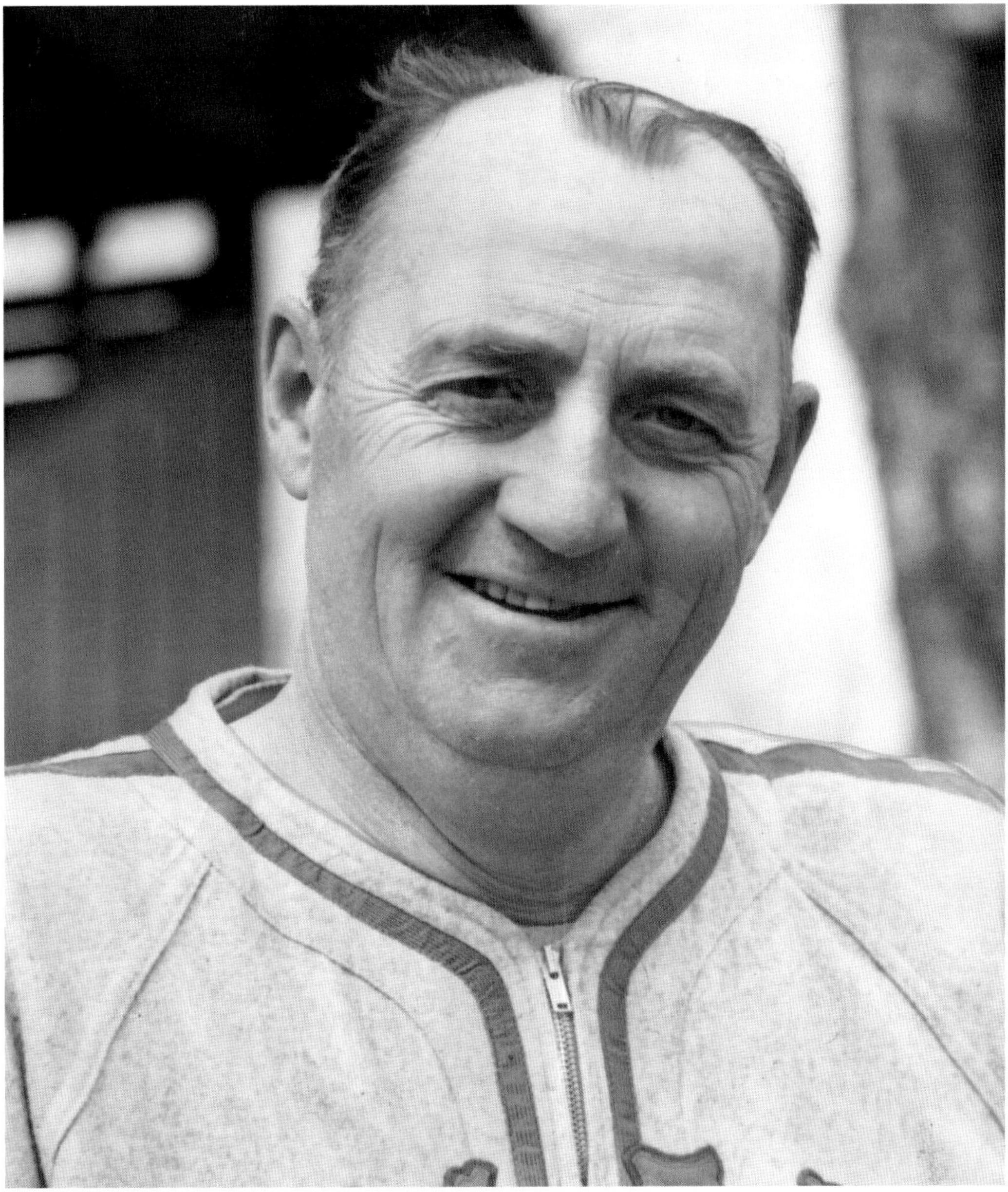

Tom Sheehan (1939–1943, 1946–1947). After making his mark in the American Association as a star pitcher for the St. Paul Saints and Kansas City Blues, Sheehan came to the Millers in 1931 at the age of 37, posting a combined record of 4-9. He then headed west to pitch in the Pacific Coast League as a member of the Hollywood Stars, putting the frosting on a 15-year minor league pitching career to the tune of 250 wins and 152 losses. The six-year major leaguer returned to Minneapolis in 1939 to manage, helping drive the team to a 99-55 second-place record that year. He managed the San Francisco Giants for a portion of the 1960 season. Sheehan appears optimistic in this 1941 photograph, but the team finished in fourth place, 12 games behind the Columbus Red Birds. (Courtesy of Hennepin County Library Special Collections.)

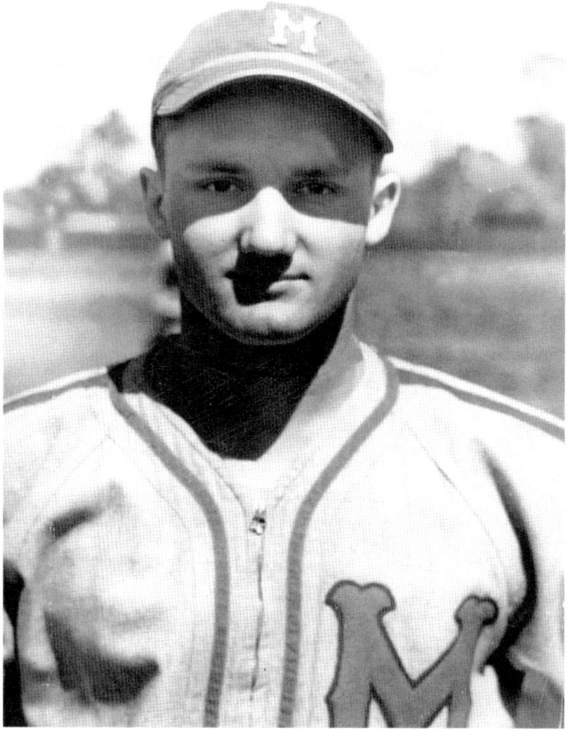

BILL BARNACLE (1940–1942, 1946, 1952). Barnacle played 359 of his total 1,504 minor league games (13 seasons) with the Millers. The outfielder/third baseman put in a pair of solid seasons before entering the Merchant Marine, batting .302 in 92 games in 1941, then hitting .274 in 148 contests the following year. With Tom Sheehan's sixth-place club, Barnacle ranked third with 223 total bases. Returning to Minneapolis after a three-year stint with the Toledo Mud Hens, he appeared in just 10 games, the swan song of a substantial professional ball career. (Courtesy of Hennepin County Library Special Collections.)

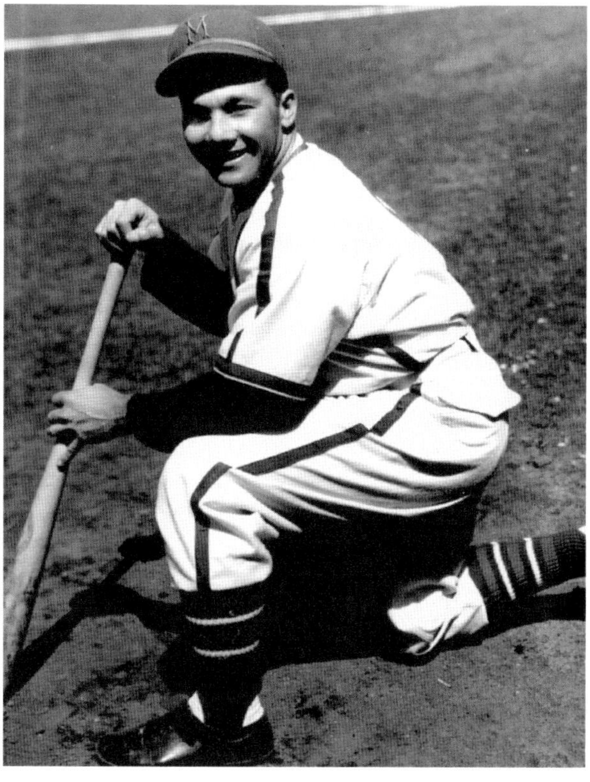

BOBBY ESTALELLA (1940). Cuban-born Roberto Ventoza Estalella, 29, came to the Millers after spending part of the 1939 season as a Washington Senators outfielder. The following numbers were a factor in his becoming one of seven Millers to play on the 1940 American Association All-Star team: 181 hits, 36 doubles, five triples, 32 home runs (second-ranked in the league behind teammate Ab Wright), a .341 batting average, a .608 slugging percentage, and 323 total bases (also second-ranked in the league behind Ab Wright). He was the grandfather of Bobby Estalella, who caught for several major league teams between 1996 and 2004. (Courtesy of Hennepin County Library Special Collections.)

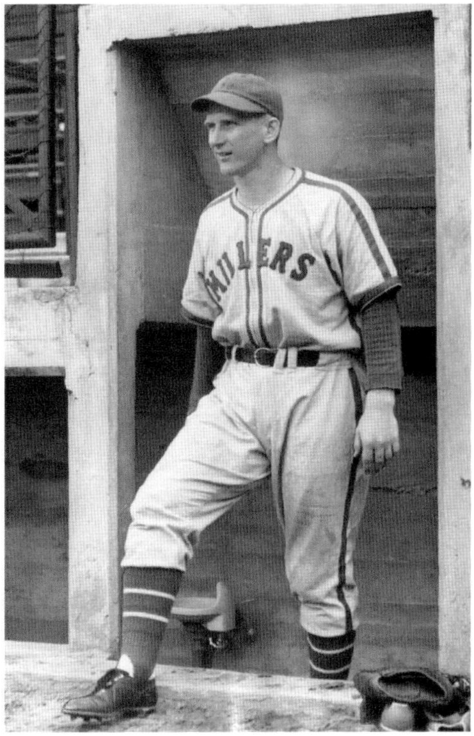

OWEN SCHEETZ (1942–1943). A right-handed pitcher from central Ohio, Scheetz had an exceptional win-loss record in 13 minor league seasons, but his first year with the Millers at age 28 showed he was a work in progress, going 15-16 with a 3.73 ERA. His work ethic was nothing to scoff at, with 251 innings of work that year, more than in any other season of his career. (Courtesy of Hennepin County Library Special Collections.)

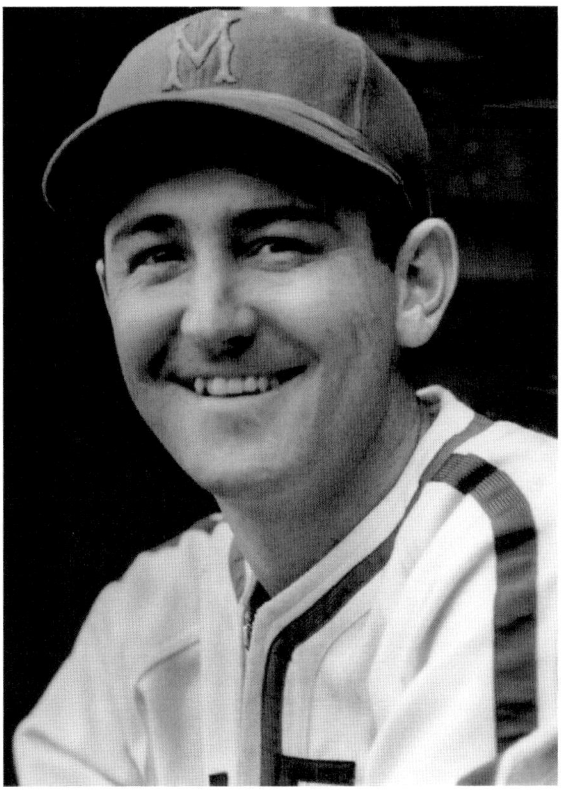

HUCK GEARY (1940–1942, 1947). Geary, a 23-year-old native of Buffalo, New York, already had considerable minor league experience when he joined the Millers in 1940. As their everyday shortstop for the first two years, Geary was a strong hitter, batting .308 his first season, with 31 doubles and 10 home runs. He returned to the Millers after serving a few years in the US Navy during World War II, appearing in just 10 games. Geary represented Minneapolis as the American Association All-Star shortstop in 1940. (Courtesy of Hennepin County Library Special Collections.)

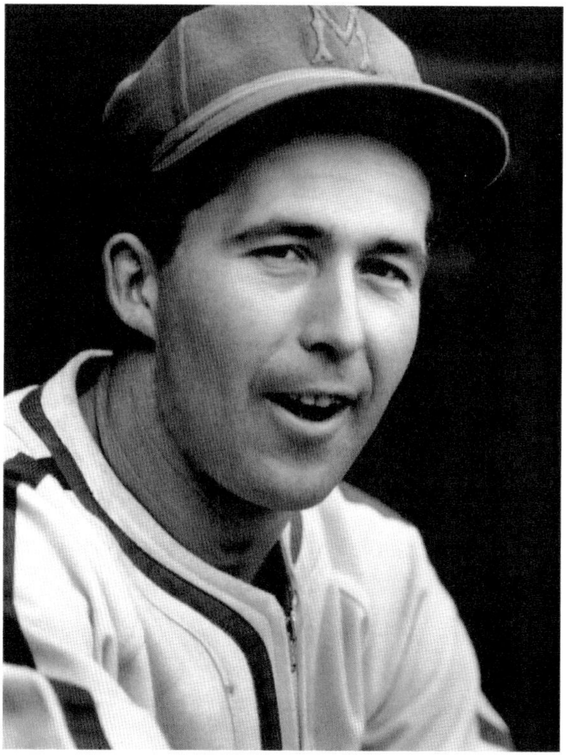

Mickey Haefner (1940–1942). In three seasons, portsider Milton Arnold Haefner, age 27, collected 44 wins against 41 losses for the Millers just before being called up to pitch for the Washington Senators in 1943. Haefner worked an eight-year career at the major league level (78-91 record), but he had his best years with Minneapolis. Breaking in with Tom Sheehan's third-place club, Haefner won 14 games against eight losses in 1940 and tied for the team lead in starts (29) with Harry Kelley and Red Evans. He was a Minneapolis representative to the American Association All-Star squad in 1942, along with catcher Bob (Claud) Linton and outfielder Joe Vosmik. (Courtesy of Hennepin County Library Special Collections.)

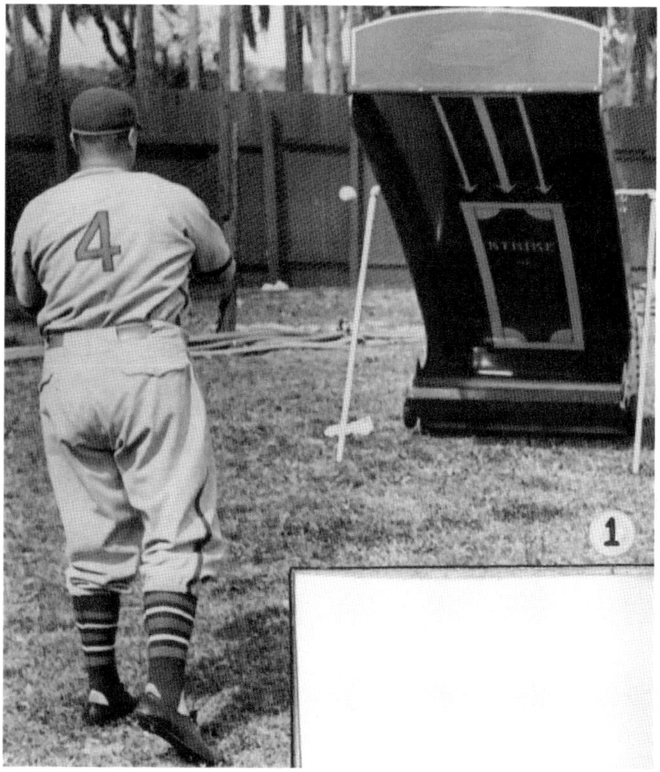

Rosy Ryan's "Bal-Bak" Machine. Rosy Ryan demonstrates the use of his unique pitching machine for the benefit of rookies during spring training at Daytona Beach, Florida, in 1940. According the news item captioning this photograph, Ryan is using "his bal-bak machine, a gadget of his own invention which is designed to improve a twirler's control and which also returns the ball to him." (Courtesy of Hennepin County Library Special Collections.)

3

THE WAR YEARS TAKE A TOLL 1941–1960

Not once in the history of the franchise did the Minneapolis Millers finish in last place. But during the lean war years, they came close on two occasions. The worst of those came in 1944, when the club, headed by former ace pitcher Rosy Ryan, mustered a meager 54-97 (.358) record. It was not quite their worst showing in club history; that honor belonged to the 1903 Millers, who won 50 games while losing 91 (.355) under two managers, Walt Wilmot and George Yeager. It was their third-straight second-division finish, but later in the decade, the club reversed its fortunes, posting the identical record of 77-77 in 1947 and 1948 while ensconced in fourth and fifth place, respectively, before finally shedding the chains of mediocrity in 1950 under manager Tommy Heath.

Heath, a former catcher, helped push the Millers to their first league championship since 1935. With 90 wins against 64 losses, Minneapolis supplanted St. Paul in 1950 as the league champion, inspiring even the most skeptical Twin Cities fans to newfound elation. On the road to the flag, the Millers were accompanied by the Indianapolis Indians, who made the chase a taut affair under future Hall-of-Fame skipper Al Lopez. Heath's men grabbed the gonfalon by just four games.

After four subpar seasons, the Millers claimed the championship again in 1955 under manager Bill Rigney, winning 92 games, the most since 1939's second-place season of 99-62. It was a fitting way of departing from Nicollet Park, where they had played since 1902. By this time, the reconstituted league included the Denver Bears, Omaha Cardinals, and Charleston Senators, along with these remaining clubs from the original circuit: Indianapolis, Louisville, St. Paul, and Toledo. Riding the bat of Rance Pless, voted the league's most valuable player that year, "Miller Magic" once again carried the club through a successful postseason swing and into the Junior World Series for the first time, where it faced the Rochester Red Wings.

During their final two-decade stretch, the Millers won 1,570 and lost 1,498 for a winning percentage of .512. This compares to the 1921–1940 span, the organization's best, when they posted 1,714 victories against 1,489 losses, achieving a winning percentage of .544. All told, the Millers won exactly 4,800 regulation games during their 59 seasons in the American Association, losing 4,366 (.524).

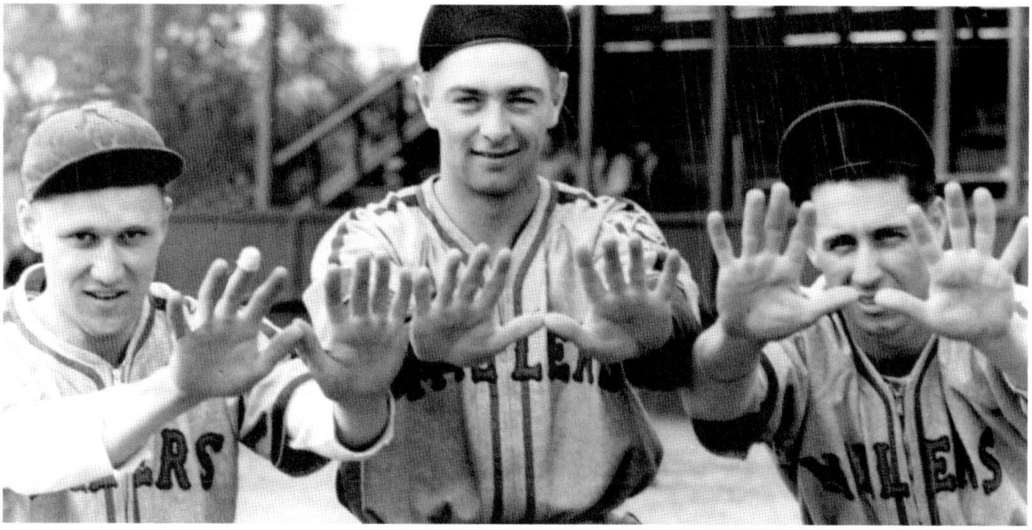

FRANK DANNEKER (1941–1946). A St. Paul, Minnesota, native (left), Danneker's ship came in during the 1941 season with Minneapolis, when he hit .276 at the plate. His best season came in 1945, when he rapped 12 home runs and 21 doubles while batting .308 with a .429 slugging percentage for the second straight year. He accepted more chances than any Association second baseman in 1945, producing a notable .966 fielding percentage. He represented the Millers as an American Association All-Star in 1945. At right is Frank Trechock, and in the center is a player identified only as "Schroeder." (Courtesy of Hennepin County Library Special Collections.)

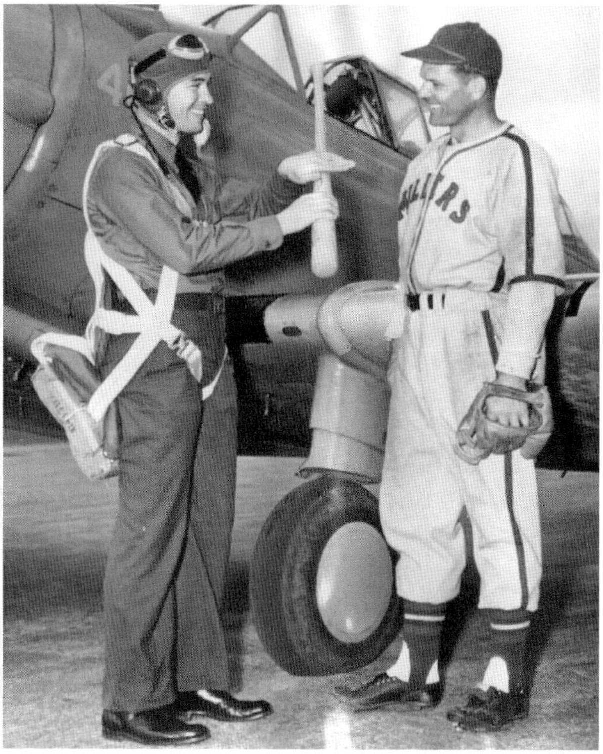

WILD BLUE YONDER. Ab Wright, whose batting numbers as a Miller bordered on stratospheric, appears to be getting a kick out of the lesson being taught by this fully equipped fighter pilot. Or was it the other way around? As the country prepared for World War II, baseball did its part to engage with the public in order to boost the war effort on a variety of fronts, including the staging of such theatrical poses as this entertaining promotion. (Courtesy of Hennepin County Library Special Collections.)

TOM SHEEHAN AND ZACK TAYLOR (1941). While the pregame discussion appears deadly serious as these two confer before the batting cage, the two managers—one a former pitcher, the other a former catcher—may be swapping stories from their many seasons in professional ball. Taylor (right) yielded to Fred Haney as manager of the Toledo Mud Hens in 1941, while Sheehan (left) stayed the course with his men of the upper Mississippi. Taylor, who caught 856 games during a 16-season major league career, later managed the St. Louis Browns for several seasons. (Courtesy of Hennepin County Library Special Collections.)

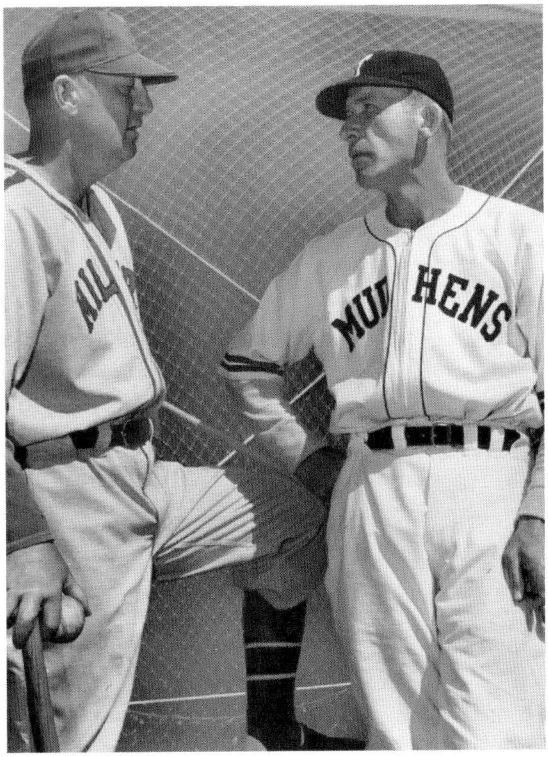

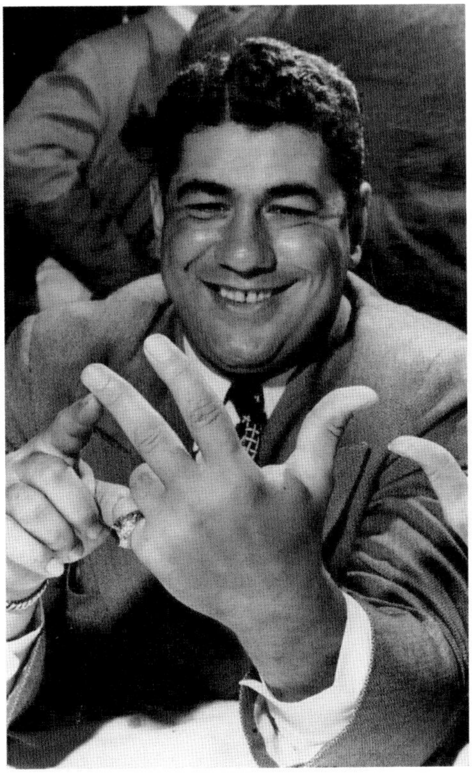

BABE BARNA (1941, 1944–1948). Left-handed batter Barna swatted more than 20 home runs in each of his six seasons as a Miller. The Clarksburg, West Virginia, native came aboard the Miller Express at 26 as an outfielder. Barna outdid himself on the base paths in 1941, stealing a league-leading 29 sacks and walloping 24 home runs. His .336 average indicated an inclination toward Association pitching. But even with his club-high 275 total bases, the Millers could not get above fourth place in the standings. Barna was the Millers' lone representative as an Association All-Star in 1946. (Courtesy of Hennepin County Library Special Collections.)

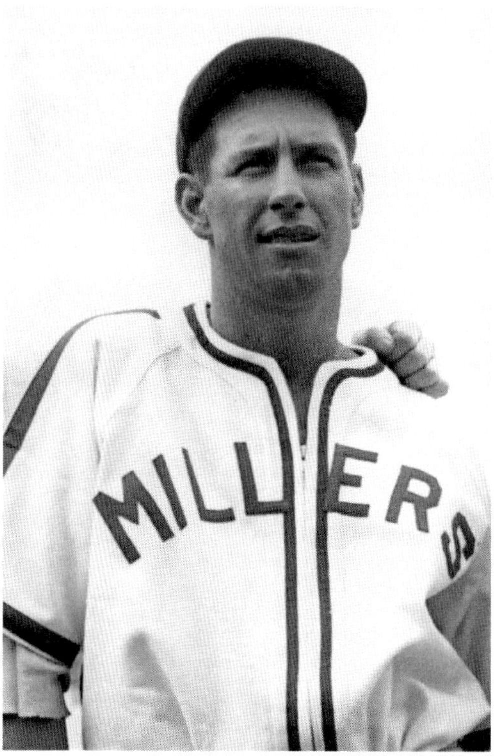

FRANK TRECHOCK (1940–1943, 1946–1948). In his first season with Minneapolis, playing 90 games at second base and 14 at shortstop, the 24-year-old Trechock batted just .248, considerably lower than the club's other starting position players. The following year, his average dipped to an anemic .229 in 145 games. But his tenacity prevailed, and he drove his average up to .272 the year after. Returning to Minneapolis after two years in the US Army, the Pennsylvania native batted .290 two years straight. He died at the age of 73 in Minneapolis and is buried at Fort Snelling National Cemetery there. (Courtesy of Hennepin County Library Special Collections.)

BOB LINTON (1942). Claud Clarence Linton was born in Emerson, Arkansas, on April 18, 1902, just five days before the first games in the American Association got underway. Appearing in 81 games in 1942, Linton batted .306, demonstrating the same consistency of high-quality hitting at the Double-A level as he had shown with the Toledo Mud Hens in 1937–1938, his best years in baseball. Despite playing in a low number of contests, Linton had the club's third-best home run total, tied with third baseman Bill Barnacle's 12 for Tom Sheehan's "Grain Grinders." (Courtesy of Hennepin County Library Special Collections.)

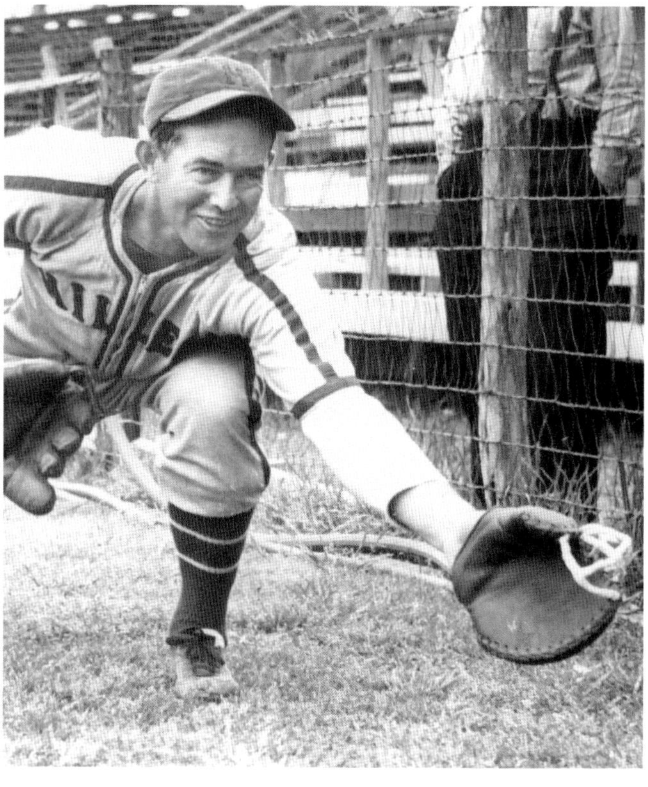

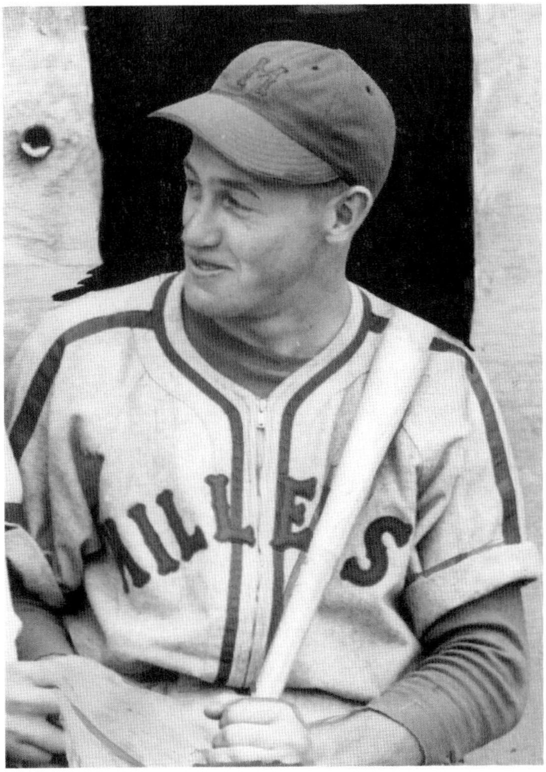

DON "SCOTTY" WHEELER (1942, 1946, 1948, 1960). Wheeler first came to the Millers at the age of 19 as an outfielder, then returned to the team after serving in the US Army as a draftee during World War II. A local product who attended South High School in Minneapolis, Wheeler spent nine seasons in the minors and finally broke into big-league ball in 1949 with the Chicago White Sox. His best season with Minneapolis came in 1948 at the age of 25, when he batted .302 with 11 home runs and 15 doubles in 111 games. (Courtesy of Hennepin County Library Special Collections.)

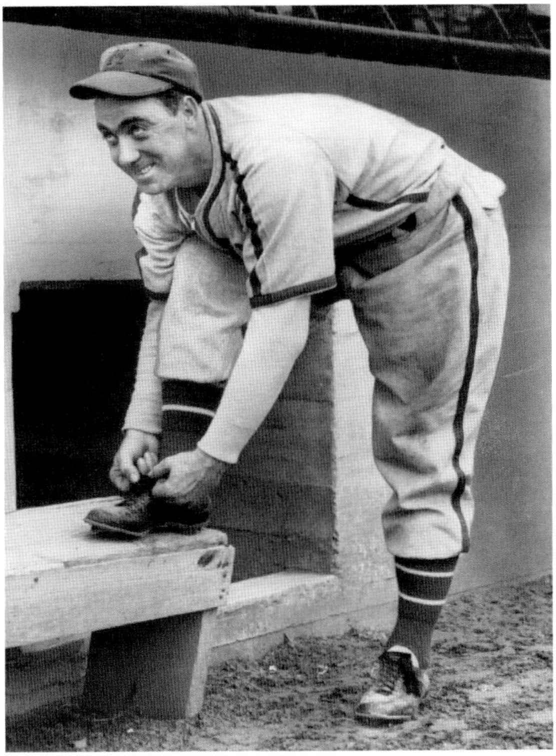

VAN LINGLE MUNGO (1942). Just after his decade with Brooklyn, 1937 National League All-Star pitcher Mungo joined the Millers in 1942, going 11-3 with a 4.57 ERA. It was the 31-year-old's only season in the American Association. A former strikeout king as a Dodger, he whiffed 72 batters and walked 61 as a Miller. Known for his off-field antics as a Dodger, Mungo was in the Army in 1944 before returning to his South Carolina home, later managing the Clinton (North Carolina) Blues (Class D). He went on to operate a dry goods store, a movie theater, and a trucking line in Pageland, South Carolina. (Courtesy of Hennepin County Library Special Collections.)

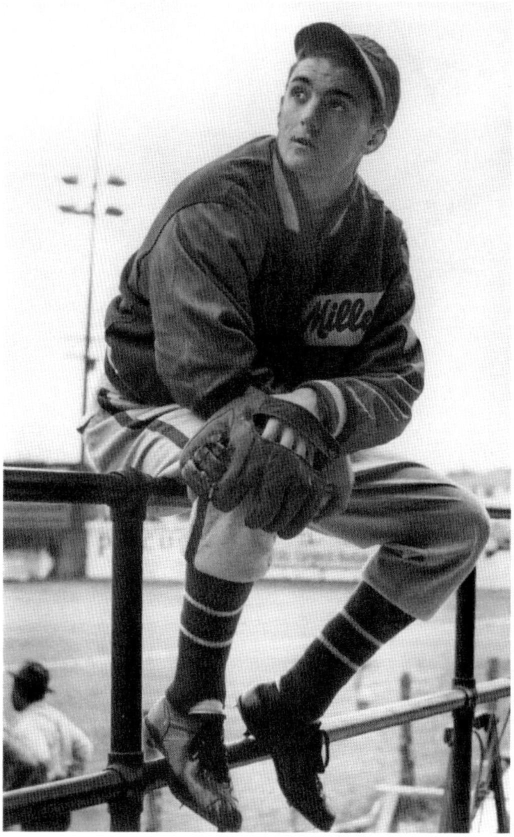

Don Schoenborn (1942, 1946). Born in St. Paul, Minnesota, on January 24, 1922, Schoenborn was a right-handed hurler whose stints pitching for the Millers sandwiched a war in between. In 1942, Schoenborn appeared in 41 games, going 2-7. He joined the US Army in 1943 and was released in late March 1946, when he resumed his relationship with Minneapolis at the age of 24, posting a 4-8 record in 38 games that year. (Courtesy of Hennepin County Library Special Collections.)

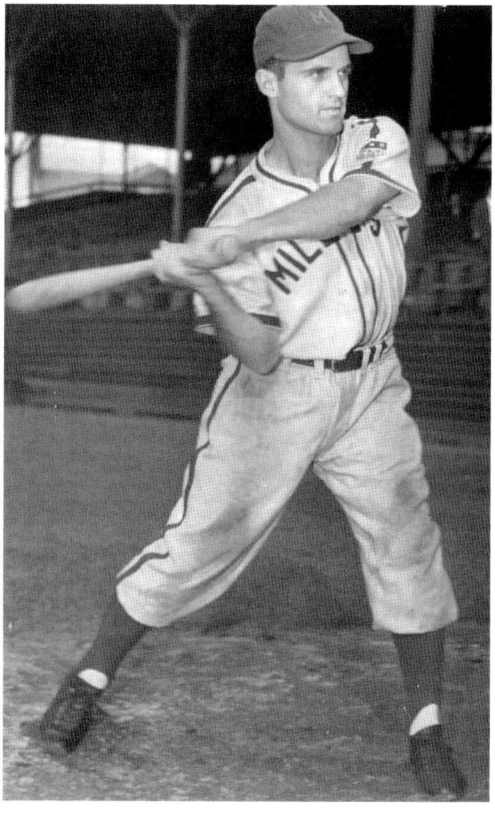

Nick Picciuto (1945). Third sacker Nick Picciuto played much of the season for Minneapolis but appeared in a combined 99 games between the Eastern League's Utica Blue Sox and the Millers, with exactly 400 plate appearances (336 at-bats), batting .262 with eight home runs and 40 RBIs. The 23-year-old made his major league debut that year with the Philadelphia Phillies, appearing in 36 games. (Courtesy of Hennepin County Library Special Collections.)

ERNIE RUDOLPH (1943). The Millers were the diminutive right-hander's fourth team in three years. Splitting the 1943 season between Minneapolis and St. Paul, the five-foot-eight Wisconsinite won a combined three games against three losses. He became a full-time member of the Saints' pitching staff the following season. On June 16, 1945, the 36-year-old made his rookie debut for the Brooklyn Dodgers as a reliever. (Courtesy of Hennepin County Library Special Collections.)

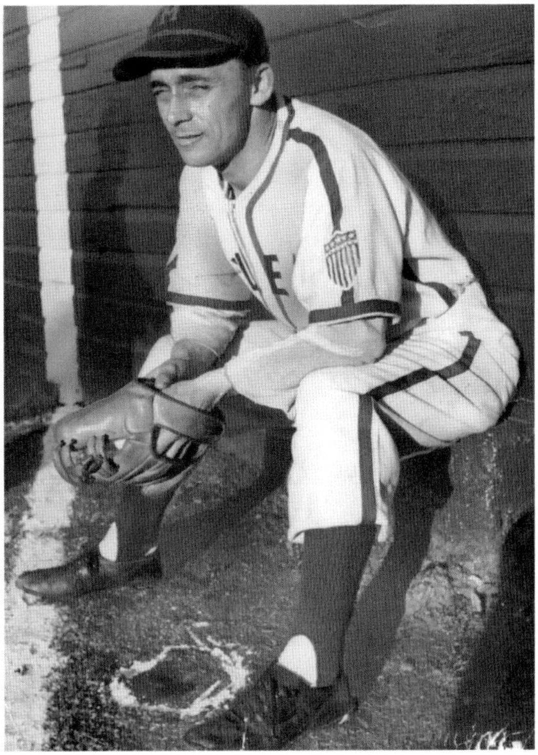

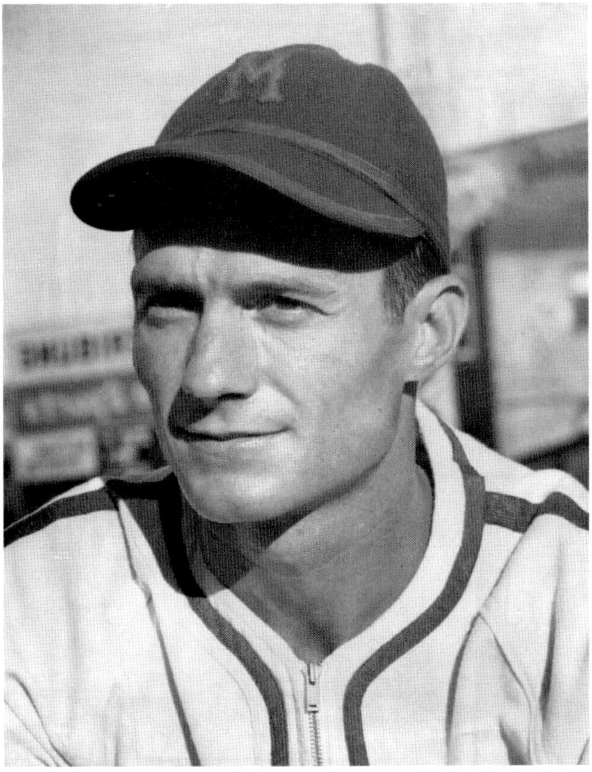

EWALD "LEFTY" PYLE (1943). Pyle was 5-9 as a member of Tom Sheehan's sixth-place Millers in 1943, appearing in 17 games. He spent five years at the major league level, his best season coming with the New York Giants in 1944 with a record of 7-10. Getting his start in professional ball in 1935 at 24, the St. Louis, Missouri, native pitched 14 seasons. During his time in the American Association, he started as a Toledo Mud Hen in 1939, went on to Minneapolis, then became a Milwaukee Brewer before finishing as a Louisville Colonel. His combined minor league record was 122-137, and he appeared in nearly 400 games with more than 2,100 innings pitched. (Author's collection.)

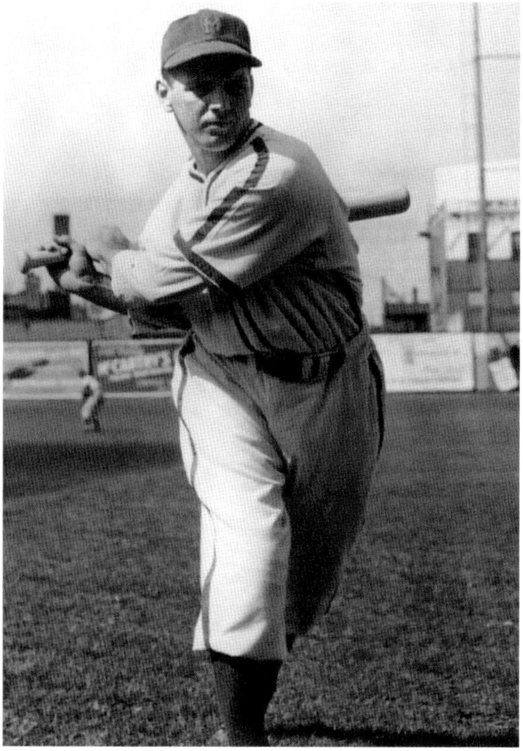

HANK NOWAK (1945–1946). Nowak, at 27, burst upon the American Association scene as a Miller with a hot bat in 1945. He never made the majors, but he spent nine seasons in the minors, averaging .293 at the plate. The Miller outfielder likely exceeded all expectations as a hitter in 1945, batting .329 with nine home runs and 33 doubles in 150 games that year. He came back down to earth the following season in only 34 games, batting .245, when the Millers became affiliated with the New York Giants. (Courtesy of Hennepin County Library Special Collections.)

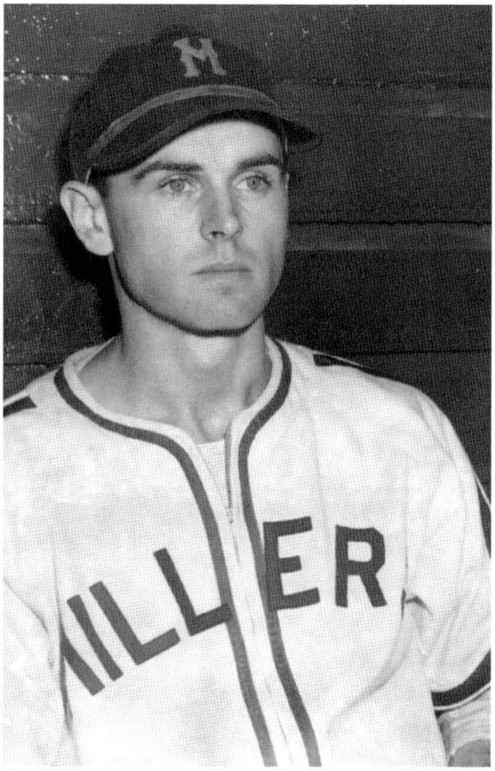

JACK "BUDDY" BREWER (1946). After returning stateside from serving his country, Brewer joined the Millers under the purview of the New York Giants. While his major league career was now in the rearview mirror, the Californian had one of his best seasons on the mound, leading the squad with 14 wins against nine losses. He placed second in the league in complete games (16) and in starts (26), tied with Milwaukee Brewer (and former Miller) Ewald Pyle. Minneapolis finished fourth in 1946, losing to Indianapolis in the first round of the playoffs. (Courtesy of Hennepin County Library Special Collections.)

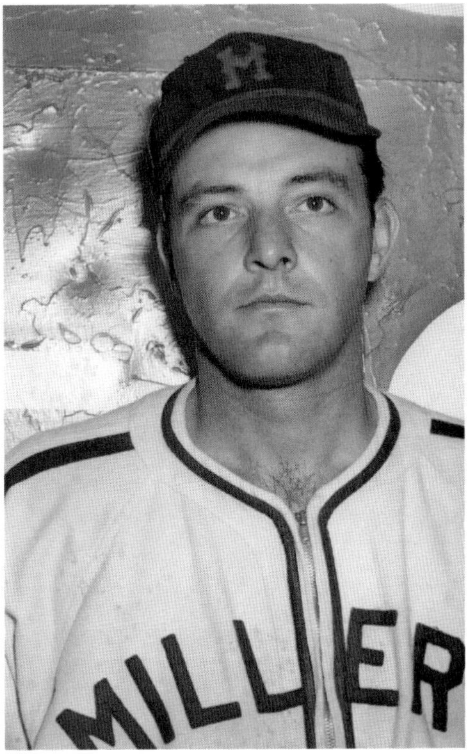

Ernie "Junie" Andres (1946). After playing in three seasons with the Louisville Colonels, a Boston Red Sox farm, Andres joined the US Navy. Returning from military duty, the 28-year-old Indiana-born righty batted .287 in 90 games, becoming a highly regarded "hot corner hero" in 76 games and playing first base in 14. The Millers played "musical managers" that year, with three commanding the ship: Zeke Bonura, Rosy Ryan, and "Long" Tom Sheehan (since May 7), in that order. (Courtesy of Hennepin County Library Special Collections.)

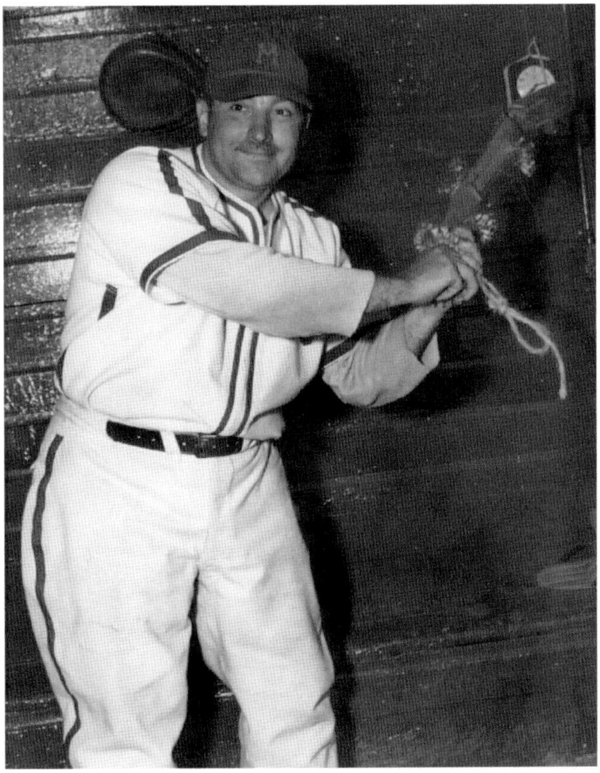

George "Skeets" Savino (1945–1946). A glimpse into the dugout at Nicollet Park in 1946 yields a look at Miller catcher George Savino, 36, who is preparing for his turn at bat by wielding a banana stalk, perhaps as a method of getting his timing down. Split between Minneapolis and St. Paul during the 1946 season, Savino batted .221, down considerably from the year before, when his combined average was .298 with Louisville and Minneapolis. He represented Minneapolis as a member the American Association All-Star squad in 1945, along with second baseman Frank Danneker. (Courtesy of Hennepin County Library Special Collections.)

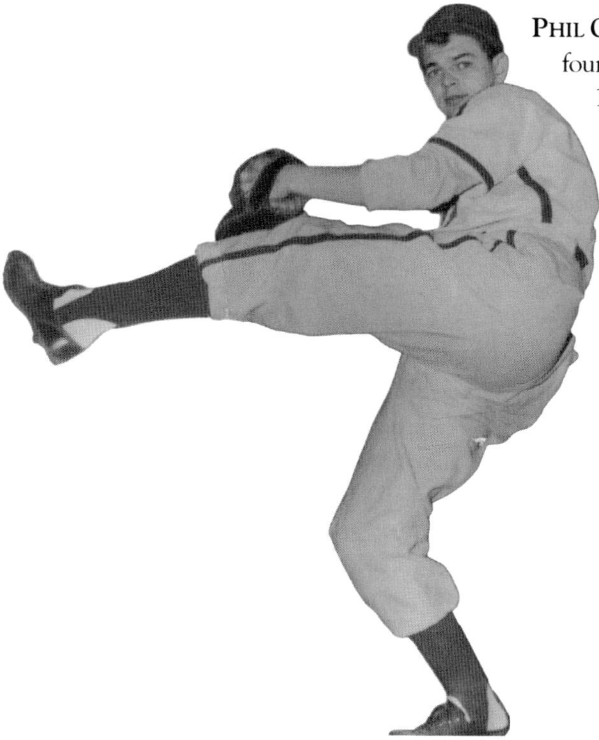

PHIL OATES (1946). Delivering five wins for the fourth-place Millers, 23-year-old Oates made 16 starts in 24 appearances, owned an ERA of 5.07, and had three shutouts to his credit. (Courtesy of Hennepin County Library Special Collections.)

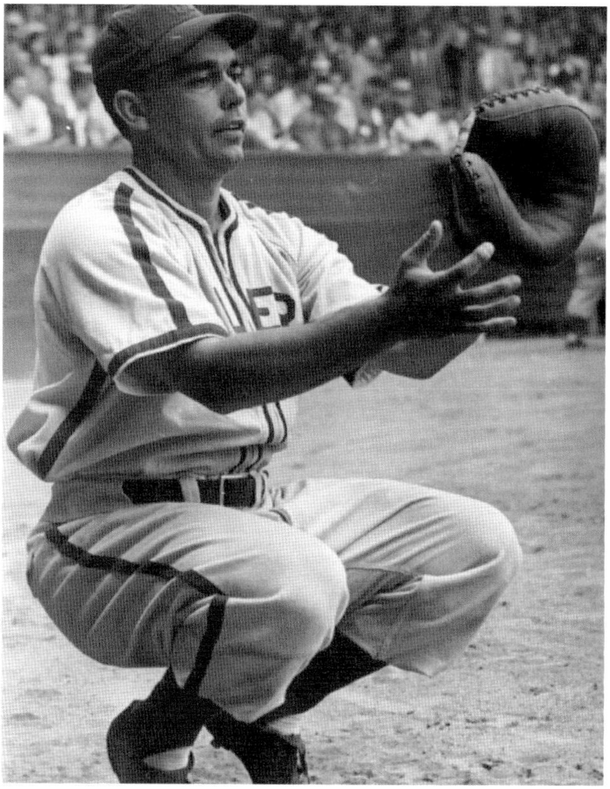

JIMMY PRUETT (1946). After two solid seasons as the catcher for the Milwaukee Brewers, Pruett joined the Toronto Maple Leafs in the Philadelphia Athletics organization and had an exceptional season. In 1946, he became a Miller, catching in 56 games with 63 appearances. The 28-year-old from Nashville, Tennessee, platooned with Minnesota native Russ Rolandson and Don Wheeler behind the plate. (Courtesy of Hennepin County Library Special Collections.)

Bill Lillard (1946). Returning stateside after a deployment in the Pacific theater of operations during World War II with a Purple Heart received for sustaining a wound from a mortar round, Lillard was property of the New York Giants. He resumed his baseball career as a Miller at the age of 28. The younger brother of Pacific Coast League standout Gene Lillard, Bill batted .269 as the club's shortstop in 60 games, filling in at second base in 19 tilts. (Courtesy of Hennepin County Library Special Collections.)

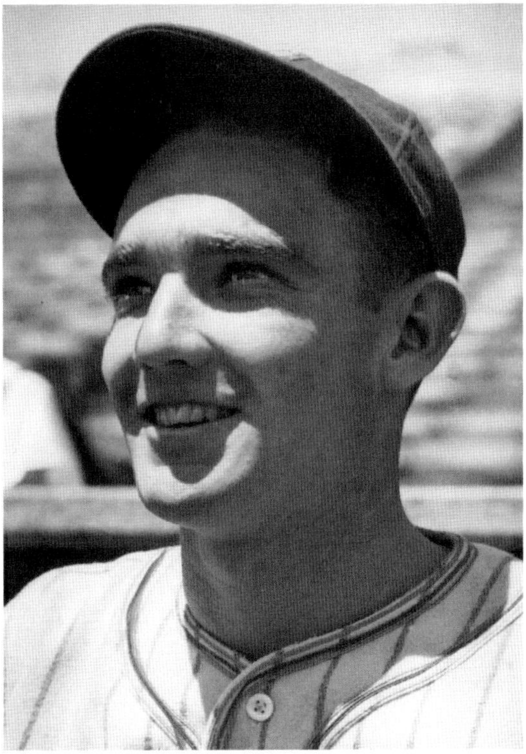

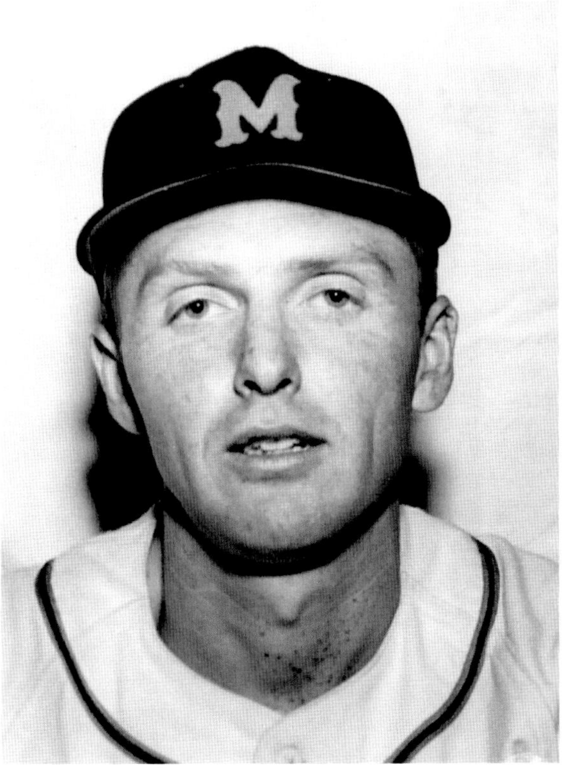

Red Hardy (1946–1949). Born Francis Joseph Hardy in Marmath, North Dakota, the righty attended South High School in Minneapolis. After serving in the US Navy, he received a brief introduction to the Millers in 1946 at the age of 23, but the following season, he put in a full slate of work with 33 games in 24 starts, compiling a record of 9-9. His Minneapolis numbers were neutral; in 1948 he went 10-10, and in 1949, 4-4. Even at Jersey City (AAA-Giants), his record stayed in balance: in 1949, 8-8, and the next year, 13-13. He finally got a call-up to the New York Giants in 1951, appearing in two contests. (Courtesy of Hennepin County Library Special Collections.)

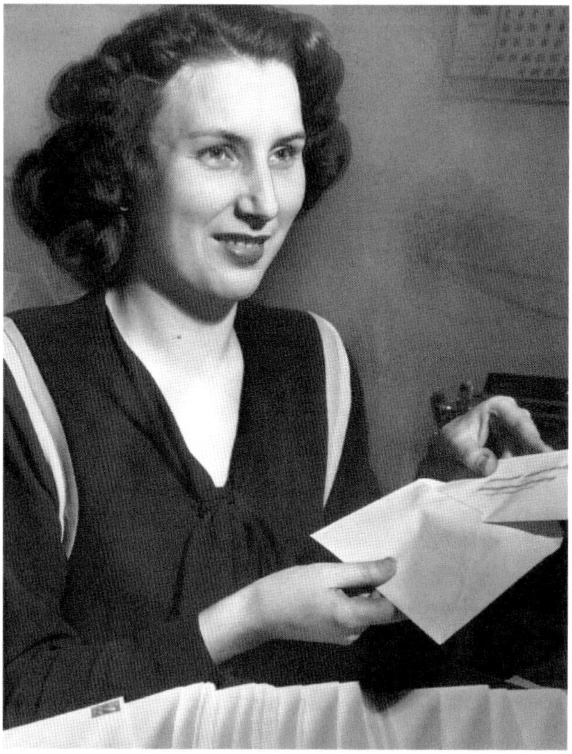

NORMA SEVERSON. Norma Severson was secretary to Mike Kelley, president of the Minneapolis Millers in 1946. (Courtesy of Hennepin County Library Special Collections.)

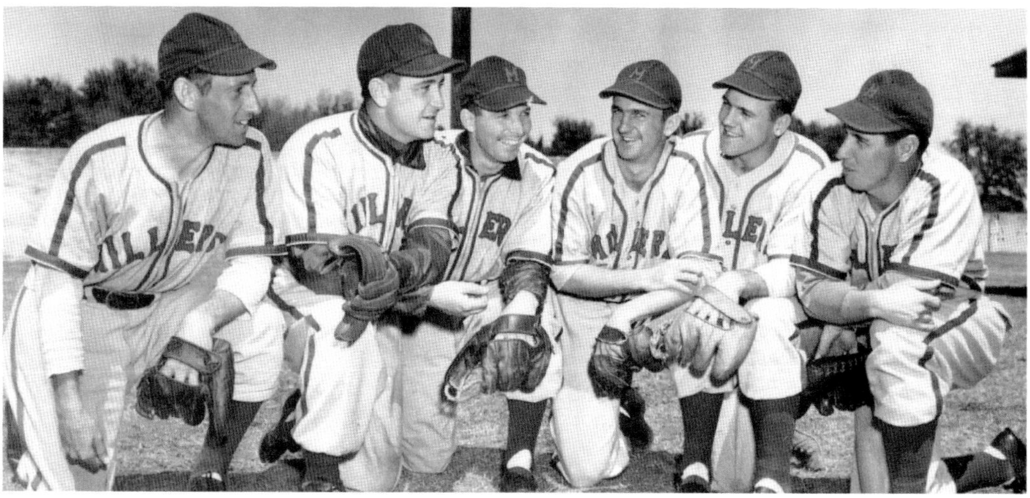

1947 INFIELD HOPEFULS. Hoping for a spot on the Millers short list during spring training at their site in Ocala, Florida, are, from left to right in this March 20, 1947, Associated Press photograph, Mel Harpuder, a Minnesota native who played in 90 games for Minneapolis in 1946; Huck Geary, who was with Pittsburgh in 1946; Bob Rhawn, formerly of the Columbus Red Birds; Dick Klaus, with Jacksonville (Florida) the previous season; Chicagoan Ray Carlson, who played for Greenville (North Carolina) of the Coastal Plains League in 1946; and Frank Trechock, another perennial favorite at Nicollet Park. Klaus did not make the squad that year, but he played a full slate of games for Minneapolis in 1954. (Author's collection.)

Bobby "Rocky" Rhawn (1947–1948). In his first season as a Miller, Rhawn, a 28-year-old third baseman/shortstop from Catawissa, Pennsylvania, hit .302 with 14 home runs. That performance led to his major league debut with the New York Giants on September 17, 1947. Rhawn was a Minneapolis representative of the American Association All-Star squad in 1947, along with catcher Wes Westrum. (Courtesy of Hennepin County Library Special Collections.)

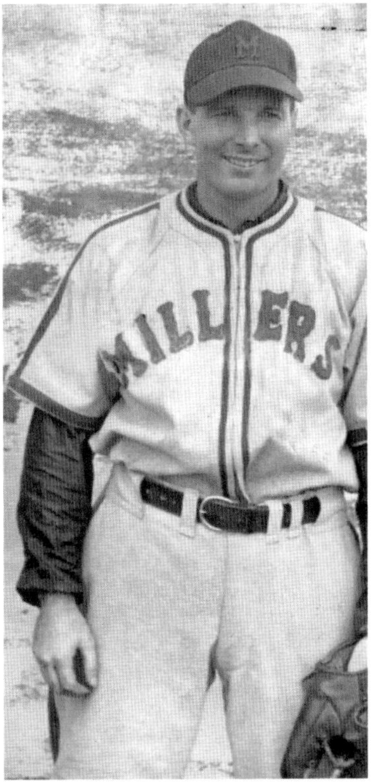

1947 Pitching Prospects. In this March 20, 1947, Associated Press photograph, the stage was set at the Millers' spring training grounds at Ocala, Florida, for some new arms to surface. Taking instruction from manager Tom Sheehan are, from left to right, Nick Andromidas of Jamaica, New York; Ed Wagner of West Pointe, Nebraska; Sheehan; North Dakota native Red Hardy (with Minneapolis the year before); and US Army veteran (and native German) Werner "Lefty" Strunk of Kenosha, Wisconsin, who pitched for the Millers in 1942 and 1946. Hardy went 9-9 that year with 24 starts, and Wagner appeared in one game; the others did not make the team. (Author's collection.)

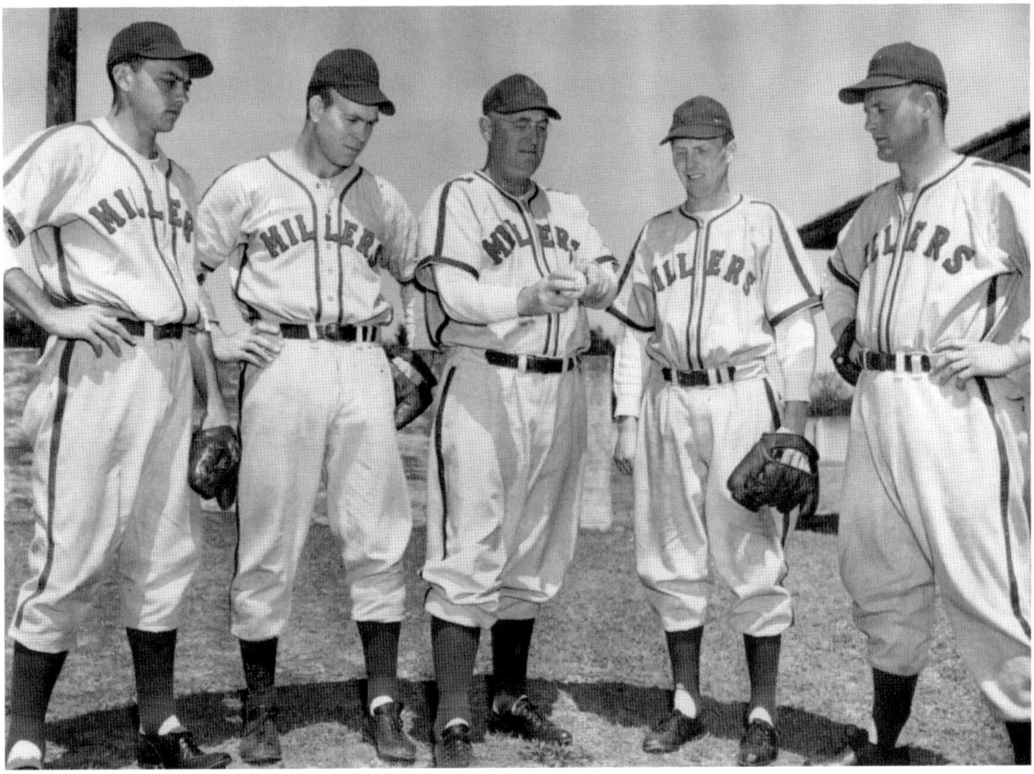

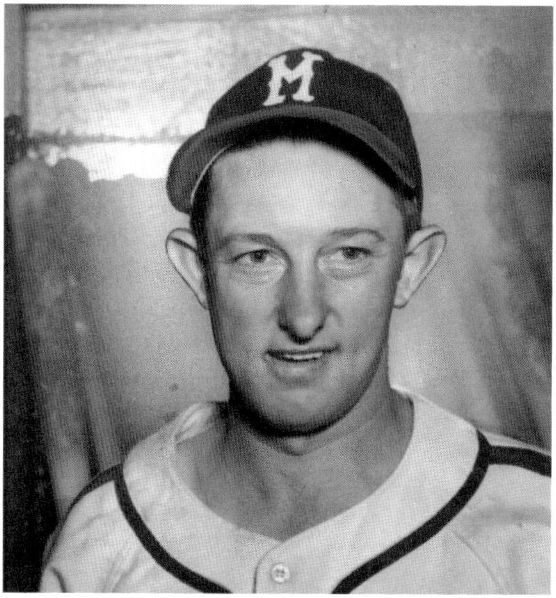

Len Schulte (1947–1948). Schulte came to Minneapolis at age 30 after a three-year association with the Toledo Mud Hens and spending the 1945 season as a St. Louis Brown. Schulte joined the Millers (still a New York Giants farm) for the 1947 season, appearing primarily as a second baseman and batting .282 in 104 games. The following season, the native of St. Charles, Missouri, played 76 games at third base, 43 at the keystone sack, batting .276 with 23 doubles for the fifth-place Millers, who finished the season with a record of 77-77. (Courtesy of Hennepin County Library Special Collections.)

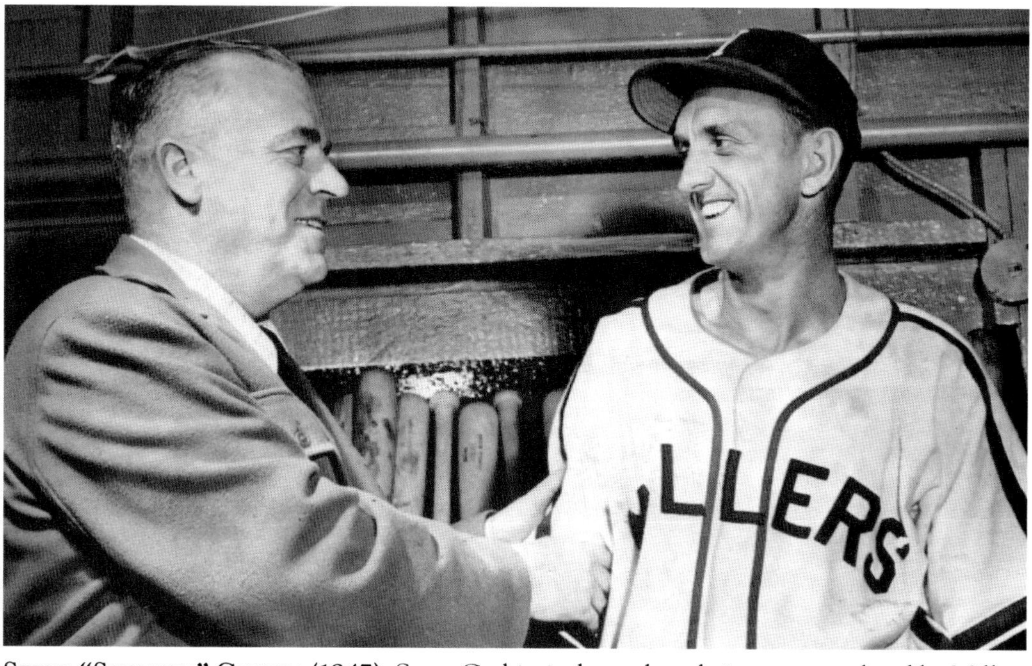

Steve "Splinter" Gerkin (1947). Steve Gerkin is shown here being congratulated by Millers general manager Rosy Ryan after his 75th appearance of the season through August 21, 1947. Gerkin posted a 10-2 record as a relief specialist for the Millers that year. The West Virginia native was the definition of lanky, standing six foot one and weighing 162 pounds. Gerkin came to Minneapolis after a forgettable season with the 1945 Philadelphia Athletics, where he went 0-12. He appeared in 83 tilts (175 innings) with Minneapolis in 1947, a new American Association single-season record. It just so happened that Ryan, who appeared in 60 games in 1932, was the record's previous owner. (Author's collection.)

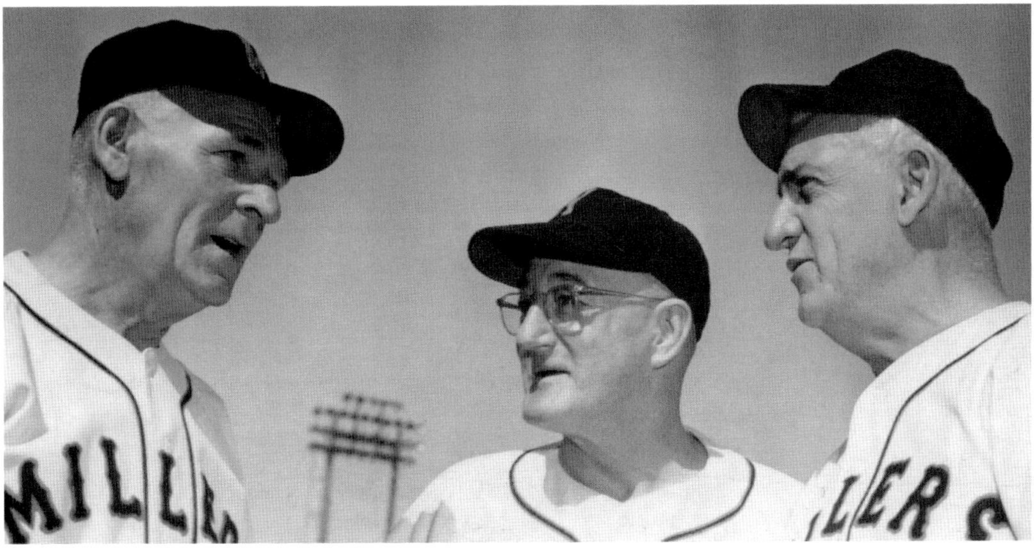

THE OLD GUARD. Three former Millers from a previous generation gathered at Nicollet Park on April 28, 1949, to help celebrate the Minneapolis opener against Louisville. The Millers won the game 4-3, boosting their record to 6-3; they would finish in fourth place with a record of 74-78 under their new manager Tommy Heath. From left to right are former pitcher Rube Schauer (1919–1923), age 58, catcher Wally Mayer (1920–1925), age 59, and pitcher Jess Petty (1932–1935), age 55. During the early 1920s, Mayer and Schauer were battery mates. (Author's collection.)

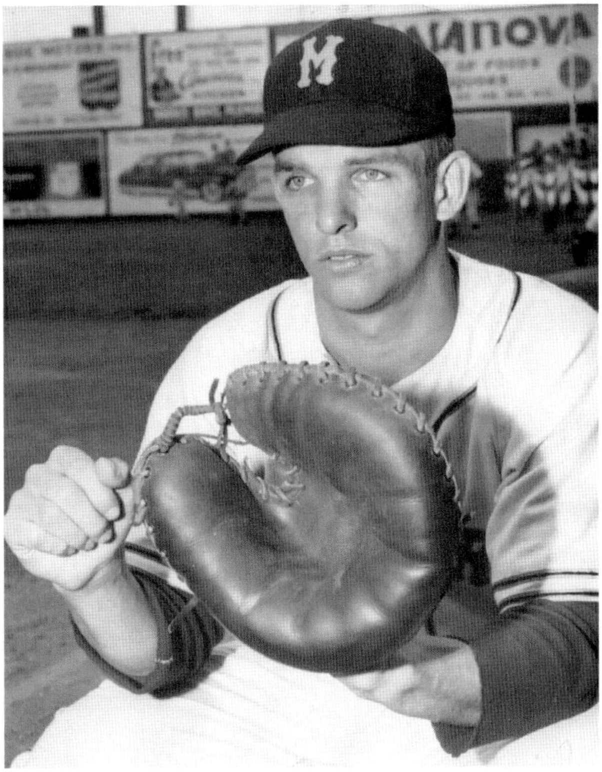

PHIL "PAT" TOMKINSON (1949–1950). The opening-day newspapers around town identified the Millers' opening-day lineup at Louisville's Parkway Field on April 16, 1949, listing a new starting catcher, Phil Tomkinson, who had played for the Jacksonville Tars the previous year. Millers freshman manager Tommy Heath picked Tomkinson over the right-handed throwing veteran receiver Bob Brady, 26, for the opening chores, but Brady soon took over the starting role, finishing the season having appeared in 77 games catching and batting .281 from the left side, while Tomkinson played in only seven games for Minneapolis in 1949. The following year, Tomkinson was back in harness with Minneapolis. (Author's collection.)

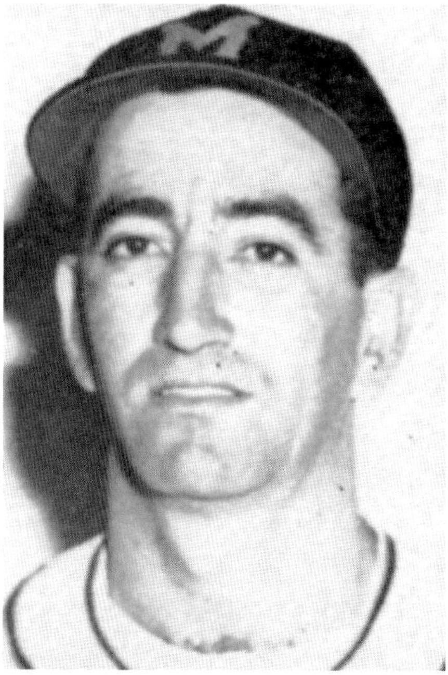

Adrián "Sugar" Zabala (1950–1953). After serving in the Cuban army during World War II, Zabala came back to the States and pitched for the New York Giants. In 1950, he received his first taste of Triple-A ball as a Minneapolis Miller. The lean lefty was key to the club's run to the pennant that year, winning 11 games while losing just four, with 14 starts. In 1951, Zabala blew the doors off the barn with a .375 batting average in 50 at-bats, going 14-12 from the mound with a 3.97 ERA. (*Who's Who in the American Association*, 1950; author's collection.)

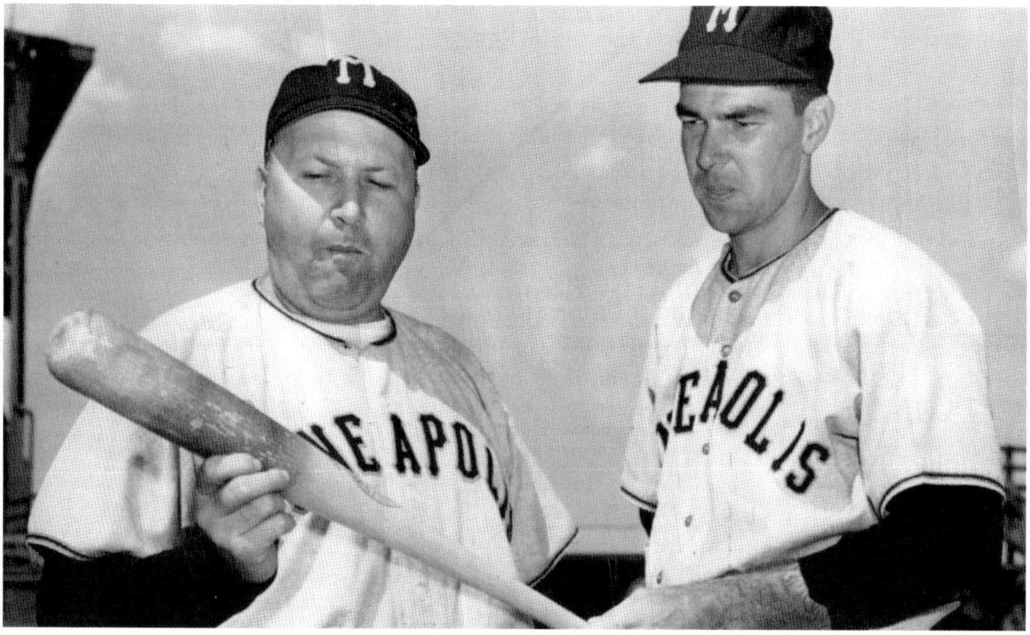

Tommy Heath (1949–1951) and Tookie Gilbert (1947, 1950–1951). After Heath (left) became manager of the Millers in 1949, the club showed improvement in the standings with a fourth-place finish despite a worse record by four losses. But in 1950, Heath led Minneapolis to its first championship since the 1935 season with a record of 90-64. He is shown here in conference with Miller first baseman Harold Joseph "Tookie" Gilbert, who first appeared in a Minneapolis uniform in 1947 at the age of 18. In 1951, Gilbert played 145 games, missing just seven, batting .273 with 29 home runs and 23 doubles. (Author's collection.)

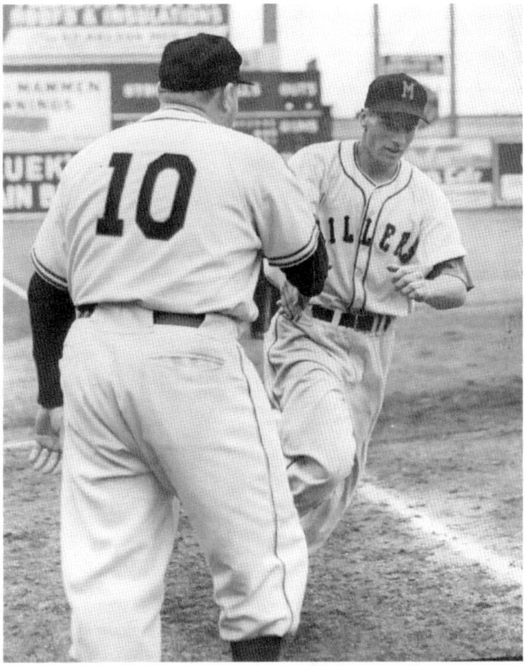

JACK HARSHMAN (1949–1950, 1952). Harshman, a six-foot-two Californian, became a fan favorite during his first year in the Mill City, swatting 40 home runs and 22 doubles as a 21-year-old phenomenon. Here, he receives congratulations from manager Tommy Heath (No. 10) after homering against Indianapolis at Nicollet Park on July 9, 1950, one of two long balls he crushed that day (and one of 17 that year). The Millers won the tilt 7-6. (Author's collection.)

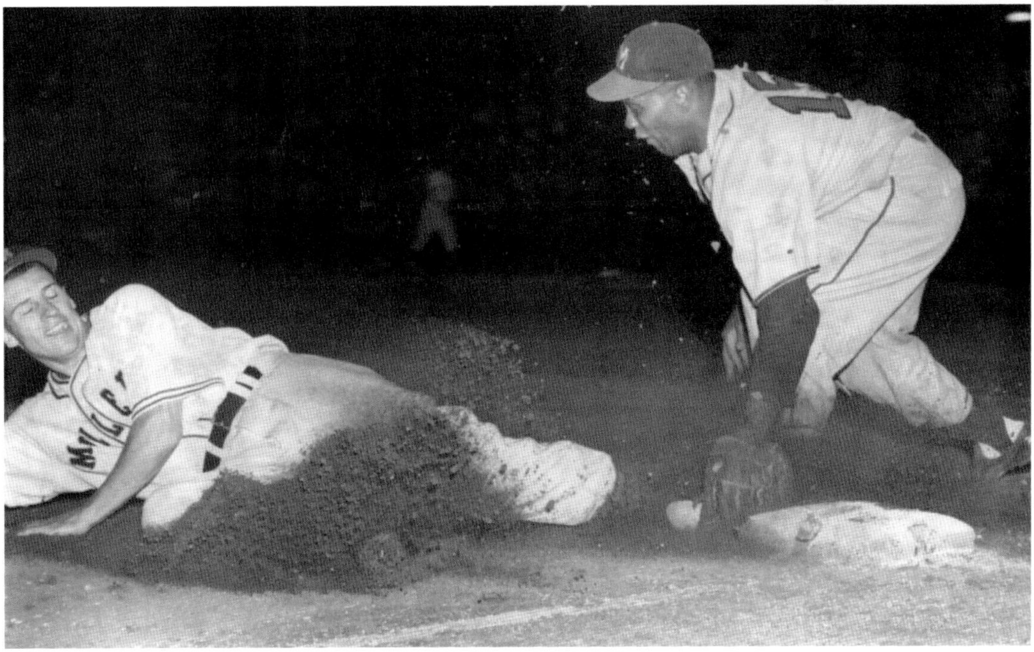

JOHNNY KROPF (1950–1953). Here, 23-year-old Millers outfielder Johnny Kropf attempts to reach third base from first on pitcher Bill Ayers's single, sliding into third and creating a shower of dirt, but Milwaukee Brewers third baseman Buzz Clarkson is just in time with the tag. The play occurred in the third inning of the first game of a Saturday night doubleheader played September 9, 1950, at Nicollet Park. The Brewers won 8-3, but the Millers came back in the nightcap with a 7-3 victory, securing their 90th, and final, win of the season. (Author's collection.)

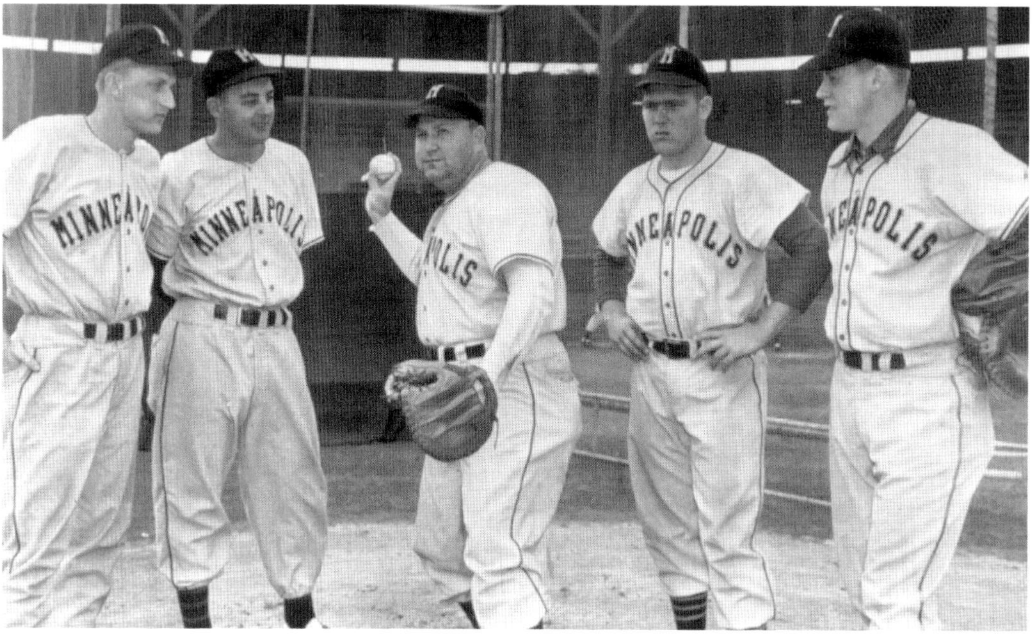

SPRING TIME SEMINAR. Manager and former catcher Tommy Heath (center) provides a few pointers to the prospective catching staff for the Millers at the Sanford, Florida, spring training site in this photograph dated March 16, 1950. From left to right are Ernie Yelen, Bob Brady, Heath, Ted Forsythe, and Joe Konitzki. Brady, 27, became the club's regular catcher, while the 25-year-old Yelen spent the season with the Jacksonville (Florida) Tars that year. Konitzki, 22, played just seven games for Minneapolis in 1950. Forsythe did not develop a record in professional baseball. (Author's collection.)

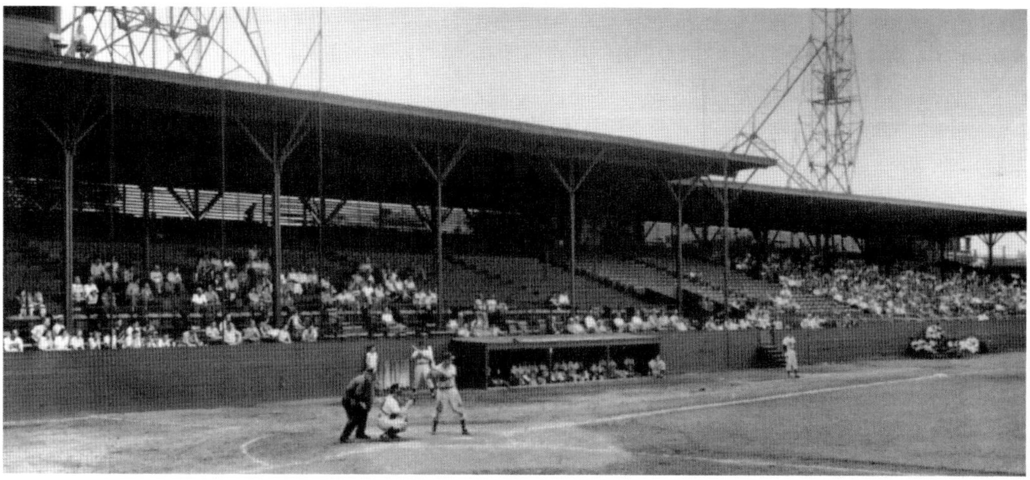

BATTER UP! This c. 1950 sweeping view of the interior of Nicollet Park, home of the Millers from 1902 to 1955, shows a sparse, laid-back, but intent crowd taking in a lazy summer's day at the Millers' friendly confines. One can almost hear the reverberating cry of the vendors as they hawk peanuts, popcorn, crackerjack, and the local favorite, Grain Belt beer. (Author's collection, gift from Don Palmer.)

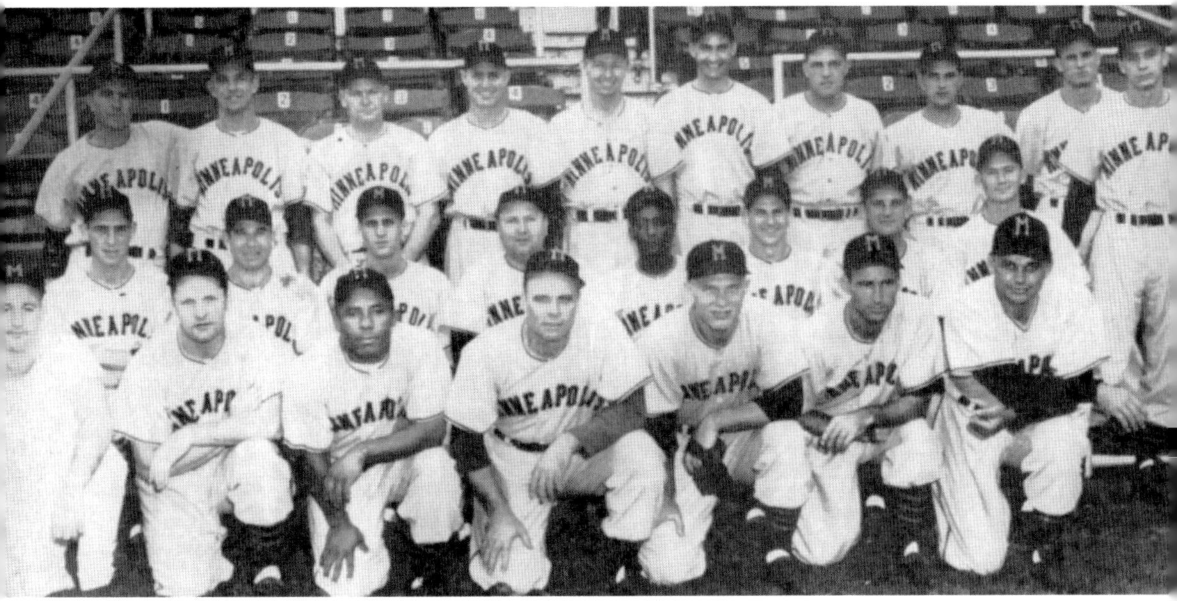

THE 1950 AMERICAN ASSOCIATION CHAMPION MINNEAPOLIS MILLERS. Tommy Heath piloted the club to a 90-64 record and its first league championship since 1935. But the Columbus Red Birds put a quick stop to their joy, knocking the Millers out of the playoffs in the first round, four games to two. During the regular season, Bert Haas led Minneapolis with 24 home runs, 276 total bases, and a .536 slugging percentage. The 27-year-old Hoyt Wilhelm, destined for baseball's Hall of Fame, won 15 games to lead the staff, while 30-year-old Dixie Howell had the club's best record at 14-2. Pictured here, from left to right, are (first row) Tommy McKenna (trainer), Bert Haas (outfielder), Ray Dandridge (third baseman), Kirby Higbe (right-handed pitcher), Alex Konikowski (right-handed pitcher), Spider Jorgensen (outfielder), and Ike Pearson (right-handed pitcher); (second row) Jack Harshman (first baseman), Bama Rowell (outfielder), Joe Lafata (outfielder), Tommy Heath (manager), Dave Barnhill (right-handed pitcher), Johnny Kropf (outfielder), Frank Fanovich (left-handed pitcher), and Davey Williams (second baseman); (third row) Bill Ayers (right-handed pitcher), Phil Tomkinson (catcher), Jake Early (catcher), Ed Wright (right-handed pitcher), George McDonald (outfielder), Wes Bailey (right-handed pitcher), Dixie Howell (right-handed pitcher), Hoyt Wilhelm (right-handed pitcher), Bill Jennings (shortstop), and Mike Vukemire (shortstop). (Author's collection.)

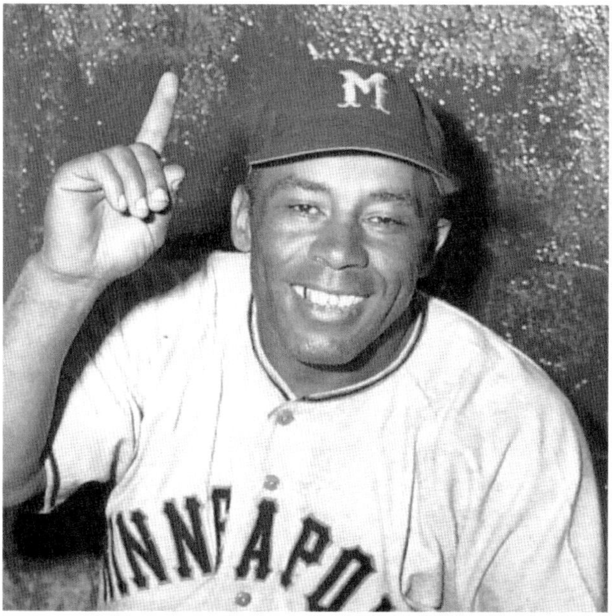

Ray Dandridge (1949–1952). Known as "Dannie" or "Dandy," Hall of Famer Dandridge was one of the first African American players on the Millers. Dandridge honed his expertise at the hot corner in the Negro Leagues. During his first season as a Miller in 1949, the 35-year-old appeared in 99 games, batting .362 while playing 83 games at third base and 16 at second. His 22 doubles qualified him as the runner-up among the club's leaders. Dandridge was the Millers' envoy to the American Association All-Star team in 1950. (Author's collection.)

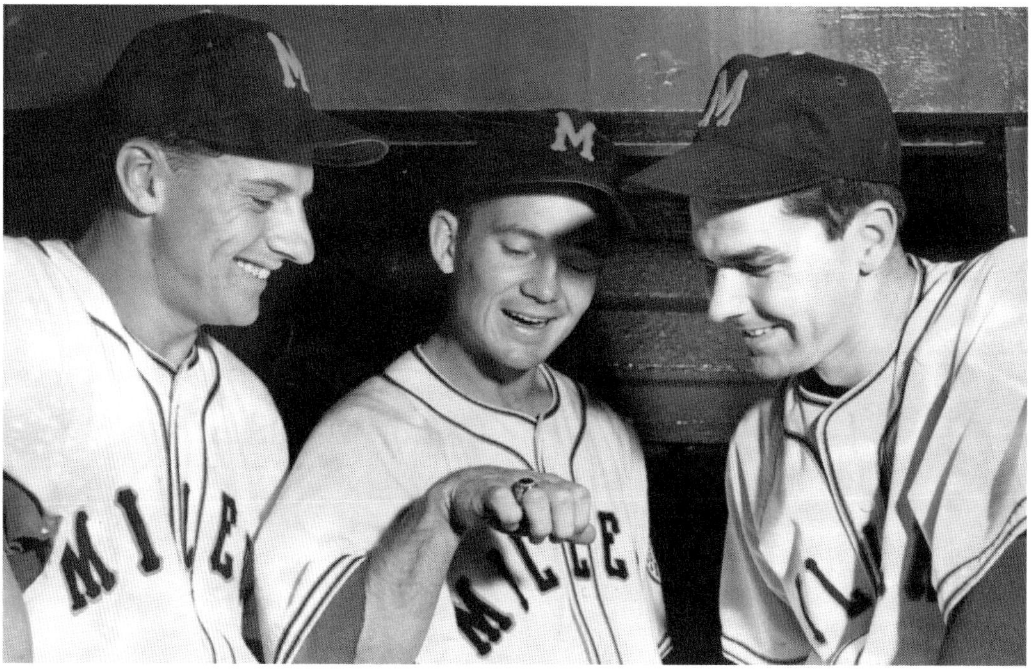

Show Off! Miller second baseman and future National League All-Star Davey Williams shows off the championship ring he earned as a member of the 1950 club, which captured the flag by four games over Al Lopez and the Indianapolis Indians. Looking on in this photograph taken May 28, 1951, are Miller outfielder Johnny Kropf (left) and first baseman Tookie Gilbert. Celebrating flag-raising day to signify its 1950 championship reign, Minneapolis took one on the chin that day as Milwaukee won 16-11, walloping nine home runs, a new record. Williams grounded into four double plays. (Author's collection.)

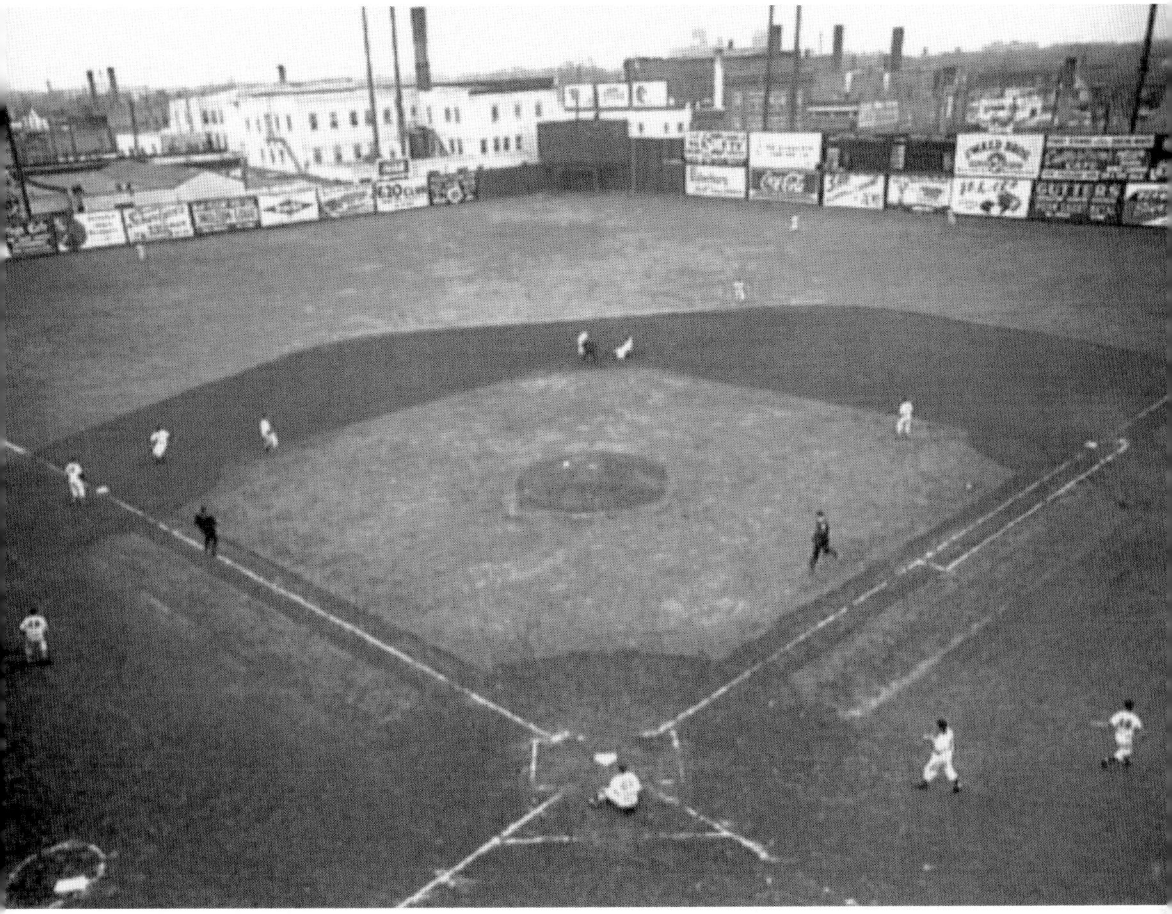

GAME ON! Nicollet Park is the scene of live action during a battle between the Minneapolis Millers and an American Association opponent. The advertisements along the outfield wall lent a colorful dimension to the expanse of green, and a few of the advertisers, such as Grain Belt beer and Ewald Bros. Automotive, remain in business today. Note the Minneapolis skyline (north of the location) at far left and the National/American League scoreboard on the right. (Author's collection.)

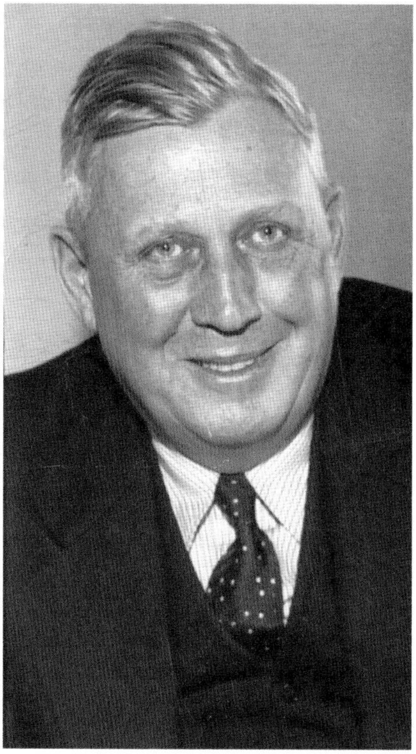

Michael Joseph Kelley (1924–1931). Long associated with the Minneapolis Millers as manager and club owner, Kelley (pictured around 1937) was under contract with archrival St. Paul for several years prior to supplanting Joe Cantillon at the helm in 1924. With 723 wins to 711 losses for Minneapolis, Kelley claimed a combined 2,203 victories (including Minneapolis, St. Paul, and Indianapolis), more than any other American Association manager. Known for the dalmatians he kept at Nicollet Park, Kelley was a true Twin Cities legend. He passed away June 6, 1955, at Minneapolis and is buried at the prestigious Lakewood Cemetery there. (Author's collection.)

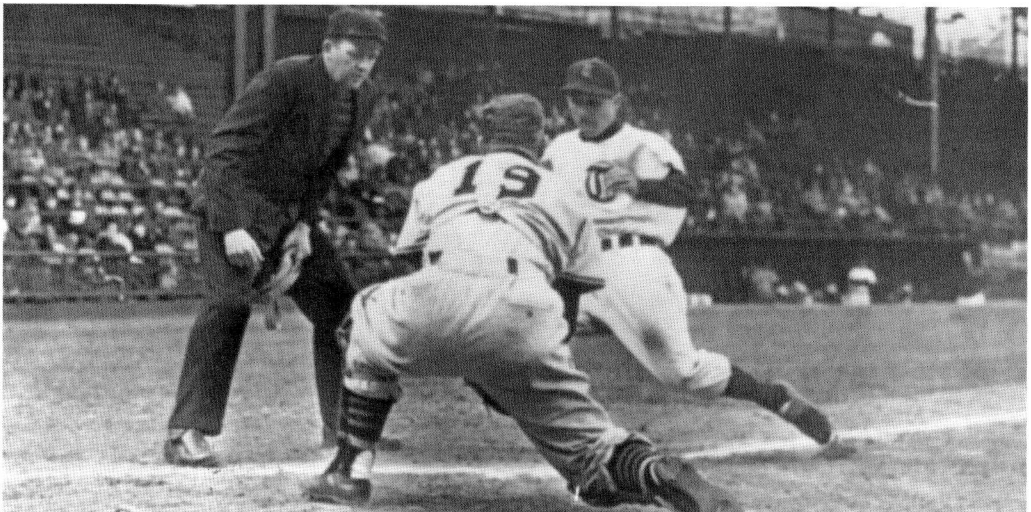

Mays Guns 'Em Down! "Katt-Nipped" is the word of the day as former Miller Bill Barnacle is cut down at the plate on a perfect throw from center fielder Willie Mays at Toledo's Swayne Field on Saturday, April 21, 1951. Minneapolis catcher Ray Katt is in position to make the tag, and Barnacle is a dead duck in the first inning. The Millers won the game 2-1 in 10 innings, ending Toledo's three-game winning streak and bringing the Millers' record to 2-2 on the young season. Katt was a three-time Minneapolis representative to the American Association All-Star squad (1951–1953). (Author's collection.)

WILLIE MAYS (1951). Inducted into the Hall of Fame in 1979 for his electric bat and adeptness in the outfield, Mays, the "Say Hey Kid," became a Miller at the age of 20. He was not with the club long before the parent club New York Giants brought him up. In 35 games with Minneapolis, the Alabama-born outfielder batted .477 with eight home runs, 18 doubles, and 30 RBIs. With numbers like those, the Millers likely regretted letting the youngster go, but in his short swing through Minneapolis, Mays made his mark on the Mill City. (Author's collection.)

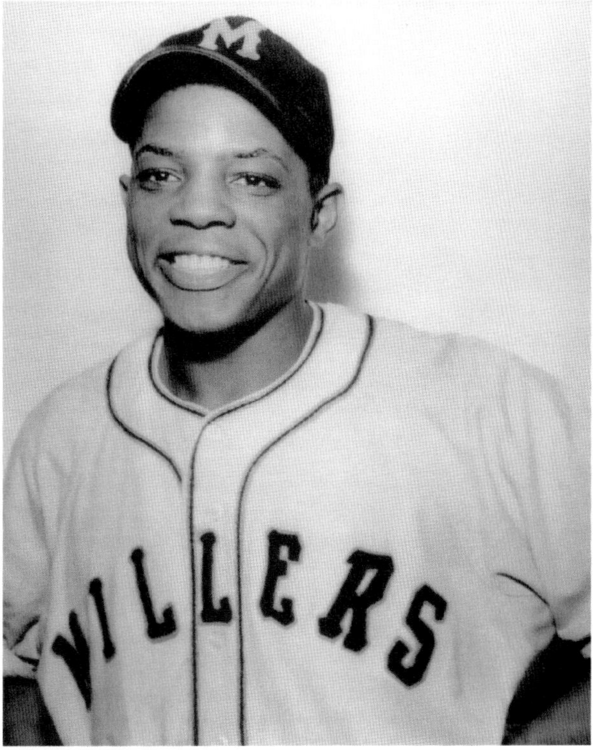

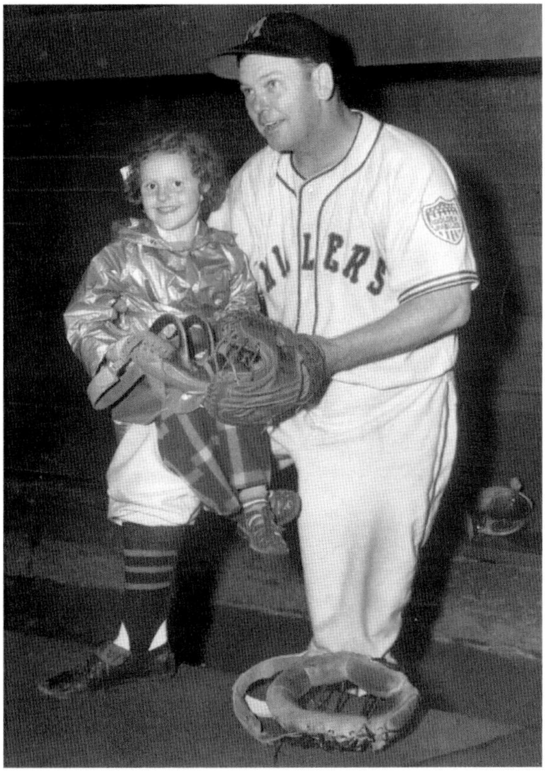

JAKE EARLY (1950–1953) AND YOUNG ADMIRER. Looking every bit like little Zuzu Bailey (Karolyn Grimes) from the 1946 film *It's a Wonderful Life*, four-year-old Minneapolis resident Terry Jean Hanson, described as a "rabid baseball fan," sits tight in good company after the game she attended between the Millers and the Indianapolis Indians was rained out. The 36-year-old Jake Early, a former American League All-Star and the Millers' backup catcher to Ray Katt, appears delighted to have been chosen as the young lady's chaperone for the evening. The photograph was taken Friday night, June 22, 1951, at Nicollet Park. (Author's collection.)

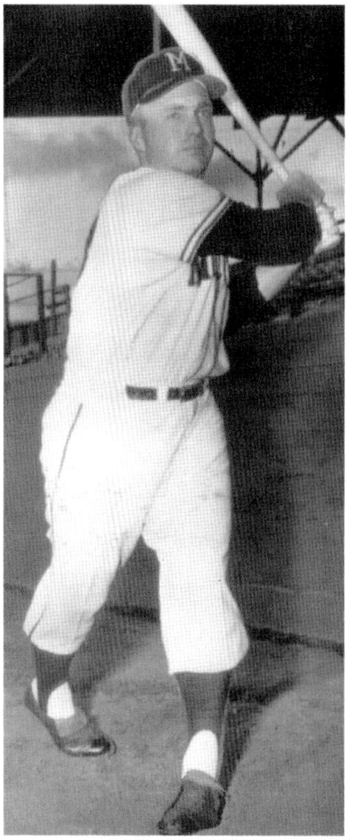

Rance Pless (1953–1955). Known as a team leader who was always behind his fellow players, Pless, primarily a third baseman, was the spearhead behind the Millers' championship in 1955. That year, Pless, 29, appeared in all 156 games played by Minneapolis, one of only two players to do so in the league (Marv Throneberry, age 21, did it with Denver). He joined elite company when he reached the 200-hit plateau, becoming one of only 40 hitters in Miller history with such a distinction. His .337 batting average and .550 slugging generated 326 total bases, the most in the Association. Pless was a three-time Minneapolis delegate to the American Association All-Star team (1953–1955). After baseball, he returned to work his family's farm in south-central Tennessee. (Author's collection.)

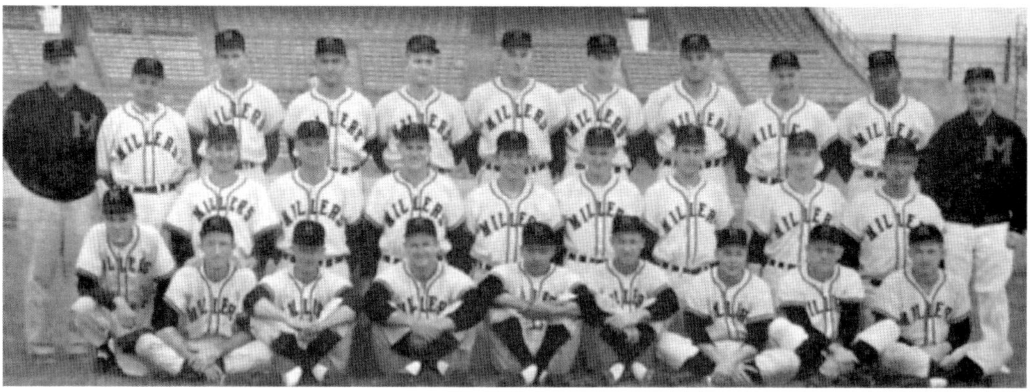

The 1956 Minneapolis Millers. The club finished fourth with a record of 78-74. From left to right in this photograph are (first row) Tom Obinger (batboy), Bob Stephenson (catcher), Roger Bowman (left-handed pitcher), Bob Lennon (outfielder), Ozzie Virgil (third baseman), Wayne Terwilliger (second baseman), Lee Tate (second baseman/shortstop), Gil Coan (outfielder), and Jake Jenkins (catcher); (second row) Dave Garcia (coach), Bill Bradford (right-handed pitcher), Don Grate (outfielder/third baseman), Dick Strahs (right-handed pitcher), Mel Held (right-handed pitcher), Phil Paine (right-handed pitcher), Al Corwin (right-handed pitcher), and Gail Harris (first baseman); (third row) Art Ruane (clubhouse), Eddie Stanky (manager), Ed Bressoud (shortstop), Ramón Monzant (right-handed pitcher), Jim "Sheriff" Constable (left-handed pitcher), Curt Barclay (right-handed pitcher), Pete Burnside (left-handed pitcher), Bill Taylor (outfielder), Vern Rapp (catcher), Willie Kirkland (outfielder), and Tommy McKenna (trainer). (Author's collection.)

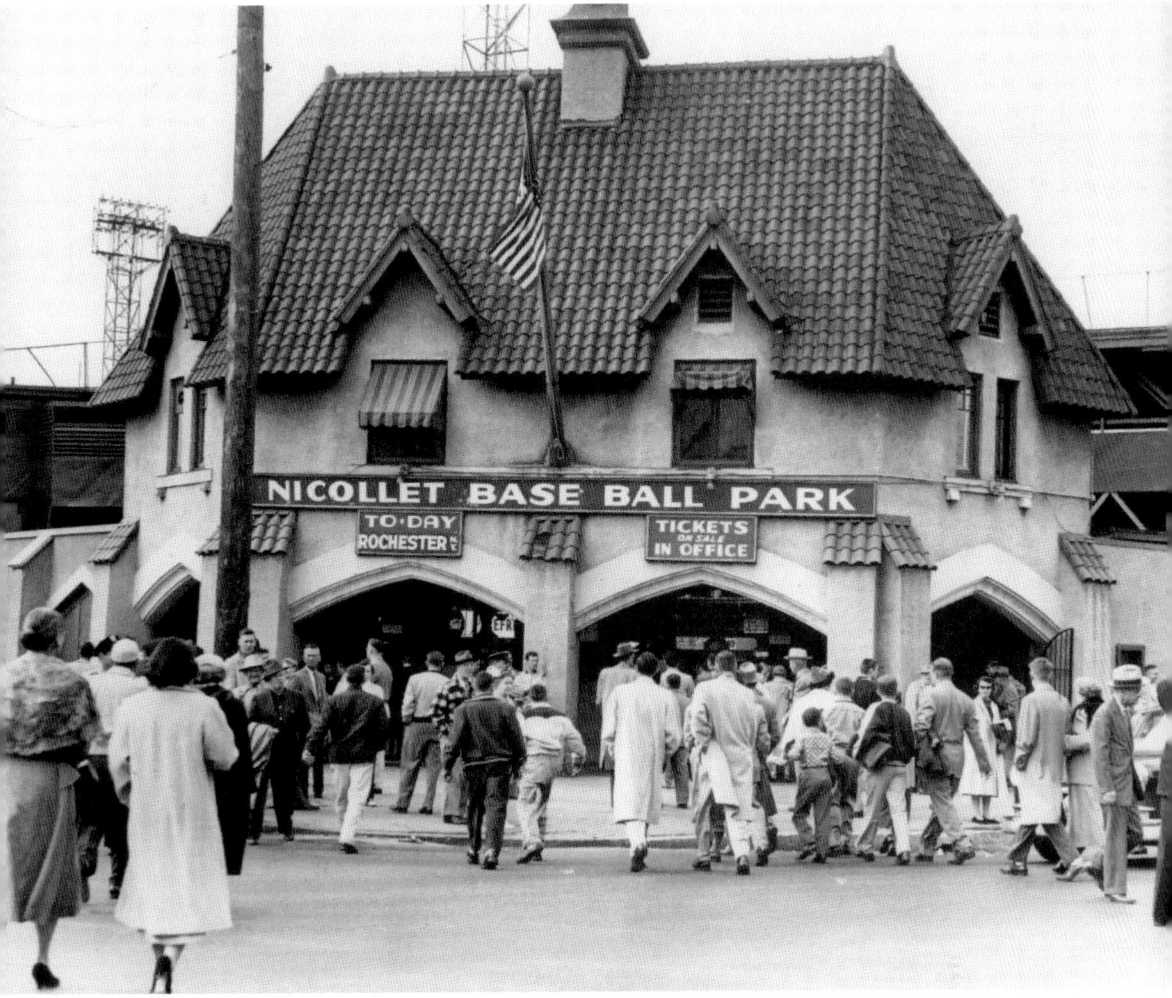

NICOLLET SWAN SONG. As the American Association champion Minneapolis Millers prepared to face the Rochester Red Wings for the Junior World Series title in September 1955, the colorful signage adorning the old ticket office beckoned fans for what became the final series at the run-down facility. The charming edifice was added during the park's first comprehensive renovation in 1912. With its dignified Tudor styling, the building sported a clay tile roof and stucco siding. Long a fixture at Thirty-first and Nicollet Streets on the near south side of Minneapolis, the building was, perhaps, the premier icon of Millers baseball, one that served as the primary portal for Twin Cities fans seeking access to their beloved boys of summer. The Millers relocated to Metropolitan Stadium in suburban Bloomington the following year, calling it home from 1956 to 1960, before the Minnesota Twins moved there in 1961. The Metropolitan Stadium site later became the home of the Mall of America. (Author's collection, gift from Don Palmer.)

Discover Thousands of Local History Books Featuring Millions of Vintage Images

Arcadia Publishing, the leading local history publisher in the United States, is committed to making history accessible and meaningful through publishing books that celebrate and preserve the heritage of America's people and places.

Find more books like this at
www.arcadiapublishing.com

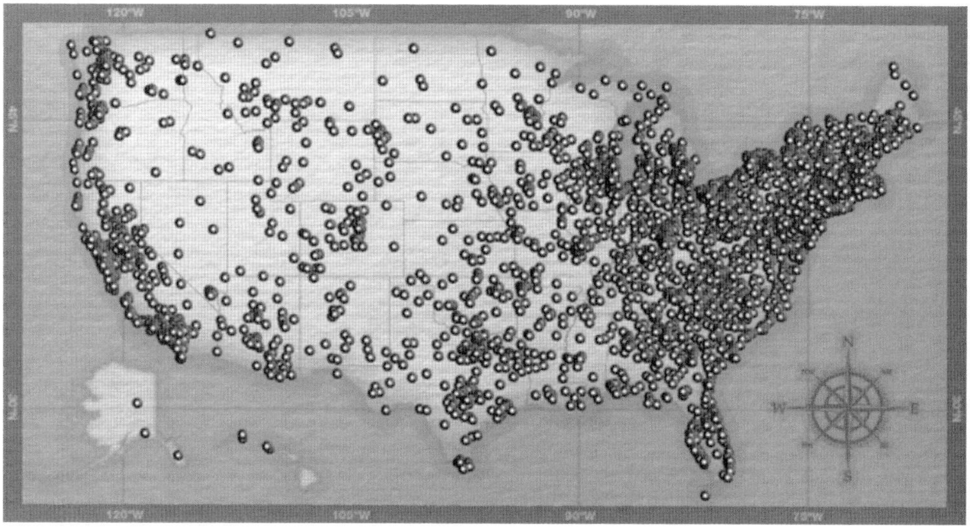

Search for your hometown history, your old stomping grounds, and even your favorite sports team.

Consistent with our mission to preserve history on a local level, this book was printed in South Carolina on American-made paper and manufactured entirely in the United States. Products carrying the accredited Forest Stewardship Council (FSC) label are printed on 100 percent FSC-certified paper.

MADE IN THE USA